Praise for *Hell's Witness*

"Brilliant journalism … An excellent portrait of an informant's relationship with the cops."

—*National Post*

"The book that was crying out to be written about the Quebec biker wars. Not since Mick Lowe's *Conspiracy of Brothers*, published almost twenty years ago, has a book about Canada's biker-gang underworld been as ambitiously researched and carefully crafted as *Hell's Witness*."

—Derek Finkle, author of *No Claim to Mercy* and editor of *Toro* magazine

"*Hell's Witness* exposes a criminal-justice system in free fall with the searing intensity of a blowtorch cauterizing a wound … chilling in the breadth of carnage it chronicles; disturbing in what it says about the shadow wars that law enforcement agencies must fight … A brooding indictment of a failed justice system."

—*The Globe and Mail*

"With wry humour, impeccable style, and carefully recreated splashes of brutal action, *Hell's Witness* [brings] to life a complex character, a disturbing criminal milieu, and the behind-the-scenes handling of a significant police informant. Who knew such an ugly story could be told so beautifully?"

—Adrian Humphreys, author of *The Enforcer* and senior national correspondent for the *National Post*

"Near faultlessly executed and throroughly engrossing … never does Sanger succumb to sensationalist temptation."

—*Hour* (Montreal)

"Intelligent and measured …"

—*Toronto Star*

PENGUIN CANADA

HELL'S WITNESS

DANIEL SANGER has worked as a newspaper and magazine journalist in Quebec for two decades. He is a regular contributor to *The Economist* and has written for a wide variety of other publications in North America and Europe, including *Saturday Night*, *L'actualité*, *The New York Times Magazine*, and *The Telegraph Magazine*. His article on Dany Kane won the gold medal for investigative reporting at the 2002 National Magazine Awards. He can be reached by email at danielsanger@canada.com.

HELL'S WITNESS

DANIEL SANGER

PENGUIN
CANADA

PENGUIN CANADA

Published by the Penguin Group

Penguin Group (Canada), 90 Eglinton Avenue East, Suite 700, Toronto, Ontario, Canada M4P 2Y3
(a division of Pearson Penguin Canada Inc.)

Penguin Group (USA) Inc., 375 Hudson Street, New York, New York 10014, U.S.A.
Penguin Books Ltd, 80 Strand, London WC2R 0RL, England
Penguin Ireland, 25 St Stephen's Green, Dublin 2, Ireland (a division of Penguin Books Ltd)
Penguin Group (Australia), 250 Camberwell Road, Camberwell, Victoria 3124, Australia
(a division of Pearson Australia Group Pty Ltd)
Penguin Books India Pvt Ltd, 11 Community Centre, Panchsheel Park, New Delhi – 110 017, India
Penguin Group (NZ), cnr Airborne and Rosedale Roads, Albany, Auckland 1310, New Zealand
(a division of Pearson New Zealand Ltd)
Penguin Books (South Africa) (Pty) Ltd, 24 Sturdee Avenue, Rosebank, Johannesburg 2196,
South Africa

Penguin Books Ltd, Registered Offices: 80 Strand, London WC2R 0RL, England

First published in a Viking Canada hardcover by Penguin Group (Canada),
a division of Pearson Penguin Canada Inc., 2005
Published in this edition, 2006

1 2 3 4 5 6 7 8 9 10 (OPM)

Copyright © Daniel Sanger, 2005
Map of Montreal and surrounding area copyright © Paul Sneath, free&Creative, 2005

Manufactured in the U.S.A.

LIBRARY AND ARCHIVES CANADA CATALOGUING IN PUBLICATION

Sanger, Daniel (Daniel K.)
Hell's witness : the many lives and curious death of Dany Kane, Hells Angels informant / Daniel Sanger.

Includes bibliographical references and index.
ISBN 0-14-301545-1

1. Kane, Dany. 2. Hells Angels. 3. Motorcycle gangs—Québec (Province)—History.
4. Gang members—Québec (Province)—Biography. 5. Informers—Québec (Province)—Biography.
I. Title.

HV6491.C32Q4 2006   364.1'092   C2005-906356-4

Visit the Penguin Group (Canada) website at **www.penguin.ca**

CONTENTS

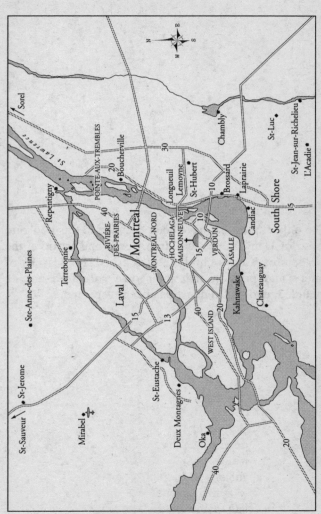

Montreal and Surrounding Area

The only names that have been changed in this book are those of Dany Kane's children. Josée and Patricia, the mothers of Kane's children, also asked, for reasons of safety and privacy, that their own surnames not be included, and that request has been respected.

THE END

Cities, like people and gems, have their better angles and aspects, approaches that show them at their most handsome, most beguiling, or simply most imposing. The city of Montreal, afloat on an island in the St. Lawrence River, looks its best from what's known as the South Shore, the patchwork of towns, suburbs, and farms that sprawl across the flat, fertile land on the southern bank of the river that leads to the Great Lakes and the heart of North America.

Seen from the South Shore, Montreal's downtown office towers rise behind the ships, harbourside parks, and historic buildings of the Old Port. Beyond the towers looms the extinct volcanic cone that Montrealers call—affectionately, if ambitiously—the Mountain, its flanks encrusted with the stone houses of the rich or heavily indebted. Perched on its brow is a giant electrified cross. On any day, Montreal looks like a city should, like a drawing from a children's book; on the right day and in the right light, it looks like a magical kingdom, at once irresistible and intimidating, there, just in front of you yet always out of reach. It's a sight people on the South Shore see regularly as they go about their business on any given day. Montreal's skyline will pop unexpectedly into view across a field or in the space between two low-rise buildings, a constant reminder to the South Shore's inhabitants of what they might aspire to or wish to leave behind.

The South Shore itself is a sprawling mix of old and new, remnants of once-isolated villages, vast cornfields still cultivated, hastily built and featureless suburban developments, and interminable stretches of strip malls, gas stations, and big-box stores. In winter every corner is whipped by snow and cold, in summer blasted by the sun. Never does the South Shore feel like anything close to a magical kingdom.

Dany Kane was born and spent almost all his life in and around the South Shore. It's also where he seems to have died, aged thirty-one, at the end of a weekend in August 2000.

At the time of his death, Kane lived on the outskirts of the town of St-Luc, twenty-five kilometres from downtown Montreal, in an upscale split-level house set on a large wooded lot on the banks of the river L'Acadie. He had quietly purchased the property for $250,000 just a year earlier. One day, he'd telephoned his long-time girlfriend, Patricia, and told her there was a house he wanted her to see. They hadn't been discussing the purchase of a home and she was surprised, but she went to have a look. Kane asked if she liked it; she did. "That's good, because that's the house I've bought," he replied. The transaction had already been taken care of.

Kane had moved in that July, and Patricia, busy in her job with a downtown research firm, had followed in September. During their first months there, with Kane frequently out of town and Patricia commuting every day, the house hadn't felt lived in. But the couple had a child together in April 2000, a stepbrother named Jesse for Kane's three children from an earlier relationship and Patricia's eight-year-old son. The baby's arrival prompted Kane to put $60,000 worth of renovations into the house, and by summer it was beginning to feel like a real home. Rooms for Kane's eldest children, who lived most of the time with their mother in nearby St-Jean-sur-Richelieu, were set up in the basement. An above-ground pool was installed in the backyard. Patricia's son, Steve, finished his school year in Montreal, where he stayed during the week with Patricia's mother, and came out to live with the couple permanently. The warm weather also helped. Winter's cold and snow had made the place seem all the more remote from the vibrancy of Montreal, but summer's birdsong and flowers and the flowing L'Acadie River made its isolation not just worthwhile but a blessing.

The weather that summer had been mixed, but the first week of August was pleasantly sunny with none of the oppressive heat and humidity that sometimes made the South Shore feel like the South Seas. Saturday, August 5, was a perfect day for a wedding, precisely what Kane and Patricia planned to attend that afternoon. Along with three hundred other guests, they were to witness the nuptials of René Charlebois, a full member of the elite Nomads chapter of Quebec's Hells Angels and a close friend of the Nomads' leader, Maurice "Mom" Boucher, Canada's most notorious biker. Indeed, the no-expense-spared reception was to take place at Boucher's luxurious estate in the South Shore community of Contrecoeur, fifty kilometres northeast of St-Luc. Dany Kane and guest would be welcome because for the better part of a decade he had been a trusted Hells Angels underling.

Patricia hadn't been keen to attend when Kane first showed her the invitation. She felt ill at ease at the gang's social events, where the men tended to chat among themselves and the women were left to make small talk, searching for interests they might have in common. In Patricia's case, these were few. While almost all the biker women, be they wives or mistresses, lived lives of leisure, Patricia insisted on working, even when Kane said he'd happily take care of her.

There was also the fact that Patricia's was often the only black face in the crowd. Although Quebec's Hells Angels are generally more tolerant than their brethren elsewhere, the larger organization is virulently racist, and its formal rules bar blacks from membership. Patricia hadn't been sorry to miss an earlier biker wedding when the local dry cleaners had closed early for the weekend, leaving them without anything to wear. She told Kane that if he was intent on attending the Charlebois event, he should take another date.

"But they know I'm with a black girl," he said.

"Then find another black girl," responded Patricia.

After weeks of coaxing, however, Kane had won her over to the idea, and she bought a flattering new dress and three different pairs of shoes to choose from. On the morning of August 5, they went to the gym in St-Jean-sur-Richelieu, a ten-minute drive from home, where Kane took a boxing lesson and Patricia worked out, sweating off the last ounces so the dress would fit perfectly on her slim, petite frame. Then, on the way home, Kane abruptly announced they wouldn't be going to the wedding after all. Patricia was baffled and annoyed.

"I have to handle a few things" was all he would say. Shortly after they arrived home, Kane got back in the car and drove off again, this time to Ontario on a quick trip to the towns of Kingston and Belleville.

Kane was back in his bed late Saturday night, and on Sunday their usual weekend routine of family obligations resumed. He didn't wake early and take the children out for breakfast so Patricia could sleep in, as he sometimes did, but before noon, after a new bed for the baby had been delivered, he took Steve and a neighbour's child in-line skating. Then it was over to his sister's place in St-Jean for a visit, Jesse in his arms. Later in the day he and Steve, to whom Kane had been a father figure since he was little more than a toddler, rode off on Kane's motorcycle to the gym. They returned soon afterwards: Steve, they'd been told, was too young to be admitted. Kane fumed that they'd boycott the gym in future.

He also told Patricia that he was expecting two visitors to the house that evening and that she, along with Steve and Jesse, should spend the night at her mother's apartment in north-end Montreal, an easy forty-five-minute drive away. Because of his secretive and unsavoury line of work, Patricia was accustomed to making herself scarce on such occasions. When they had rented an apartment together in downtown Montreal she found herself doing a lot of walking and shopping when Kane's gang associates dropped by. Still, it was rare that Kane asked her to spend the whole night away, and Patricia objected. Her mother had just had her apartment painted and the fumes might harm the baby, she said. But Kane was adamant and her mother dismissed her concerns. The matter was settled.

In the afternoon, Kane had a phone call from Josée, the mother of his three eldest children. They had a rare, pleasant conversation but it deteriorated when Josée got to the point: was he still planning to drive the thirty kilometres up the Richelieu River to pick up their middle child, Nathalie, from camp that day? Kane told Josée he wouldn't be able to make it and they argued. When she told him he couldn't be depended on, he hung up.

Kane had bailed out of another obligation that evening. He was supposed to meet the flight of Normand Robitaille, a Nomads member and favourite of Mom Boucher's, for whom Kane had recently been serving as gofer and chauffeur. Invoking one excuse or another, he had managed to pass on the job to another flunky.

After the conversation with Josée, an uneasy calm descended on the household. Patricia spent the early evening watching a cartoon video with Steve and Jesse while Kane stretched out on the couch in the living room listening to a Doors album. Patricia and Steve had been told not to answer any of the phones—the house was wired with two land lines, and Kane had three cell-phones—because he was either waiting for an important call or avoiding one. It wasn't clear.

The telephone had been nothing but a source of stress that weekend. It had started on Friday when Kane got into a shouting match with a man for whom he had guaranteed a substantial loan from a Hells Angels loan shark. Not for the first time the debtor was unable to make his weekly payment, and Kane was on the hook. He was furious and intent on driving to Laval, an island suburb on the other side of Montreal, to have it out with the deadbeat. Frightened of what Kane might do, Patricia talked him out of it.

Later on Friday afternoon, when Kane's younger sister, Gisèle, dropped by for a visit, the two women overheard another heated conversation about money. This time it wasn't clear who was on the other end of the line, only that Kane and his interlocutor were negotiating about who would shoulder some substantial financial burden. At one point Kane declared that he didn't want to dig into his rainy-day fund to cover the cost. Patricia made it a point not to ask, or even think much, about Kane's financial affairs; she wasn't aware of the existence of any rainy-day fund. She simply assumed that this conversation had something to do with the earlier call and that one or both might be related to their cancelled social plans on Saturday.

Forty-eight hours later, as Kane lay listening to the bleak lyrics of Jim Morrison and the pressures of the week loomed ahead, Patricia suspected he was still brooding over these telephone confrontations. Kane was not his usual ebullient and energetic self, but neither did he seem to be seriously depressed. Patricia had seen him despondent before, most worryingly the previous Christmas when he'd refused to see anyone or leave the house for almost two weeks. This wasn't anything like that. Since those dark days, Jesse had brightened his life and he was determined to be a better, more involved father than he had been with his other children. He was even making noises about giving up the biker life and starting fresh somewhere else.

More cryptically, he hinted that soon enough, perhaps in just weeks or months, he would have enough cash that neither he nor his children would ever have to work again. Indeed, that very Sunday he'd boasted to his family about how rich he would be. He'd told Gisèle that he would buy Josée the house in the country she wanted for herself and their children, and he'd promised his father a new pickup truck. They'd take a road trip to Florida together, just father and son, do some fishing.

Patricia interpreted his glum silence as passing cranki-ness. At one point in the evening she went in to see him. She lifted his legs off the couch, sat down, and then laid his feet in her lap.

"What's wrong?" she asked.

"Nothing," Kane replied in a cold voice.

Patricia rose to go back to the children.

"I'm sorry," he apologized. "It's not you."

"Do you want to talk about it?" Patricia asked.

"No."

Kane had arranged for his parents to drive Patricia and the boys to Montreal; at about eight-thirty, after a dinner of veal prepared by Patricia, Kane told her they were on their way over. Jean-Paul and Gemma Kane lived in St-Jean, just a few minutes away. Patricia packed an overnight bag and started tidying the living room, collect-ing the baby things that were scattered about. Kane told her not to bother. The next day was Monday, the day Gisèle, whom they paid for cleaning services, was due to visit.

Kane's parents arrived in the late-model VW Beetle that he had leased for his mother. They transferred to Kane's minivan, loaded the kids and Patricia and, after the son slipped his father $50 for gas, made for the city. The Sunday-night cottage-and-country-place traffic was heavy. It started to rain and there was congestion on the bridge connecting the South Shore to the island of Montreal. Patricia and the boys weren't dropped off until after ten, and Kane's parents didn't linger; by the time Kane called Patricia shortly after her arrival, they were well on their way back to St-Luc. Kane said he was call-ing to say good-night and to tell Patricia he loved her. But he seemed concerned to know when he could expect his parents at the house.

Jean-Paul and Gemma saw their son shortly after eleven, when they exchanged vehicles before heading home to their own beds. He was out on the front porch, sitting in a lawn chair. It wasn't a place he normally chose to relax, not with the inviting back garden available, but it seemed logical once he answered his parents' question concerning the whereabouts of his Mercedes 500 SEL. The car, which Kane had leased a month earlier, had been parked in his driveway when his parents came for Patricia. A friend had taken it for a drive, Kane said. He'd be back any minute.

Patricia went to sleep that night with an uneasy feeling, a sense that something was wrong. When Jesse, a sound sleeper from the age of two weeks, woke screaming in the middle of the night and remained inconsolable for half an hour, her apprehension was hardly relieved.

Before eight the next morning Patricia called the house and tried Kane's cellphones several times but could not reach him. She also paged twice, once affixing 911 to her number—their code for "Call me or else." Still no response. She assumed Kane had left the house early and was going about his business, too preoccupied to call. She would have liked to be sure, however, since a pool repair crew was scheduled to arrive shortly after nine. Leaving Jesse with her mother, Patricia and Steve headed back to St-Luc at about eight-thirty, driven by one of Kane's gang associates. She was both worried and annoyed.

At the house her irritation grew. She had asked Kane the night before to make sure the front door was not dead-bolted because she didn't have the key; all she carried was the device that opened the remote control lock. It didn't work. With Steve and the driver, Patricia marched around to the rear of the house to try the back door of the garage. Something was holding that door closed, but together they pushed it open just enough for Steve to squeeze through. As they did so, the household cat dashed past their feet and out. Patricia was struck by the smell of gas but thought it was Kane's motorcycle. The garage was eerily quiet, the Mercedes sitting silent. Then Steve cried out, *"Dany est tombé dans les pommes!"* Kane "had fallen in the apples"—he was unconscious in the car.

Patricia's driver forced the door farther, allowing her to slip inside. The Mercedes' windows were down. Kane was in the driver's seat in jeans and a white muscle shirt, his arms at his side, head back, leaning toward his right. He was rigid, and Patricia couldn't find a pulse. Still, he didn't feel cold and his skin was pinkish. She thought he might yet be resuscitated.

Patricia dialled 911 at 9:22, but not before sending Steve back to her mother's with the driver. Then, between pacing about the house, she made two telephone calls, one to Gemma Kane, the other to Patrick Lambert, the man who almost a decade before had introduced Kane to the world of outlaw bikers. Police and firefighters were the first to arrive at 9:27; the ambulance followed. No effort was made to revive Kane. Rather, after the briefest of examinations, the ambulance attendants told Patricia, *"Lui, il est fini."* He's gone.

Patricia soon found herself barred from the house. When the local St-Luc police plugged Kane's name into their computer, they discovered that he was associated with the Hells Angels and assumed he must have been involved in the violent gang war that had plagued Quebec, the Montreal area in particular, for more than six years. They did what any sensible small-town constabulary would do: they contacted the joint RCMP, Sûreté du Québec, and Montreal police task force that had been created to deal with the warring bikers.

With the special squad on its way, Patricia was taken to the St-Luc police station to give a statement and answer questions from both St-Luc police and Sûreté du Québec officers. The procedure took several hours and was not characterized by much compassion for her distress. Rather, Patricia remembers a mocking callousness from her interrogators. "Poor you. Your life is going to change now," they told her.

Afterwards she returned to the house but was allowed back in for barely five minutes, just long enough to be served with a warrant allowing the coroner and police to search the premises and "examine or seize any objects and documents considered pertinent." In the end they left with very little: a bill from the car dealer who held the Mercedes lease; the Mercedes itself; a ten-metre length of swimming pool hose that Kane had apparently tried to run from the car's exhaust pipe to one of its windows; a laptop computer; and a Jennings Model 48, a down-market .38-calibre semi-automatic pistol and its charger, which was jammed. Kane's body was transported by a local funeral home to the Montreal morgue for autopsy.

When Patricia was given full access to the house again at about 6:30 p.m., she knew exactly what to do, almost by reflex. Kane had told her often enough, since they first lived together almost four years before, that in the event of his death her first task was to go through all his possessions and separate out any item associated with the gang. Into two green garbage bags went T-shirts, patches, papers, photos, anything that connected Kane to either the Hells Angels or its affiliates the Rockers, the Evil Ones, the Demon Keepers, or the Road Warriors. Purge completed, Patricia placed a call to a member of the Rockers gang, who dispatched an underling to collect the bags that night.

That evening too, another Rocker telephoned her to discuss funeral arrangements. She didn't want a circus, a parade of patch-wearing bikers astride their Harleys and car after car of gaudy wreaths—a display that did double duty as a show of force as well as respect. She wanted something simpler, more intimate. Fulfilling her wishes wouldn't be a problem. Mom Boucher had already let it be known that Kane wasn't eligible for a lavish send-off. Dying by one's own hand precluded that.

The funeral, paid for by a senior member of the Rockers, was held the following Friday at the Lessieur et Frères funeral home in St-Luc. The chapel was crowded with the gaudy wreaths Patricia had dreaded, tributes from the Rockers de l'ouest and the *gars du nord,* from Kane's lawyer, Danièle Roy, and from Agence Aventure, Patrick Lambert's stripper agency. There was a respectable showing of bikers, though Mom Boucher didn't attend.

None of the bikers seemed to question the conclusion of suicide, despite the absence of an obvious motive. Since he had a new baby, a beautiful girlfriend, and what seemed a happy home life, it was assumed that financial pressures lay behind his death. In a culture as materialistic and money obsessed as the bikers', such an escape was comprehensible. At the funeral, a procession of bikers approached Patricia, Josée, and the family. They offered their condolences along with assurances that they would have helped Dany if only they'd known, if only he'd asked. The man Patricia took to be the loan shark who had lent the money that Kane had guaranteed also came forward. He said there were other ways that Dany could have worked things out, giving Patricia the distinct impression that the money had not been repaid.

The funeral was a closed-casket affair. Jean-Paul Kane had inquired about an open-coffin ceremony, the Québécois tradition, but was told by the mortician that his son's corpse was not in a state to be displayed. Likewise, the police had not allowed the family to view the body while it was in their custody, claiming its condition would upset them. "You don't want your last memory of him to be like that," they'd said. This explanation puzzled the Kanes: why, if he died of carbon monoxide poisoning, would his body be so *"magané,"* so disfigured? But they didn't insist. They were accustomed to submission in the face of authority. The family was also persuaded by Patricia—later they would say coerced—to cremate the body. Soon, all that was left of Dany Kane was a litre or so of ashes in a square red urn.

In the week following the funeral, Patricia and Gisèle sorted through those of Kane's effects that, in Patricia's words, "we didn't recognize or understand." Papers, letters, photos of strangers—all were piled into Gisèle's fireplace and burned. Among them were several cheques, including one from the government of Quebec to a company Patricia had never heard of for more than $500,000.

During that week too, Patricia was offered her pick of three Montreal apartments by the Rockers. They knew she couldn't keep up the mortgage payments of more than $1600 a month on the St-Luc property, and they understood she probably wouldn't want to stay there anyway. As the common-law widow of one of their own, Patricia would be looked after. She chose a high-ceilinged walk-up in Hochelaga-Maisonneuve, the east-end working-class neighbourhood that had bred Mom Boucher and had been one of the flashpoints of the biker war. While the apartment was being fixed up, Patricia and the boys stayed with her mother. On moving day, the gang organized a crew of hangers-on to do the heavy lifting. That was essentially the end of Patricia's contact with Dany's former world, and she didn't greatly mind.

Despite the lurid fascination of the Quebec media with the long-running biker war, Dany's death wasn't noted by the major daily newspapers or counted among the war's casualties. Only *Allô Police,* the weekly newsletter of Quebec's criminal community that was read as faithfully by cops as crooks, gave his passing any coverage. On the Friday of the funeral it ran a brief item buried on the inside pages, easily overlooked amid the eight pages devoted to the René Charlebois wedding. Ginette Reno and Jean-Pierre Ferland, two over-the-hill icons of Quebec song, had performed their standards. The photo that generated the most chatter was that of Reno being hugged by the province's foremost crime lord, Mom Boucher, looking smug in a tux.

Dany Kane was largely forgotten as the winter of 2000–2001 set in, dead and buried figuratively if not literally. The red urn was still in his parents' living room, the family too strapped to pay for a cemetery plot or headstone. Patricia went about her life on auto-pilot, focusing on her boys' well-being, not allowing herself time to grieve. Yet there were regular reminders of the world she'd recently left behind when the biker war burst back into the news. In the fall of 2000 a Montreal journalist was gunned down by a Hells Angels trigger man; a bar owner who refused to allow the gang's dealers to do business in his establishment was beaten to death; a special squad of prosecutors was created to go after the bikers, and there were almost weekly arrests of Hells Angels members and affiliates. These events brought consoling telephone calls from her mother, the essence of which were that maybe Dany had chosen a good time to go.

Then, in the spring, came the police sweep that would grant Kane an extraordinary, posthumous renown. Early in the morning of Wednesday, March 28, 2001, some two thousand officers from local, provincial, and federal forces descended on Quebec's Hells Angels and their associates. By the end of the day, 128 people had been arrested and millions of dollars in cash and assets seized or frozen. Virtually every member of the elite Nomads chapter and all the Rockers—the Hells Angels warrior units—were in jail. The scope and success of Opération Printemps 2001 (Operation Springtime) countered persistent criticism that the authorities had been soft on the Hells Angels or somehow even complicit in their crimes. In the deluge of newspaper stories that detailed almost every aspect of the operation in the days following, there was no shortage of police gloating.

One story, which appeared on page 10 of the March 30 edition of Quebec's largest circulation daily, the tabloid *Journal de Montréal,* revealed that an insider had provided the police with "dynamite" evidence against his former gang-mates before taking his own life eight months earlier. "Danny Boy" Kane, as he was identified, had given sworn videotaped testimony about the gang's illegal activities, and he had planted hidden microphones and cameras at their clubhouses and meeting places. The fact that Kane was deceased shouldn't jeopardize the prosecution's case, the *Journal* assured its readers: a recent Supreme Court of Canada decision had decreed that videotaped testimony provided by a witness who was "no longer available" was admissible in court. No source for the story was cited, but the information clearly originated with the police or Crown prosecutors.

The day the article appeared, Patricia was telephoned by either Gisèle or Josée—she can't remember whom. It wasn't a long conversation.

"Have you seen the *Journal*?" she was asked.

"No," she answered.

"Then go buy it."

The news that Kane had lived a double life was like a blow to the head. After the Opération Printemps 2001 sweep, Patricia had thought, like her mother, that the timing of Kane's death might have spared him from arrest, trial, and many years in prison. Now she didn't know what to think.

That same day a gang associate stopped by her apartment to ask if she had known that Dany was a police informant and agent.

"Hell, no!" she exclaimed, and the man had no trouble believing her. The shock of the revelation was still evident in her face.

In the days following, Gisèle repeatedly dialled the toll-free police hotline that existed to solicit tips concerning the biker war. She wasn't offering information, she was seeking it. She and her family wanted to know whether the story was true and what other surprises might await them. They made repeated and fruitless trips to SQ headquarters, hoping to see the police photos of their dead son and brother.

Finally, they were visited by Det. Sgt. Benoît Roberge and Cpl. Gaétan Legault, investigators with the joint anti-biker task force and Kane's handlers at the time of his death. They confirmed the story but little else. "The best thing you can do is find yourself professional help, a good therapist," Kane's mother remembers the cops telling them. "When it all comes out at trial, it will be painful."

The next day the two policemen delivered the same message to Patricia. They added that they had frequently tailed her without her knowledge, that they had often spoken to her on the phone without disclosing their identities. Dany, they said, had been "a good guy."

Good actor was more like it, she thought. Patricia found herself questioning virtually everything Kane had ever told her or led her to believe. The fact that he had been working for the police cleared up some mysteries: where his money came from; why he had always left the house so early in the day for unspecified appointments; what those hints of imminent wealth had been about. For his superstitious parents, it confirmed what a seer they had consulted after his death had been talking about. She had spoken of a secret at the centre of his life; now it was revealed.

As for Kane's suicide, however, the information aroused all sorts of new questions and revived more than a few nagging inconsistencies. When Patricia and Steve had made their way into the garage, the cat had run out. How had it survived? What was a silk pillow, recognized by no one, doing on the floor of the garage? Why was there a footprint halfway up the garage door? And why would a guy who was forever penning handwritten notes

to Patricia and his family decide to tap his suicide note
into a laptop computer he barely knew how to operate?
They wondered why Kane, in the days just before his
death, had bothered to keep a dentist's appointment, or
spent $650 to have the suspension of his driver's licence
lifted, or bought himself new in-line skates. Why had he
devoted so much time to the organization of Jesse's baptism, scheduled for August 27, and told family and friends
that he was going to propose formally to Patricia at the
event?

Patricia and the Kane family weren't alone in
wrestling with these puzzles. Some among his criminal
cohorts, many of them stewing in prison thanks to Kane,
thought his suicide a well-staged piece of police theatre
designed to protect an immensely valuable informant.
Such speculation was widely dismissed as the idle conjecture of a paranoid milieu. But the conjecture and the
theories didn't abate. As the Hells Angels lawyers bored
their way through the Crown's volumes of evidence,
Kane's complicated relationship with three police forces
was chronicled in exquisite, shocking, and damning detail,
arousing even more difficult questions about his mysterious
life and convenient passing.

THE
BEGINNING

The **strongest selling point** of the house that Dany Kane lived in during the last year of his life was its lot: more than forty-six hundred square metres, larger than a football field, dotted with mature evergreens and sloping down to a bend on L'Acadie River. The opposite bank, perhaps fifteen metres away, rises steeply and is more densely wooded. Largely undeveloped, that side has no easy access to the river. It all makes for a private and bucolic backyard for 18 Rue Letourneau where, during the warmer months, Kane conducted his business, strolling down to the river and standing by its bank with fellow gang members, his customers, and quite possibly his police handlers.

L'Acadie River had flowed through much of Kane's life. He was born in Greenfield Park, a suburb closer to Montreal, and his first home was about seven kilometres upstream from his last, in the small farming village of the same name, L'Acadie, itself named after the original Maritimes homeland of the Acadian people. In the late eighteenth century many of those once-exiled families flocked back from the United States, drawn to a place where their own language was dominant and to the most fertile farming land in Quebec.

Dany's mother, Gemma, was an Acadian from New Brunswick who migrated to the Montreal area almost two centuries after the Acadians were run out of Canada. There she met Jean-Paul Kane, who had grown up in a large family on the South Shore at a time when its rural villages could not have imagined their futures as Montreal's bedroom communities. By the latter half of the 1960s, however, when the couple settled down to start their family, the transformation was under way.

It was the time of Quebec's Quiet Revolution, ushering in the decline of the Catholic Church's power and the blossoming of secular culture and Québécois nationalism. Montreal was the movement's vibrant centre. After decades of cronyism, the city had elected a reformist mayor, and Expo 67, as the jingles put it, was bringing the world to town. L'Acadie and other towns around St-Jean-sur-Richelieu were just a short drive from Montreal's excitement but offered the security and familiarity of rural life.

The Kanes didn't have the leisure or the resources to enjoy many urban temptations. Jean-Paul Kane had to chase bricklaying work, and none of it paid well. Their eldest child, Jacqueline, was born in July 1967, at the height of Canada's Centennial celebrations. She was followed fifteen months later by a son, Daniel, known immediately as Dany. He was an energetic but not particularly difficult baby. Along with his sister Jackie, however, he made a handful, especially after Gemma became pregnant with a third child in 1972 and began suffering both physical and emotional problems.

Like any rambunctious four-year-old, Dany demanded a level of attention that Gemma and Jean-Paul didn't always have time to grant. When the idea of sending Dany to live with Jean-Paul's elder brother and his wife was proposed, it seemed the ideal solution. They were much more secure financially: Gérard Kane was a technician with Radio-Canada, the French-language arm of the Canadian Broadcasting Corporation, and his wife, Jeanne, taught elementary school. They lived nearby, in the suburb of Lemoyne, just over the Jacques-Cartier Bridge from downtown Montreal but near enough to L'Acadie that Dany could easily return home for weekends and holidays. Despite years of trying, Gérard and Jeanne were unable to have children of their own. They happily took in their lively nephew.

At Gérard and Jeanne's the material benefits were readily apparent. Dany was given his own room and didn't lack for toys or books. As the only child in the household, he was naturally doted on. And with regular weekend visits home, he had, it seemed, the best of both worlds. Locals in L'Acadie remember Dany eagerly tagging along after Jean-Paul as he went about his chores or completed brickwork contracts in the area.

Shuttling back and forth, young Dany could compare the life of relative ease enjoyed by his aunt and uncle with that of his parents, and he soon appreciated the differences that money could make. He saw that long hours of honest labour barely allowed his father to get by, an understanding that appears to have marked him. Years later, Kane would tell people how poor his parents had been and that he had to sleep on the couch when he came home on weekends. The seeds of an obsession with money—the more easily secured the better—had been planted.

Two or three years after Dany took up residence with Gérard and Jeanne, Gemma's health improved, and the baby, a daughter named Gisèle, was a healthy toddler. Family lore has it that when his parents suggested Dany could return home permanently, he chose to stay with Gérard and Jeanne. He would enjoy their indulgence for the next decade.

The couple treated Dany as their own, enrolling him in Scouts and swimming classes, taking him on expensive vacations, and providing him with everything he needed and most of what he wanted. Academically, however, he didn't shine, despite having a schoolteacher waiting for him at home. The problem had nothing to do with his intelligence or quickness and everything to do with his lack of self-discipline and aversion to authority. When Dany was ready for high school, Gérard and Jeanne registered him as a day student at a nearby private college. The increased regimentation was met with increased resistance. Under his uncle's watchful eye, Kane would depart the house in the morning in his school uniform. Once clear, he'd change into the casual clothes he'd hidden in his knapsack. At school, he smoked cigarettes and flouted the rules openly, simply as a show of defiance. To no one's surprise, he didn't last long and soon found himself at the local public high school, Polyvalente Monseigneur Alphonse-Marie Parent. The school offered various technical programs, and Kane studied printing, but he made little impression on his classmates. Slight and boyish, he wasn't involved in sports or drawn to extracurricular activities, and almost every weekend—thus, much of his social life—was spent back in L'Acadie.

It was at a community dance in L'Acadie in 1983 where Kane first encountered the girl with whom he was to have a volatile relationship for the rest of his life. Josée was thirteen at the time, Kane two years and two days older. They didn't talk that evening; they simply stole glances at each other. Enough mutual notice was taken, however, that recognized each other immediately when they met again almost two years later at the baseball diamond in L'Acadie. Josée and a group of girlfriends were playing an evening game of softball, with Josée's mother pitching. Chatting after the game as night slowly fell, Dany and Josée began making up for lost time. Short and skinny, Kane didn't look the stuff of schoolgirl fantasies. Josée didn't care. She was attracted to his energy and sense of fun; he made her laugh. His quick smile and bright blue eyes compensated for his diminutive stature. They shared eclectic tastes in music, everything from Kenny Rogers to Iron Maiden to the Québécois rocker Plume Latraverse. Then, of course, there was the motorcycle.

To the teenagers and young adults of L'Acadie, *bicyclettes à gaz,* as the older residents still call them, symbolized freedom far more than music, drugs, or education. As soon as they turned sixteen, most teenage boys traded their ten-speeds for small, starter motorcycles that transported them beyond the village and its suffocating confines and out over the straight country roads. Heading north and west, the motorcycles took them to the city, opening up all of Montreal's delights and dangers. South or east, they raced past the hills of Mont-Bruno and Mont-Ste-Hillaire, sitting on the flat farmland like loaves of bread on a table, and into the rolling Eastern Townships and the Adirondack chain.

Kane had a 250 cc Honda Rebel, bought for him by Gérard earlier that year. The bike was designed to look like a small Harley-Davidson, the bike of choice for North

American motorcycle gangs, and Kane carefully added Harley decals to further the illusion. It didn't have much in the way of horsepower; 250 cc Rebels are pushing their limit at a hundred kilometres an hour. Still, it was big enough for two restless teenagers, and Kane spent much of the summer beetling around the region with Josée clasped tightly behind.

In September Kane returned to Gérard and Jeanne's in Lemoyne. Though less than twenty kilometres from L'Acadie, it was a long-distance telephone call, so during the week Josée resorted to letters, page after page of rounded script, full of hearts and doodles. Kane didn't write back as often or as romantically, but he did return every weekend. During these visits he complained to Josée about his uncle's attempts at discipline and how they made him bristle.

Blow-ups were frequent and predictable: his performance at school, the state of his room, his taste in music, and the volume at which he listened to it. Drugs and alcohol weren't serious issues. Kane was asthmatic, and marijuana and hashish had never appealed to him, though, like his parents and sisters, he smoked cigarettes. As for drinking, he could nurse a single beer for hours. His antics at school—in particular his rebellion against rules of any kind—sparked the most rows. During one dispute with Gérard, Kane was asked why he couldn't be like other students. "I'm not like the others," he shouted, adding prophetically, "someday books will be written about me."

The situation in Lemoyne deteriorated, and before the school year was done, Kane was plotting to flee his uncle's home. He'd jump on the Rebel and head south. The American border was only seventy-five kilometres away, and beyond it was a new world, even for a unilingual francophone. But Kane couldn't keep his plans to himself and soon Gérard got wind of them and decided to force the point. If Dany didn't want to live with them, well, neither was he welcome any more. At the age of seventeen, Kane dropped out of school and moved back home to live with his parents.

Shortly after his return to L'Acadie, Jean-Paul and Gemma sold their house and moved into a trailer park. Camping des Cèdres, on the road out of L'Acadie toward Napierville, catered mainly to summer vacationers, but there were some year-round residents, and Dany, along with his parents and sisters, joined the group. Around this time, he concluded that he and Josée weren't cut out for each other—at least not exclusively for each other—and he ended their relationship. Three months later he had a change of heart, but Josée kept her distance. She was still in high school and serious enough about her studies that she planned to attend junior college and university. Dany, on the other hand, was intent on having fun—a lot of it, Josée suspected, with whoever came along.

Now that he had few fetters, the next twelve months were Dany's wild year. He worked with his father when Jean-Paul had a contract and Dany couldn't avoid it, which meant he didn't work much at all. He partied as often as possible, and used recreational drugs as heavily as he ever would. They weren't hard to find: Jacqueline's boyfriend was a dealer and an enthusiastic user himself, not that Kane had to be coaxed. He paid for his vices by committing the odd house burglary. These were small-time jobs and infrequent enough that he was never caught; neither did he make much money from them.

So when he developed a particular fondness for cocaine, it wasn't long before he found himself deeply in debt. The situation was serious enough that he had to ask his parents to bail him out, something they could hardly afford to do. But Kane seems to have learned his lesson: he wouldn't have problems with street drugs or alcohol ever again.

After that episode, Kane slowed his pace slightly, and in the fall of 1987 Dany and Josée got back together. He sent her a birthday card, she phoned to thank him, and one thing led to another. It didn't concern Josée's parents. Even though Kane was two years older and a high-school dropout without a job or any obvious interest in holding one, they found his charm and sense of humour endearing. From the start they had let Josée go out more often and stay out later as long as she was with Dany. He had won them over with his good-natured banter and willingness to laugh at himself. At five foot seven and barely 130 pounds fully dressed, Kane was obsessed with becoming bigger, stronger, more formidable. Her parents would poke fun at him when he assured them that one day he'd acquire the muscles. "How? By mail order?"

Josée finished high school in the spring of 1988 and that fall headed off to study literature and film at a junior college in northeast Montreal. She and a friend took an apartment together. Dany, still living at his parents' house, only sporadically employed, was a regular visitor. It was an exciting year, marred to a small degree by a burglary at the apartment in which Josée and her roommate lost all their possessions of any value.

The following September, appreciating that living with her parents was not only safer but cheaper, Josée decided she would commute to the college from L'Acadie, a drive of an hour each way. Dany found a place of his own in the village of St-Jacques-le-Mineur, a two-street farming community about ten kilometres southwest of L'Acadie. The village was dominated by an imposing grey stone church, complete with adjoining cemetery. Dany struck a deal with the owner of a small house directly across from the graveyard. He would rent it with an option to buy when his finances permitted. The couple would soon need their own home: Josée became pregnant that fall. She soldiered on with most of her college courses, driving the winter roads with her bulging belly crowding the steering wheel.

Josée's condition wasn't a novelty to the Kane family. Dany's younger sister, Gisèle, had given birth to a child the previous February, just days after she turned sixteen. Jackie followed with her first less than a year later, when Josée was in her fifth month. Jean-Paul and Gemma, both in their forties, were quickly being surrounded by grandchildren. Financially or otherwise they weren't in a position to help greatly, although their situation improved when Jean-Paul landed a full-time job as a mason at the Canadian Forces Base in St-Jean. The days of living from contract to contract, from hand to mouth, were behind them, at least for a while.

Josée's parents had always been more comfortable. For years her father had worked at Tissus et fibres d'Amoco, a textile and thread plant in an industrial area of St-Jean. Seeing that Dany would soon have a child—his grandchild—to support, Josée's father put in a good word on his behalf at Amoco. Soon Dany was on the shop floor, minding a thread-making machine. It looked as if he and Josée would follow the path taken by countless young working-class couples before them: an unplanned pregnancy leading to reduced expectations, truncated schooling, thwarted ambitions, and a lifetime of factory employment.

Josée was well into her eighth month when her final college course ended. Dany was living in the St-Jacques-le-Mineur house with his first Harley, a 1946 knucklehead model, temporarily parked in what was to be the baby's room and awaiting a bright yellow paint job. Josée stayed at her parents', planning to join Dany shortly after the baby's birth. That event came in June 1990, at a hospital in Montreal. Dany attended, along with what seemed like a small mob of doctors, residents, and medical students. One of them was black and Dany raised a fuss. He had displayed his share of small-town bigotry in the past, but on this occasion it was resisted. Kane backed down.

They named the child Benjamin. With the baby doing well, they became a family under one roof in the house in St-Jacques-le-Mineur. But gazing out her window at the graveyard every day didn't elevate Josée's postpartum spirits. She was isolated in the village. St-Jean-sur-Richelieu might be a mere twenty-minute drive away along country roads, but it was too far for most of her friends. None had children, nor were they interested in training for them. Tiny St-Jacques offered few distractions and little opportunity for friendships. The village had a credit union, a butcher shop, a seed dealership, and a *dépanneur*, the community's social hub. There gossip was traded as briskly as beer, chips, and lottery tickets. The new couple in town—she so young and *flayée,* he away so much of the time—proved as fertile a subject for chatter and speculation as the surrounding fields were for corn. Josée, just eighteen, hated it.

So when Dany lost his job after telling his boss that he wasn't interested in weaving a lifelong career out of thread, and the couple could no longer afford the rent on the little house, Josée was hardly heartbroken. Nor was she surprised when, newly unemployed, he began gravitating ever closer to the Condors, a motorcycle gang based in the nearby South Shore suburb of St-Hubert. For as long as she had known Dany, the only real ambition he had ever expressed was to be a biker, ideally a Hells Angel.

THE BIKER
DRAW

The late 1980s were an odd time for a Québécois to be nursing a desire to join the world's most notorious motorcycle gang. Nowhere were the Hells Angels in such disarray as they were in Quebec in those years.

The gang had arrived in the province in 1977, when the Popeyes, a Montreal-area club that enjoyed enough of a reputation to be noticed and sponsored by the New York chapter of the Hells Angels, was "patched over," or absorbed by the larger organization. Like virtually all motorcycle gangs in North America, the Popeyes had formed in the post-war era of complacency and conformity, though unlike many of the Hells Angels founders, its members were not disgruntled repatriated servicemen looking to recapture the thrills and camaraderie of war. Rather, they were overwhelmingly working-class youth kicking against the constraints of a stifling society.

In some respects, the Popeyes had the least cause for rebellion among the dozens of motorcycle gangs that were established in Quebec in the 1950s and 1960s. Montreal had long boasted a vibrant demimonde of brothels, illegal gaming houses, and nightclubs open to anyone so inclined. Elsewhere in the province such temptations were scarce or non-existent. For clubs like the Missiles of the Saguenay–Lac-St-Jean area, the Gitans and the Atomes of the Eastern Townships, or the Drageurs and the Flambeurs of the Laurentians, the environment was more suffocating, and the thrills—legal or otherwise— were harder to come by.

All of Quebec's gangs owed a creative debt to the early outlaw bikers, especially the Hells Angels, who had emerged amid a blaze of sensational media attention in California in the immediate post-war years. This debt was acknowledged through the aesthetic, the rituals, and, frequently, the names of the Quebec clubs. How else could a francophone club from the Quebec City region come by the moniker Pacific Rebels? Or a club from Havre-St-Pierre call itself the Beatniks?

For shock value more than anything else, many American bikers appropriated images and references from Nazi Germany. Some Quebec gangs followed suit: the Missiles displayed a giant swastika flag on the wall of their clubhouse, and the east-end Montreal gang, which was to spawn both Mom Boucher and the Rock Machine's founder, Salvatore Cazzetta, called itself the SS. But other clubs put a peculiarly Québécois stamp on the outlaw biker template, one that reflected the spirit of the times. The flourishing of biker gangs in the province coincided with the rise of militant Québécois nationalism and the whole-sale rejection of a Church- and anglo-dominated society. While the intellectual class embraced international libera-tion struggles abroad and the *indépendentiste* movement at home, some of their working-class contemporaries joined biker gangs in a no less fervent, if less well articulated, protest against the established order. One intriguing if short-lived motorcycle club attempted to bridge the divide.

Les Citoyens de la terre—Comrades of the Earth—roared around the Île d'Orléans, east of Quebec City, fuelled by drugs, alcohol, and revolutionary Marxist rhetoric. Their leader, Raymond Cardinal, called himself Che Raymond.

Les Citoyens was just one of hundreds of independent motorcycle clubs established in Quebec and Canada in the 1950s, '60s, and '70s, one of thousands across North America. The dominant mythology for all these clubs was that of the free man, unshackled by career, family, or conventional values, refusing to conform, doing whatever he wanted whenever he wished. The archetypes that outlaw bikers were compared to and often appropriated for themselves came from other, epic ages—marauding Vikings, the Mongol hordes, pirates, and gunslingers of the Wild West.

The single institution that demanded unquestioned loyalty was the club itself. As the anthropologist Daniel Wolf wrote in his remarkable study of one biker gang, *The Rebels: A Brotherhood of Outlaw Bikers,* "If one chooses to view the club as a form of social mutiny, then the brotherhood is its cause." The club came first for every member; otherwise, it wasn't worth signing up. Obligations to wives, children, friends, or employers were no excuse for failure to appear at meetings or join group motorcycle trips or "runs," or hang around the clubhouse. The irony that individualistic bikers joined a club with often rigid rules and a highly formal hierarchy in order to flout the norms of the larger society was usually lost on them. When it wasn't, such contradictions were dismissed as a small price to pay for the support and brotherhood offered by an organization of like-minded iconoclasts.

In most clubs, aspirants started as "friends" before graduating to "hangarounds." These stages were the biker club's equivalent of boot camp, during which initiates proved their dedication by, in Wolf's words, "being willing to do just about anything he's asked to do … without bitching." In some clubs this meant performing cleaning chores or running errands; for more criminalized gangs, it could mean committing crimes as serious as murder. Only then, perhaps several years later, was a biker considered for "striker" status, given his "patch" and allowed to wear the colours of the gang on his jacket. In some clubs, striker is the last rank before full member; in others, such as the Hells Angels, there is also the "prospect" rung to climb. Each of these stages almost invariably required a full year's service.

It's an arcane organizational structure, and in the early years one such hierarchy was usually enough. Few clubs had more than a chapter or two, confined to well-delineated territories, and most were unknown outside their province or state. There was contact between gangs, of course, but these were largely social relationships and limited to club runs, motorcycle shows, field days, or parties. In the late 1960s and early '70s, however, several American gangs expanded their territory by either opening new chapters or absorbing independent clubs. To a large degree, this expansion was spurred by the increasing criminalization of the biker milieu and the inevitable conflicts over drug and prostitution turf.

Originally, outlaw motorcycle gangs were just what many of their spokesmen still claim them to be: special-interest social clubs not all that unlike the Elks or the Lions. Their criminality, if any, wasn't institutionalized or structural; rather, it varied from member to member. The "outlaw" qualifier had as much to do with their image as their actions. One biker might deal pot or hash to supplement the paycheque from the plant. Another might fence stolen goods. Often, bikers exploited their own intimidating image and reputation by renting themselves out as muscle to organized crime for debt collection or extortion purposes, not to mention security to rock stars and other celebrities.

Gradually, as the potential for profit from a burgeoning drug culture became apparent and the realization took hold that working for criminal organizations was much less lucrative than running them, many outlaw gangs began to shift their focus from wild partying and hard living to the business of crime. They found their structure perfectly designed for it. The clubs were inclined to a simplistic insularity that dictated that all fellow gang members were above suspicion while everyone else was untrustworthy until proven otherwise. They held straight society and its values in contempt, and above all, they had no time for police. Whether they were perpetrators or victims of crime, they settled their own scores. Under no circumstances was an outlaw biker allowed to cooperate with the state justice system.

In the late 1960s and first half of the '70s, the only Canadian club with anything close to a national renown was the Satan's Choice. Founded in 1965 to resist the predatory ambitions of a now-forgotten Toronto club, Satan's Choice grew to include ten chapters within five years. Only one of these was outside southern Ontario, and it wasn't far, hailing from west-end Montreal. There had been short-lived chapters in British Columbia as well as western and northern Ontario, however, giving the Choice the highest profile of any outlaw motorcycle club in the country.

Testament to this was the fact that the Hells Angels, who themselves had only a dozen or so chapters, sent an emissary north to discuss a merger of the two clubs in 1968. The Choice, perhaps reflecting a growing Canadian nationalism, met the Hells Angels delegate at the Toronto airport, listened to his pitch, rejected it, and sent him on his way.

The Choice's confidence and cohesion didn't last. Ontario police cracked down hard on the gang in the 1970s, using methods legal and less so. Its founder and charismatic leader, Bernie Guindon, was jailed, and no succeeding club president was able to fill his boots. Many of the gang's aging riders decided it was time to settle down and go straight—or relatively so. Finally, internal tensions boiled over when members of one chapter were hoodwinked by two newspaper reporters into cooperating on an intimate and damning profile of the club. By the spring of 1977, only the chapters in the Toronto area continued to wear the Satan's Choice patch. Windsor, St. Catharines, Hamilton, and Ottawa had switched over to the Outlaws, American rivals of the Hells Angels, who had also been looking north to establish outposts. The Montreal chapter, sensing the inevitable, patched over to the Outlaws as well.

The Popeyes took notice. Overwhelmingly francophone, they were based in the area to the east and north of downtown Montreal known as the Plateau. The Choice-turned-Outlaws were in St-Henri, south and west of the downtown, and in the suburbs referred to collectively as the West Island. They were largely anglophone. Relations between the two gangs had never been cordial and had grown uglier as the 1970s progressed. When the Popeyes saw their cross-town competition merge with an expanding

American club, they decided that the best way to ensure their own survival was to follow suit. The Hells Angels, whose expansion drive had seen their chapter tally triple since 1969, were happy to welcome the Popeyes on board. On December 5, 1977, Canada got its first Hells Angels chapter.

The Popeyes were already considered to be among the harder core of the biker community. While their business operations were limited primarily to drug dealing and petty crime such as burglaries and car theft, several members had displayed a disturbing capacity for murder. Chief among these was a Popeye founder, the short, slight, and deadly Yves "Apache" Trudeau. In the early 1970s he had shot and killed at least four men who had crossed him or the gang.

Other members had taken to using dynamite as a score-settling weapon of choice. The benefits of their bomb making were debatable: by the time of their patch-over, the Popeyes had done as much damage to themselves as their enemies with explosives. "Tiny" Richard, a future national president of the Hells Angels in Canada, had lost an eye and been permanently disabled by a bomb that went off as he was assembling it. Two other Popeyes fared even worse: they were killed by the premature detonation of a bomb that was intended for Montreal's subway system, a protest against the prison conditions of colleagues who were doing time. Nonetheless, these incidents did little to diminish the gang's enthusiasm for explosives. Dynamite would continue to be the Quebec Hells Angels' favourite way to send a message almost two decades later.

The absorption of Montreal's Satan's Choice by the Outlaws and the Popeyes by the Hells Angels only escalated the hostilities between them. Apache Trudeau alone murdered another seventeen people, most of them rival bikers, over the next four years, during which time the Outlaws largely faded from the scene. The Quebec Hells Angels won themselves a reputation as the wildest of the wild in the annals of Canadian organized crime and throughout the gang's expanding worldwide network.

Some of that expansion occurred in Quebec itself, when the Montreal chapter found itself overflowing with members after recruiting the best—that is, the most ruthless—bikers from other clubs in the region. Pressured by police to relocate from their downtown clubhouse, they divided into two chapters in September 1979, one based in Sorel on the South Shore, the other in the northern suburb of Laval. Most of the original Montreal members ended up in the northern chapter, where they were soon at odds with their Sorel brothers.

Bad debts and personality conflicts caused some of the friction, but there was also a deeper philosophical divide over what it meant to be a Hells Angel. The Laval chapter embodied the nihilistic archetype—living for the moment, not worrying about the future, consuming copious amounts of drugs, and having no qualms about selling their murderous services to the highest bidder. The Sorel members were much more in tune with the club's evolving operating model—a vertically and horizontally integrated organized crime outfit with a specialization in drugs and prostitution but an interest in anything that could make them money.

The first major conflict occurred in early 1982 when Denis "Le Curé" (The Priest) Kennedy, a Laval member with a heavy cocaine habit, found himself heavily in debt to Frank "Dunie" Ryan, a leader of Montreal's largely Irish West End Gang and one of Canada's major drug lords at the time. Kennedy, like Trudeau a prolific killer, concocted a scheme to kidnap one of Ryan's children and then turn around and use the ransom money to pay off his debt to Ryan. Rumours of the hare-brained plan reached Ryan, who ordered several friendly Hells members, eager to maintain good relations with a major importer, to take care of Kennedy and his accomplices. In short order, Kennedy and three others were executed and their bodies disposed of in the Quebec Hells trademark manner: wrapped in sleeping bags and chains, weighted down with concrete blocks, and dumped into the St. Lawrence River.

After the housecleaning, the Sorel chapter tried to restore order by pushing through a bylaw decreeing that cocaine could be bought and sold but not snorted by Quebec's Hells Angels. This attempt to bring the Laval chapter to heel was ignored; its members voted among themselves to allow cocaine use.

No member's appetite for coke was more prodigious than Apache Trudeau's, and his killing rampage kept pace. Over the next three years he took part in the murders of at least eighteen more victims. Some were rival bikers or drug dealers, some were former accomplices whose silence he wanted to ensure. Some were executed at the behest of the West End Gang, for whom the Laval chapter had resumed contract work after getting rid of Kennedy. None of the deaths was of great concern to the police: they were seen as settlings of accounts among people who had chosen a dangerous lifestyle and ended up paying for it.

Trudeau's conduct was unsettling to other Hells Angels, though. On November 13, 1984, Dunie Ryan was killed by a rival in his own mob. The rival foolishly bragged about it, and less than two weeks after the murder, Trudeau was engaged by Ryan's lieutenant, Allan "the Weasel" Ross, to exact revenge. He delivered a booby-trapped TV and VCR to the man at his high-rise hideout near the Montreal Forum. The terms of the contract Trudeau had negotiated with Ross were generous: $200,000 cash and the erasure of a $300,000 debt owed by various Laval chapter members. But after the bomb went off, killing the intended target and three other men, Ross told Trudeau that he wouldn't pay anything beyond the $25,000 already advanced. Trudeau, he said, could collect the balance from debts owed to Ryan at the time of his death by the Sorel Hells Angels and Halifax's 13th Tribe, a club that was on the verge of becoming Atlantic Canada's first Hells Angels chapter.

The Sorel Hells told Trudeau to forget it, but he managed to extract about $100,000 from the Halifax bikers before they complained in early 1985. The 13th Tribe were by then full-patch Hells Angels. Hells Angels weren't supposed to lean on other Hells Angels—this was a brotherhood. The Sorel chapter could only agree; indeed, they decided that Trudeau's behaviour and that of the whole Laval chapter could no longer be tolerated. They were causing too much trouble, and with two new chapters up and running—in Halifax and in Sherbrooke where the Gitans had been patched over—they were dispensable.

The word went out that in late March 1985 there was to be a Hells gathering at the Sherbrooke chapter's large clubhouse in the nearby university town of Lennoxville. All members of the four eastern Canadian chapters were directed to attend the meeting and subsequent party. In reality, what was scheduled was a massacre. At least six

Laval members were slated for summary execution, including Apache Trudeau. Two others were to be forcibly retired and another two offered membership in the Sorel chapter. The Laval chapter, less than five years old, was to be dissolved, a bad experiment terminated.

Suspecting trouble, or simply too wasted to make the 150-kilometre trip to Lennoxville, most of the Laval members were no-shows on Saturday, March 23; only three of those on the hit list turned up. The meeting was put off for a day while the missing bikers were contacted and told their attendance was mandatory. On Sunday, a couple of the absentees arrived, but Trudeau was not among them. A week earlier he had checked himself into a detox centre in Oka, Quebec, after a cocaine binge that even he had determined was excessive.

The targeted Laval members were dispensed with by gunfire as they entered the clubhouse for the afternoon meeting. Those slated for retirement or reassignment to the Sorel crew were given their options at gunpoint. The bodies were dumped in the Hells Angels' usual grave—the St. Lawrence—and over the next week the Laval clubhouse and the dead bikers' apartments were emptied, the loot divided among the three remaining chapters. Contracts were put out on Apache Trudeau and another Laval biker who had stayed away. Outside of the Hells Angels, no one knew for certain that the massacre had occurred until early June, when the bodies began floating to the surface.

The ensuing media coverage was exhaustive and ghoulish, with Quebec's crime tabloids taking every opportunity to print the police photos of the bloated, decomposing corpses. The Hells had always made good copy but never as good as this. Never before had an entire chapter been wiped out; never before had bikers been so cold-blooded with their own.

Police and prosecutors figured out what had happened in short order but struggled to make their case until they persuaded Trudeau and a gang prospect to inform against their brothers. Charges were laid in October 1985. Then, four months later, another Hells Angel, one who had actually witnessed the massacre, agreed to testify. The Crown's case was finally solid.

The resulting trials would take several years to wend their way through the courts, all of the proceedings assiduously chronicled by *Le Journal de Montréal* as well as the crime weeklies *Allô Police* and *Photo Police*. Those publications were the reading material that Dany Kane had been raised on. They seem to have provided him with not only information and entertainment but also inspiration.

CONDORS, KIDS, AND
A STRETCH IN THE CAN

The Condors were a small club with none of the history or profile of the Popeyes, the Gitans, or the Satan's Choice. It had formed in the early 1980s, a period when the number of clubs in Quebec was in freefall. The best estimates suggest that 350 motorcycle clubs operated in the province at the end of the 1960s; twenty years later, fewer than a tenth of that number were in existence.

The decline was part of a continent-wide trend and one analogous to the shakeouts that occur in many young industries. In the car business, dozens of independent manufacturers sprang up in North America in the first two decades of the twentieth century; by the outbreak of the Second World War, the Big Three—General Motors, Chrysler, and Ford—had squashed or swallowed almost all the competition. Similarly, the motorcycle gangs were being rationalized into oligopolies.

New clubs such as the Condors were allowed to exist only because they were affiliated from the start with one of the Big Three of the biker world—the Hells Angels, the Outlaws, or the younger, Texas-based Bandidos. They were the equivalents of wholly owned subsidiaries, satellite units serving specific functions or territories. The Condors belonged to the Hells Angels, and their assignment was to extend the gang's control over drug distribution on the South Shore.

Although the police raided their clubhouse in 1984 and again in 1991, the Condors are not remembered for much more than bar fights by the cops who worked their area. They were regarded as relatively tame compared with the Hells Angels, who were dominating the headlines at the time. "They didn't give us much trouble," says a veteran St-Hubert detective who began working in the area in the early 1980s. "They were just a bunch of guys with motorbikes."

In fact, whether the police knew it or not, the Condors controlled a substantial share of the street-level drug trade on the South Shore and in the towns and villages that extended south to the American border. One of their most effective dealers was Patrick Lambert, also from the St-Jean-sur-Richelieu and L'Acadie area. Kane and Josée had known Lambert for several years by 1990, during which time he had been building his drug-dealing enterprise within the gang's territory. Josée first met him when she was in Grade 10 and on her way to an Iron Maiden concert in Montreal with a friend. The friend had arranged that Lambert give them a lift into the city, but when they arrived at his house, they weren't the only visitors: it was being turned upside down by police. The girls missed the show.

Lambert became a frequent presence in Josée's and Dany's lives as well as a fixture in the bars and clubs of St-Jean. He was instantly recognizable, with long dark hair worn loose and falling over his face. Soft-spoken and very guarded, he was in many ways the antithesis to

Kane—which may well have accounted for the pair's easy friendship.

That friendship was strong enough that when Kane lost his job at Tissus et fibres d'Amoco, Lambert offered him another. This was no entry-level position, serving as an on-the-spot dealer in one of the bars where Lambert controlled drug sales, but a supervisor's job, going from bar to bar, making sure the frontline dealers had the inventory they needed and collecting the money they owed to Lambert. Kane was paid a weekly salary of $700 for what amounted to three nights of work. The arrangement lasted for six months while Kane developed his own sales territory in the small towns south of St-Jean-sur-Richelieu, in places like Napierville, Sherrington, Bedford, and Lacolle, on the Quebec–New York border. In time, Kane controlled the drug sales in six or seven bars, buying his supply—overwhelmingly cocaine—from Pat Lambert and distributing it to his own network of dealers. Kane also cultivated a few private clients who would contact him by pager.

This arrangement was much more profitable: before long, he was clearing an average of $3000 every week. It allowed for some indulgences. Kane bought the first of a string of flashy cars, and he was able to hire an associate to drive him on his rounds. He was licensed to drive a motorbike but not a car, and during his months working for Lambert, the chauffeuring had fallen to Josée. She would spend long Thursday, Friday, and Saturday evenings ferrying her common-law husband from one small-town bar to the next in their Hyundai Pony, Benjamin strapped in his car seat in the back. The winter months were the worst. Josée spent interminable hours huddled in the Pony in bar parking lots, the little car's engine never squeezing out quite enough heat, while Dany attended to his affairs inside.

The drug business was, of course, more lucrative and interesting than operating a thread-making machine, and it required different talents. Kane had to be authoritative and intimidating, the better to dissuade those who might be tempted to stiff or cheat him. To encourage respect and instill fear, Kane had started taking steroids in 1989, transforming his physique from scrawny street punk to bulked-up fireplug. He also took to carrying a handgun and letting it be known he was armed. Even so, he ran into problems with people who wouldn't or couldn't pay. In such cases, he had to stand his ground: a dealer who lets too many debts slide for no good reason tends to see his receivables mount quickly and insolvency loom almost as fast. On several occasions, Kane went beyond threats to blows and beatings. Once, having seen it done on television, he stuck his handgun in a man's mouth and threatened to blow his head off if he didn't produce the money Kane said he owed.

Kane not only owned a handgun during this period, he also dealt in them. He obtained the weapons from an ever-widening circle of contacts in the border area and on the nearby Kahnawake Mohawk reserve, a long-established conduit for illegal firearms smuggled in from the United States. He sold to whoever wanted a gun and had the money. By his own admission, Kane may have retailed as many as fifty in the early 1990s, mostly machine guns and silencer-equipped handguns, pocketing a profit of $300 or $400 on every one.

Guns were not his only enthusiasm. In 1992 the Bar Delphis, an isolated biker hangout just north of St-Luc, found itself on the wrong side of Kane and the Condors.

Réal "Tintin" Dupont, the bar's owner, had long been
hostile to the Hells, and that spring he paid the consequences. Perhaps Dupont kicked out one of the Condor's
dealers; perhaps he was letting a dealer from a rival gang
sell drugs on his premises; perhaps the Hells had just
lost patience. Whatever the reason, sometime around
midnight on May 2, Kane dynamited the empty bar and
burned it to the ground. It never reopened.

The incident apparently instilled an interest in explosives in Kane and a fascination with their power. Later,
through a contact who was in the Canadian Forces at the
Valcartier base near Quebec City, he bought 4.5 kilos of
C4 plastic explosive, paying $5000 for the lot. He had no
particular plans for it; he simply thought it might come in
handy or, at the very least, that he might make a good
profit selling it. Curious about its force, Kane conducted
tests with small amounts of the C4 in the countryside near
St-Jean that summer, storing the rest in Josée's fridge.

Dany and Josée were living apart, at least nominally,
at this time. Josée and their son, Benjamin, occupied an
apartment in a twelve-unit complex in St-Jean where
she acted as the building's superintendent and lived
more or less rent-free. Dany shared a house in L'Acadie
with two fellow Condors and an older man, Robert
Grimard, who'd had some run-ins with the authorities
and was considered by his neighbours as the village's
criminal element. Their separation had its practical
aspects: Kane worked late and Benjamin woke early. It
also allowed Josée, who saw very little of the revenue
that Dany's drug and arms dealing generated, to collect
more in welfare payments as a single mother on her
own. Still, they were a couple in their minds and in the

eyes of their community. And in the summer of 1992, Josée was pregnant again, expecting in November.

Kane had always been outgoing and gregarious to the point of recklessness in the eyes of his family. He would strike up a conversation with anyone, instantly become a pal, and invite the person home, no matter how marginal he was or how questionable his character. Kane's new line of work brought him into contact with a steady stream of people around whom most others would steer a very wide path.

In the summer of 1992, he brought two young hoods, Martin Giroux and Eric Baker, around to Josée's apartment. Even by the low standards of Kane's crowd, she could see the pair weren't trustworthy. After they left, she told Dany that she didn't want the men in her home again and suggested that he might want to limit his dealings with them. He brushed off her concerns.

If the two weren't welcome at Josée's, the door at Robert Grimard's place in L'Acadie was wide open. That's where, in late August, Baker and Giroux were shown an impressive arsenal of weapons belonging to the Condors living there. The two nineteen-year-olds promptly conspired to steal the guns, an easily executed theft. The firearms—about twenty of them, including at least one machine gun—were in a hockey bag that the men simply had to retrieve from its hiding place under a stairway after letting themselves into the house when no one was around. Selling the guns was a more difficult proposition. Baker and Giroux tried to fence them in St-Jean, but potential buyers weren't interested. Instead, the two were advised that they had done something very stupid and their best course of action was to return the loot.

Just hours after stealing the guns, Baker and Giroux returned to 514 Chemin des Bouleaux in L'Acadie with the hockey bag and its contents. By this time, however, the theft had been discovered, and Kane, Grimard, and two other men, including Condor Louis David, were waiting for them. Baker hightailed it across a nearby cornfield and escaped; Giroux was caught and, after some manhandling, told that he would suffer much worse if he didn't help Kane and his friends get their hands on Baker.

It took five days, but Baker was finally located in the nearby town of Laprairie. There, in the middle of the afternoon, he was grabbed off the street, shoved into Grimard's car, and driven to an isolated sandpit near Napierville for his comeuppance. First Kane shot him in the right leg, the bullet passing through into the left. Then, according to Baker, Kane put the gun barrel against his head but at such an angle that when he pulled the trigger the bullet just grazed his skull. (According to Kane, the gun went off accidentally while he was pistol-whipping Baker.) Throughout, Kane terrorized him by asking his accomplices if he should kill Baker; were it up to him, he said, he would.

By this time, Louis David and another man, identified as Richard Proulx, had arrived at the quarry in a separate car. They took over Baker's beating. David twisted one of Baker's arms behind his back until it broke. Proulx attacked him with a stick, opening a wound near an eye. They tried to burn his face on a campfire, but Baker wriggled away from the coals. Proulx then opted for humiliation over pain and urinated in Baker's face.

Kane stepped in again. "Should I shoot him? There's one bullet left," he said, according to Baker. But one of the others pointed out there were too many witnesses, so

Kane backed off. Finally, after forcing Baker to the ground, both Kane and David revved their car engines and made as if to run him over. They braked just in time. It seemed that was enough, and the others piled into the cars and drove off, leaving Baker in the sandpit.

It took more than an hour of crawling and stumbling, but Baker was able to reach the nearest house a little more than a kilometre away. Covered in blood, he asked for help but pleaded with the residents not to alert the police. Kane's last words to Baker were to forget his tormenters' names, and Baker seemed prepared to do just that. But the homeowner wasn't having any of it and called the Sûreté du Québec at once. Baker eventually spent two weeks in hospital receiving treatment for bullet wounds, the broken arm, cracked ribs, and a shattered eardrum, and many cuts and bruises. He resisted cooperating with the police and said he didn't want charges laid for fear of what might happen next time.

Police already had a good idea who was involved. An unmarked car had been tailing Grimard's vehicle the day that Baker was grabbed, and the officers had witnessed his abduction. However, they claimed to have lost track of the car as it headed toward the Napierville sandpit. Offered police protection, Baker at last agreed to testify, and two weeks after the kidnapping and beating, Kane and his cohorts were arrested.

The arrest warrant allowed police to search Grimard's house, where they discovered and seized the guns that had prompted the whole affair, as well as explosives, a remote-control detonating device, and other bomb-making equipment. The police neglected to raid Josée's apartment simultaneously, and by the time they appeared at her door she had done her housekeeping. The C4, assorted guns, and the scales and cutting powder Kane used for weighing and diluting cocaine had been stashed in an empty unit in Josée's building.

Only Proulx, the urinator, was given bail. The others were held in the St-Jean jail. After a month during which their lawyers haggled with the prosecutor, Kane, Grimard, and another man, Daniel Audet, agreed to plead guilty to most of the charges against them as long as the most serious, attempted murder, was withdrawn. Grimard and Audet, who seems to have been along just for the ride, were given ten and a half months for kidnapping, forcible confinement, and conspiracy. Kane was portrayed as the ringleader. He had used his firearm and so was given two years less a day for the same charges, plus assault and using a firearm in the commission of a crime. All received three years' probation in addition to their sentences; Kane was ordered not to possess guns or explosives for at least five years.

Josée wasn't much disturbed by Dany's imprisonment. Since she had given birth to Benjamin and Dany had become involved with the Condors, their relationship had deteriorated. Her weight had ballooned with the baby, reaching almost two hundred pounds, and losing it was difficult. Kane was hardly sympathetic. In the past, they had regularly gone out together, often to ogle motorcycles at stores like Bob Chopper or browse the bike shows in the region. But after the baby's birth, he refused to take her anywhere and at one point pressed her to try a slimming product from the same dubious source who supplied him with steroids, a Condor who ran a gym. The weight-loss drug was really a veterinary medicine for horses, and it made Josée so shaky that after a day and a half she couldn't even hold a pen.

More corrosive to their relationship was Kane's increasing crankiness and ill temper when he was with her. As a hangaround of the Condors, Kane was ordered about constantly and given whatever distasteful task had to be done, such as cleaning toilets, fetching drinks, and doing guard duty while the other members partied. There were also jobs related to the gang's criminal activities, including intimidation, assault, and the like—lessons in what was expected of him if he was to become a bona fide biker. As far as the Condors were concerned, he was at the bottom of their heap and was kicked around as part of an extended initiation rite and as a test of his mettle and commitment. Below Kane, however, was Josée, and the inevitable resentment of his daily humbling at the hands of the Condors was regularly vented on her. She compares it to an avalanche, "and I was at the bottom of it."

Nonetheless, when Kane asked Josée to move into Robert Grimard's house in L'Acadie and take care of it while he and its other regular occupants were in prison, she did so, pregnant and with Benjamin in tow. The police had trashed the house in their search, and it was up to her to restore order. Once that was done, Josée began thinking of a job. The trickle of cash Dany provided had dried up completely with his imprisonment, and she had never liked taking welfare.

As it happened, Pat Lambert needed a secretary and receptionist for a business he was running on behalf of a full-patch Hells Angel. Agence Aventure operated in that other industry that attracted outlaw bikers: the sex trade. Officially, it was a booking agency for strippers, but it also ran an escort service and was thus a front for prostitution.

Josée made an appointment to see Lambert about the job, but on the morning she was to meet him her water broke. She dropped Benjamin at her parents' home, grabbed her suitcase, and drove herself to the same South Shore hospital where Dany had been born. There, she phoned Lambert to explain her absence. Ever the reliable friend, he hurried over to be with her for the birth of Dany's second child, a girl named Nathalie.

Kane had been ordered to serve his sentence at a provincial facility in Waterloo, about sixty kilometres east of St-Jean-sur-Richelieu toward Sherbrooke, and a day or two after Nathalie's birth he was accompanied by two guards on a visit to meet his daughter. A week or two later, however, he offended Waterloo's authorities and was transferred to the gothic ruin that is Bordeaux Prison in Montreal's north end.

There, Kane became good friends with a denizen of the institution, a transvestite called Tamara. She was a member of an odd subculture that jails like Bordeaux sometimes harbour: biologically male but superficially female inmates who regard the prison as home and, once freed, commit fresh crimes to get sent back. Inside, they develop relationships with inmates who serve as their protection. As far as Josée knew, Tamara took care of Kane's hair, then shortish on top and long at the back, a style known as a *coupe Longueuil* on the South Shore, as a mullet or "hockey hair" elsewhere. She didn't suspect that Tamara might be providing sexual services to Kane. Rather, she viewed the relationship as another example of Kane's expansive embrace of new friends. But she didn't understand why he asked her to bring copies of men's fashion magazines when she visited, magazines with as many underwear ads as possible.

Kane was in Bordeaux for nine months, until the summer of 1993, when he was sent to a halfway house not far from the jail. He was given training in a field that was considered appropriate for his outgoing personality and promising as a growth industry: old-age-home attendant. The idea of such a career didn't seize Kane. As soon as he was allowed, he headed back to St-Jean and moved in with Josée.

Her time at Grimard's house in L'Acadie had been brief. With only one prior conviction, for car theft more than two decades earlier, Grimard was freed after serving four months of his sentence. When he returned, Josée left. Nathalie was only two months old, and it was the middle of January, not the time to be hunting for a place to live. When Dany's parents said she could move into the upper unit of their duplex in St-Jean, a house they had bought after a few years in the trailer park, Josée agreed.

It wasn't ideal. She had never been comfortable with Dany's mother and knew that the Kanes would always side with their son. In their eyes he could do no wrong. Josée remembers being shocked at the way Dany could talk to his parents and how they accepted it with a smile. If his father was in a chair that Dany wanted, Dany would tell him to move; if Dany felt like a Coke or a coffee, he would order his mother to fetch it. The roles seemed to have been reversed: Dany was the father, and a tyrannical one at that, and Jean-Paul was the easygoing junior. Part of Gemma and Jean-Paul's passivity may have had to do with Dany's being the only son, or with a lingering guilt at sending him away to live with Gérard and Jeanne. Almost certainly it was related to the fact that soon after the cash started rolling in from Dany's criminal activities, he regularly passed money to his parents to cover their bills and to buy luxuries they couldn't otherwise afford.

With Dany living upstairs with Josée, Jean-Paul and Gemma's supplementary income source was about as near as he could be. Unfortunately, the account was almost empty. While he was in prison, Kane's business had disappeared, his turf taken over by others. Reclaiming it would require a lot of muscle and would pit Kane against former Condor colleagues. In Kane's absence, the Condors had been absorbed by a more established club in the area, the Evil Ones. They were also a farm club for the Hells Angels, formed about the same time as the Condors, but stronger and more entrenched. In the ongoing rationalization of the biker world, it had been decided that the most promising and productive Condors would be adopted by the Evil Ones and the dead wood retired. Pat Lambert was among those invited to join, but he chose to drop out and keep the gang at arm's length. He would do business with them and maintain friendly relations; he just wasn't prepared to sign up.

When Kane was released from Bordeaux, he could easily have approached the Evil Ones, been accepted as a hangaround, and started the climb up the club's ladder. Instead, he chose to follow Lambert's lead. He hadn't lost his interest in gang life; on the contrary, Kane wanted to become a Hells Angel more than ever. He was just too impatient to work his way up through the lower ranks. Besides, Kane had learned of an interesting project that just might offer a shortcut to his full patch.

BUSTED IN BELLEVILLE

Through Pat Lambert, Kane had been introduced to and become friends with David "Wolf" Carroll, a Nova Scotian who had graduated to the Hells Angels when the 13th Tribe patched over in 1984. Along with three other Halifax members, Carroll had been charged in the 1985 Lennoxville massacre of the Laval Hells, though all four were later acquitted. A sizeable number of Quebec's Hells Angels hadn't been so lucky, and while they were serving long prison terms, Carroll had helped keep the club's flag flying in the province in the face of renewed threats from the Outlaws and other organized crime groups.

Carroll established strong links, both personal and business, in the Montreal area, while Halifax remained his base of operations. In the early 1990s, however, when Carroll was drinking heavily and facing new charges in Halifax, he decided that a change of scenery was in order, and he moved to Montreal. It would give him a chance to sober up at the centre of the action. There was also a lot of money to be made by being well-positioned between the two cities, and Carroll would eventually manage much of the drug pipeline between Montreal and Halifax. He transferred his membership to the Sorel-based chapter, but he didn't allow his Halifax interests to slide. His control over the Halifax chapter remained unquestioned.

Kane barely spoke English, Carroll's French was shaky, and there was a sixteen-year age difference between the two. Still, Kane's outgoing enthusiasm won over the older Angel, and not long after meeting, the two men became good friends. In 1991 or 1992 they took a one-day firearms-handling course together, the only continuing education Josée remembers Kane pursuing after dropping out of high school. Carroll had deposited his son, who was just a few months older than Benjamin, with Josée that day, giving her a box or two of outgrown baby clothes.

Another Hells Angel whom Kane cultivated was the small, quiet, and horribly scarred Wolodumyr—or Walter—Stadnick, another anglophone a decade and a half Kane's senior. In 1993 Stadnick was nearing the end of a frustrating term as national president, a position that sounds more powerful than it is. The post is unofficial and, rare for a biker gang, doesn't come with a patch. More important, most chapters and most members are fiercely autonomous, in keeping with the individualistic biker creed, and are loath to be ordered around, especially from a distance. Stadnick's role was one of peripatetic diplomat and facilitator, coaxing the various chapters to work together for the common good.

Nicknamed "Nurget," Stadnick had become national president sometime in the late 1980s, a period when there was little competition for the post. The gang's Quebec talent pool had been seriously depleted by the Lennoxville massacre and subsequent imprisonments, and the British Columbia and Halifax chapters were still relatively young, their members without the experience or profile required for the job. Stadnick had the years of service and near-legendary status as well.

He had grown up in working-class Hamilton in an East European immigrant family. Like Kane, he had been an indifferent student, diminutive in size and social stature, interested in little beyond auto mechanics and drug peddling. In the mid-1960s, while still in high school, he and some neighbourhood friends started a gang called the Cossacks. They pulled their long hair through holes cut in their helmets to affect a warrior-of-the-steppes look and rode around on low-horsepower, usually British-made motorbikes.

In the 1970s Stadnick moved up a notch, joining Hamilton's Wild Ones, one-time affiliates of the Satan's Choice. Like many biker gangs of the day, the Wild Ones rented out their services to other organized crime groups, planting bombs and accepting extortion and intimidation assignments. In Hamilton, historically home to one of Canada's most vibrant and entrenched Mafias, there was no shortage of work.

By 1978, however, the Wild Ones were feeling threatened by the Outlaws and their takeover of Satan's Choice chapters in nearby St. Catharines and Windsor as well as a new, uncomfortably close Choice chapter in the Hamilton-Burlington region. Stadnick and a fellow Wild One headed to Montreal to try to negotiate an alliance of their own with the Hells Angels. If the trip was meant to be a secret, it was a badly kept one. The Outlaws decided to discourage any Hells Angels–Wild Ones cooperation with a heavy and bloody hand. They sent a pair of clean-cut hit men from Detroit after the two Wild Ones, and in an east-end Montreal bar they accomplished half the job: Stadnick's companion was killed.

Nothing definitive came of the Montreal meeting, but that didn't deter the Outlaws, who mounted a campaign against the Wild Ones on their home turf. Two of Stadnick's gang were blown up—one dying, the other losing a leg—in different bombings. Two others were killed building a retaliation bomb. By 1980 the club was on its way to oblivion, but Stadnick was intent on staying in the biker game. He had maintained his contacts with the Montreal Hells Angels, and by 1982, though Hamilton was still his base and his French needed a lot of work, Stadnick was a full member of the gang.

The episode that made Stadnick famous outside the club—and gave him the derogatory moniker "French Fry" that some police still use—didn't occur until 1984. It was an incident that might have sprung from the overheated imagination of a B-movie screenwriter. Pope John Paul II happened to be holding an open-air mass in Montreal on September 11, the same day that the Quebec Hells Angels were commemorating the one-year anniversary of the slaying of their first national president, Yvon "le Boss" Buteau, with a ceremonial ride and a party. A rural priest, speeding through the countryside near Drummondville in fear of being late for the pope's performance, ran a stop sign and ploughed straight into the biker procession. One Hells Angel prospect, Daniel Matthieu, was killed. Stadnick's gas tank exploded, melting his helmet and severely burning the upper half of his slight five-foot four-inch body, leaving him short two fingers and a nose.

Members of the 13th Tribe flew in from Halifax and guarded Stadnick during his weeks of recovery in a Hamilton hospital. (They were spelled off by some of Hamilton's finest, moonlighting off duty.) That unsolicited show of respect helped the Halifax bikers win promotion to full-patch Hells Angels less than two months later, by which time Stadnick and his story were known across the country, far beyond the biker and police fraternities.

As an anglophone member of the Quebec Hells Angels, Stadnick was able to smooth relations between French and English chapters. When he was made national president, it was hoped Stadnick would go a step further and lead a Hells Angels charge into the richest market in the country, his home province of Ontario and especially the Golden Horseshoe region between Oshawa and Hamilton. In the late 1980s and early 1990s, there were several attempts to achieve this through diplomatic means—the wooing of various gangs already entrenched in the province, in particular the Satan's Choice, and not-so-subtle shows of force meant to intimidate clubs into affiliation and ultimate absorption. After incidents like the Lennoxville massacre, however, the Ontario gangs were more than a little wary. There were countless polite meetings, some partying, and a few long dinners. Months of pleasantries with the Ontario gangs turned into years, but in the end the answer was always the same: thanks, but no thanks. Ontario's bikers were content with the status quo. For a decade and a half, the Outlaws, Satan's Choice, and the assorted other gangs in the province co-existed relatively peacefully, sometimes in the same cities and markets, understanding that the pie was big and rich enough that it wasn't worth warring over slice size. Inviting a hungry new player to the table, especially one as predatory as the Hells Angels, was only asking for trouble.

In 1993 Stadnick was done with diplomacy and decided that another strategy was called for, one that required a dozen or so ambitious and reckless bikers like

Dany Kane. Stadnick had concluded that if the Hells Angels couldn't win over any existing Ontario clubs, they would set up their own gang in key Ontario cities. The first pins in the map were Cornwall, Ottawa, Niagara Falls, and the prime objective, Toronto. The plan had two elements. First, the new gang would supply high-quality drugs to independent dealers at reasonable prices and in this way build a network. Second, they would take on the established Ontario gangs aggressively, either forcing them out of existence or making them change their minds about affiliating with the Hells Angels.

Kane's bona fides were well established. He'd run his own drug sales operation, he'd bombed a nightclub, and he'd done a stint behind bars. Stadnick thought that gave him the credibility on the street for the top job, president of the new club's Toronto chapter, and a supervisory role overall. As Kane himself would acknowledge, there were few other candidates; the other recruits were unseasoned and undisciplined. So Kane was brought into the planning and recruitment for the puppet club and even came up with its name. "Demon Keepers" has a certain ring to it, Kane suggested. The Hells agreed, and as easily as that, Dany Kane had managed to make his initials those of the new Hells Angels proxies who, it was hoped, would soon conquer Canada's most lucrative market.

In late 1993 and early 1994 Kane laid the groundwork. When he was in the Montreal area, he arranged for the creation of the Demon Keepers logo and for club patches to be made. These were ready in time for the official founding of the club on January 29 at celebrations held in Sorel, an irony that escaped the bikers. Similarly, no one seems to have considered it odd that the overwhelming majority of the Demon Keepers membership came from the South Shore area and that none could claim much familiarity with Ontario.

Kane was trying to make up for that deficiency in early 1994. Often he would simply leave and be gone for a week or two, Josée having no idea where he was, whether he was alive on the other side of the country or dead in a ditch a few kilometres away. It didn't necessarily damage their relationship. According to Josée, "he was away three-quarters of the time. That's why we stayed together so long."

Most often, Kane and his driver, a gang underling, headed west along Highway 401 to Toronto, where Kane had to set up a clubhouse. Rather than follow biker tradition and find a well-protected building in an industrial area or a detached house in a rundown neighbourhood, Kane established the Demon Keepers Toronto headquarters in a small, third-floor apartment on Eglinton Avenue. Though a source of amusement and ridicule to police and the club's rivals, the apartment's location had one thing going for it: it was just a short distance away from the accommodation Pat Lambert rented for the Quebec strippers he brought into Toronto to work the clubs there.

Kane often found himself in Cornwall, Kingston, and Belleville. In these places, as well as in Toronto, he and his colleagues would try to make contacts for future drug sales and conduct intelligence on their adversaries. Both tasks were tougher than anticipated. Not only did they not know Ontario's crime community, its major players, its protocol, and its history, but Kane and virtually all the other French-speaking Demon Keepers could barely make themselves understood. Prospective clients were inclined to regard them more as oddities than serious businessmen.

As far as their intelligence work went, the Demon Keepers focused on their parent club's historic enemy, the gang whose arrival in Ontario had hastened the Hells Angels' own push into Quebec, the Outlaws. In those first months of 1994, they plotted the murders of several Outlaws, conducting surveillance on the bars the Outlaws frequented, as well as their homes, sometimes tailing them in their cars. But thanks to the amateurishness of Kane's fellow Demon Keepers, none of the plots led anywhere. The only goal the gang seemed capable of achieving was being noticed.

Stadnick had told the Demon Keepers to wear their colours prominently as a way of spreading the news and the name. There was a downside to this campaign for attention, however. The police were as aware of the Demon Keepers as any of their enemies, and they had decided on a policy of hitting them hard and often. Within a month of their founding, eleven of the eighteen members of the Toronto chapter had been busted for one minor crime or another. For those granted bail, an invariable condition was to get out of Ontario until their case came to trial. This, of course, put a serious crimp in the Demon Keepers' activities.

If things weren't going very well, Kane didn't put all the blame on his inexperienced cohorts, even though he would later describe most of them as "imbeciles who had absolutely no talent." Part of the problem originated higher up, with the Hells supposedly overseeing the project. Stadnick was preoccupied with other matters, including the expansion of the gang into Manitoba and continuing negotiations with the Satan's Choice and Para-Dice Riders in Ontario. Wolf Carroll's problems were of a different sort: he was hitting the bottle heavily again and not in any shape to provide attentive leadership. The only superior Kane didn't complain about was Scott Steinert, the quick and enterprising Hells Angels striker who was the intermediary between Kane and the mother club.

In late March the Demon Keepers fixed on a victim and decided that this time they would get their man. His name was Gregory Walsh, and he was a sometime strip-club operator and well-known drug dealer in Belleville with a reputation for stiffing his suppliers and reneging on his debts. In an attempt to build a client base, the Demon Keepers had probably fronted him some drugs that he then refused to pay for. Perhaps the Outlaws had told him they would protect him, an offer they were making to dealers in a bid to thwart the Hells Angels initiative. Whatever the case, the Demon Keepers decided it was time to pay Walsh a visit. Either he would produce the cash he owed, or he would pay with his life.

But there was a problem. As new as the club was, it had already sprung a leak; a member was on the payroll of the Sûreté du Québec. When it appeared that the Demon Keepers might carry through on one of their murder schemes, a joint anti-biker task force of provincial police from Quebec and Ontario swung into action.

In the early evening of Friday, April 1, Quebec cops tailed Kane and fellow Demon Keeper Denis Cournoyer from Sorel to Montreal, where they picked up another member of the gang, Michel Scheffer, and collected their guns. They followed the trio as they left the city in a red 1992 Corsica, heading west on Autoroute 20 toward the Ontario border. There Ontario Provincial Police picked up the tail with a relay of unmarked vehicles. The SQ knew that Kane, Cournoyer, and Scheffer were planning to rendezvous with a yellow Mustang jammed full with four other Demon Keepers at a Wendy's parking lot just off the 401 at one of the Belleville exits. That, the task force decided, was the spot for the takedown. The OPP had their men in place, and when the second car rolled in at 10:05 p.m. they struck.

The exercise was textbook perfect—so much so that the OPP later edited the grainy police videotape of the operation into an eight-minute promotional film about the effective work the force was doing against outlaw bikers. Their police cruisers easily boxed the Corsica and the Mustang, cutting off any chance of escape. There was no resistance whatsoever; the bikers were flabbergasted that the police were on to them before they'd done anything.

In the Corsica, police quickly located the two loaded handguns the SQ's informant had told them they would find: a .357 Magnum in the front passenger seat where Kane was sitting and a silver .32 under a green bag in the back seat with Scheffer. In the trunk they discovered two jean jackets and a leather jacket with Demon Keepers patches on the back. They also pulled out a Remington rifle, a large quantity of ammunition, and a pair of gloves with weights sewn into them—enforcement gloves. Then they let loose Dillon, the police dog; he located a gram of hash between the front seats. Nothing incriminating was found in the yellow Mustang or on its occupants, and they were allowed to go.

Kane, Cournoyer, and Scheffer were taken into Belleville, where they were charged with restricted firearms offences and jailed. One of the OPP officers remarked on Kane's appearance, so at odds with the biker stereotype. "He was very small and very thin. Very young-looking," remembers Sgt. Bruce Townley. Still, Kane acted the hardened criminal, hardly speaking and refusing to cooperate. It was an impression shared by Peter Girard, the Belleville criminal lawyer hired to defend Kane and his cohorts. "I remember thinking, Baby-faced assassin. He looked, well, very studious and barely said a word, even to me."

Cournoyer and Scheffer, both of whom had relatively unblemished records, were granted bail the next day and released. Kane, however, had been the ringleader in the sandpit assault and was known to be the top dog among the Demon Keepers. He wasn't going anywhere.

For seven weeks he stewed in the Quinte Regional Detention Centre, going over the arrest in his mind, wondering what had happened, who had talked. He reflected on the whole notion of establishing the Demon Keepers and began to appreciate it for what it was: an absurd endeavour, destined to fail for any number of reasons. After all, Ontario was one of the most crowded and competitive biker communities in the world. How could a bunch of young francophone Québécois, most of whom had rarely ventured outside their home province, succeed in establishing yet another gang? The more Kane thought about it, the more he suspected he had been set up. And if he had been, he would have to get his own back.

Before that, however, he had to deal with the most pressing matter facing him: the two counts of Section 91 (3) of the Criminal Code of Canada, unauthorized possession of a restricted weapon, and one count of Section 354 (1), possession of property obtained by crime. The Magnum, it turned out, had been stolen. After discussions with his co-defendants and lawyer Girard, Kane agreed to take the fall for the Magnum. Scheffer accepted responsibility for the .32. They would both plead guilty as early as possible.

The opportunity came May 19 at the pre-trial hearing. In return for guilty pleas from Kane and Scheffer, the charges against them were reduced, while those against Cournoyer, a certified organic chemist whose drug-cooking talents were invaluable to the Hells organization, were withdrawn. Scheffer received two months for unauthorized possession of a restricted weapon. Kane was sentenced to four months for one restricted weapon count and four months concurrent for the stolen property charge. Back he went to the detention centre in Napanee.

Inside, Kane became buddies with a bank robber named Steve. Steve had used little more than a piece of paper in his heists, evidence that he was a nice guy, Kane would later tell Josée, when he tried to persuade her to sponsor his new friend when he got out on parole. Other than Steve, Kane didn't have much company. Josée had gotten pregnant for the third time almost as soon as Kane was released from Bordeaux into the halfway house. She was in her final trimester when he was sentenced in Belleville. That, combined with her displeasure that Kane was in prison again and the distance to Napanee, meant she didn't visit.

So Kane had a lot of time to contemplate how he had ended up where he was, to ponder who had betrayed him and to fantasize about how he might reciprocate. The choices were endless, but one revenge seemed sweeter, more elegant than the others. It would allow him to make a great deal of money. It would let him live out his childhood fantasies of being a secret agent. And it would permit him to stay close to the gang members he had become attached to. Around the time Josée was giving birth—this time all alone—to their third child, Kane, according to a police investigator familiar with him, "raised his hand" in police parlance, and discreetly told his jailers he wanted to speak to someone from the RCMP.

CROSSING OVER

The RCMP's version of how Dany Kane became an informant goes like this: in the early afternoon of Monday, October 17, 1994, an unidentified man telephoned the offices of Interpol in Ottawa and asked to speak to someone about bikers. Interpol has little interest in biker gangs, at least as far as the gangs' activities within Canada are concerned, so the caller was transferred to the RCMP sergeant Jean-Pierre Lévesque, the force's top outlaw biker specialist and the chief analyst for the Criminal Intelligence Service of Canada, whose office was just down the hall.

CISC is a Mountie-run clearing house for information on organized crime groups collected by dozens of police forces across the country. In its annual reports, Lévesque had repeatedly warned that biker gangs, in particular the Hells Angels, were the most serious criminal threat to Canada, one whose strength was growing.

In Lévesque's experience, the Hells Angels were impervious to leaks and informants, at least in their upper ranks. A low-level hangaround with one of the puppet clubs might sometimes proffer a tidbit or two to escape a drug charge or make some extra cash, but from prospects or full-patch members of the Hells Angels proper, nothing. No one, it seemed, could be bought or leveraged, and the chances of positioning one of their own agents in the upper echelons were negligible.

Initially, Lévesque was doubtful that this caller had anything substantial to offer. As the conversation progressed, however, his curiosity grew. Though not a full-fledged member of the Hells, the man knew the identities of those who were, the names of their associates, and the nature of their business. Lévesque tried to catch him out on several details, but it soon became clear that on the subject of Quebec's Hells Angels, the man knew as much as Lévesque and a whole lot more.

The two spoke about meeting, but nothing definite was decided. The man said he would call back later that afternoon or the next day; Lévesque did not ask his name. As soon as he hung up, Lévesque called Cpl. Pierre Verdon, a twenty-year veteran of the RCMP and a close friend in the force's Montreal bureau. Lévesque knew that if the biker who had just contacted him became a regular source, he couldn't be his handler, however much he might have relished the opportunity. The biker was on the street in Montreal; Lévesque held a desk job in Ottawa. Should the man become a source to be monitored and cultivated, Levesque wanted Verdon involved. He could rely on Verdon to pass along to him any information of interest, and in Lévesque's world, reliable information was gold.

On Tuesday afternoon, the man called Lévesque again and a rendezvous was arranged for that very evening at six. They agreed to meet at a mall on Montreal's West Island, a safe distance from the biker's home on the South Shore and a slightly shorter drive than otherwise for Lévesque, coming from his office in east-end Ottawa.

On the road to Montreal, the brilliant autumn colours didn't distract Lévesque from wondering who the mystery man might be. His mind kept returning, he said later, to a photograph in his bulging files of a biker, a small, slight young man in reading glasses. The fellow's record suggested he was well down the ladder in the Hells hierarchy, but Lévesque had been intrigued by his unlikely demeanour from the first time he'd seen it. Could he be the one? Lévesque mused. After meeting up with Verdon, he drove to the appointed spot, the east entrance of a shopping centre in Pointe-Claire, just off Highway 40. There, right on time and with a copy of the highbrow *Le Devoir* under his left arm as instructed, was the young man from the photo, Dany Kane.

Between the call to Interpol and Lévesque's premonition, it makes for a good story. But that may be all it is. Kane served two months of his four-month sentence at the Quinte Detention Centre before being released in July, and Josée maintains that as soon as he was out he spoke about a lucrative deal he had struck. This deal would bring him a modest, regular income in the short term but deliver a major payday in the end. She knew not to ask about the deal's particulars and like everyone else in Kane's orbit never suspected that his benefactor might be the RCMP.

There are also knowledgeable police officials who dispute the RCMP's official version of events. They say it happened in a much more banal manner. Kane was in prison in Napanee, convinced he had been betrayed by the people whose territory he was working to enlarge—the Hells Angels, perhaps Walter Stadnick himself. The best way to avenge their treachery, he decided, was to sell them out, a risky course that nonetheless held real attractions. Unsuspected, he could continue to rise in the gang and perhaps one day realize his dream of becoming a full-fledged Hells Angel, achieving all the power and prestige that came with the patch. The secret agent element, known only to himself, added an extra frisson to the game, the kind of thrill that appealed to him. Best of all, working for the police and the bikers, he would make money at both ends, coming and going.

According to this account, after raising his hand, Kane was visited in prison by Lévesque, who had been contacted by a corrections officer at the Quinte Detention Centre. Their discussions led to an agreement that Kane would become an active informant for the RCMP once he was back on the street, perhaps after a cooling-off period of a few months. If this version of events is true, the question arises why the RCMP would feel compelled to invent a much more elaborate tale. One explanation is that corrections officers are uneasy about acting as go-betweens for police and prisoners who opt to become informants. In terms of security, it is thought to make the corrections officers more vulnerable both in their workplace and outside it. The informant's security is also compromised since the pool of people aware that the prisoner is a source—or willing to become one—is necessarily larger.

Whatever the circumstances of Kane's engagement, Lévesque and Verdon could barely contain their excitement after the West Island meeting. The Mounties had taken a room at the Dorval Best Western between the autoroute and the runways of Montreal's main airport for a comprehensive interview. They were there for more than three hours, with Kane doing most of the talking while

Verdon and Lévesque scribbled in their notebooks. It seemed they had hit the motherlode.

Off the bat, he told them he had access to several of the top members of the Hells Angels and almost all members of the South Shore farm club, the Evil Ones. Then he offered a resumé of his biker career to that point, describing at length the debacle of the Demon Keepers' foray into Ontario. Following Kane's imprisonment, the gang had been shut down, their colours pulled by their Hells Angels sponsors. All but a few Demon Keepers were told in no uncertain terms to disappear; they had no future with the Hells Angels organization and shouldn't expect to have any further dealings with them.

Kane was one of the Demon Keepers given another chance, and he told Lévesque and Verdon that since his release, he had become close to Scott Steinert, the Hells Angels protegé who had been involved with the Demon Keepers disaster. Handsome, quick, and with ambition to match his ego, Steinert had recently been promoted to prospect, having leapfrogged earlier mandatory stages. He owed his meteoric rise to the sponsorship of a gang veteran, the three-hundred-pounds-plus Robert "Tiny" Richard, who had taken over as national president from Walter Stadnick in June 1994.

Steinert didn't fit the traditional biker profile. His was what a Corrections Canada official would later deem an upper-middle-class background with good values. The Steinert family came from Beloit, Wisconsin, home of the Beloit Corporation. The company had begun as a small, all-purpose ironworks but grew to employ thousands in the specialized field of papermaking machinery. In 1970 Steinert's father was sent to help run the Beloit plant in Sorel, Quebec, the South Shore town that was known for its shipyards and heavy industry, and would soon become home to the province's most prominent Hells Angels chapter.

A small English school in the town catered to the privileged children of the managers and executives of the area's factories. Scott Steinert was considered intelligent and motivated but not academically inclined. A fellow student remembers the irate and exasperated principal lifting him off the floor by his shirtfront. From a relatively young age, Steinert fell into minor crime. He started smoking hash at sixteen and soon moved on to chemicals such as PCP and LSD. By eighteen he had made three appearances in juvenile court, dropped out of high school, and left the family home. He moved out to British Columbia, where he spent summers working as a carny at the Pacific National Exhibition and his winters collecting pogey and dealing small amounts of drugs. "In this way he was fully able to live his hedonist and marginal lifestyle," noted the Corrections Canada official. With a group of friends he formed a small, unaffiliated biker gang.

By his early twenties Steinert showed all the promise of a career criminal, albeit rather minor league: his record included arrests for breaking and entering, possession of stolen goods, possession of drugs, and assault. He moved up a notch in October 1985, when, back in Sorel, he arranged for the sale of two kilos of PCP, sometimes called angel dust, to a customer who turned out to be an undercover RCMP officer. He pleaded guilty and two days before Christmas was sentenced to five years in prison.

Steinert maintained the PCP sale was a one-off, that he hadn't wanted to be involved in the deal but couldn't resist the easy profit. He swore he didn't have any connection to the Hells, a claim another Corrections official doubted. "It is difficult to imagine that the Hells would permit the intrusion of an outsider into the drug market when one knows how tightly they control this very lucrative business."

Nonetheless, prison officials were impressed by him. "He is outgoing and has a good demeanour. He answers questions without any reticence and with a remarkable transparence!" gushed one report. He was tattooed, heavily into weightlifting, and refused to see the prison psychologist. Still, officials lauded his "interesting qualities" and "higher than average potential," deciding he was "more a marginal than a delinquent."

Swayed by the fact that he sold drugs only to adults, Corrections Canada granted Steinert full parole after he had served just over two years. By this time his parents had moved back to Wisconsin, but his long-time Sorel girlfriend promised to provide him a stable home. Steinert started up his own insulating business on money borrowed from his father, and Corrections officials applauded. "Scott spends most of his free time with Louise. He enjoys going to the movies, downhill skiing and playing soccer during the summer months. He has a very small circle of friends, 'legit' people, he tells us."

But within a year Steinert had been charged with extortion after a welfare recipient who had borrowed $300 from a loan shark complained to police of harassment. The man had repaid more than $2000 and been threatened and beaten up when he refused to pay more. Steinert, the man said, was the loan shark's muscle. Back in prison, Steinert was evaluated more skeptically. Officials noted his "elastic morality" and his "pronounced taste for luxury" and declared he was no doubt involved with outlaw bikers. He was sentenced to a month for the extortion affair and was out again by mid-1989. Over the next few years he became more adept at avoiding trouble even as he was drawn closer to Sorel's Hells. When Kane got to know him, Steinert, six and a half years his senior, was considered something of a golden boy in the club and thus a very good person for an aspirant to cultivate.

In the months following Kane's release from prison, he and Steinert became so tight that in the spring of 1995 Kane asked Steinert to be godfather to Guillaume, the son Josée gave birth to while Kane was in Quinte Detention Centre. The christening took place in May, and in photos of the event, Kane looks like an extra from a high school production of *Guys and Dolls,* wiry and youthful in a dark suit and tie, his hair slicked back, and a goofy grin below a moustache that might be pasted on. Steinert, taller and considerably beefier, exudes a mix of menace and manliness in a leather jacket, jeans, and cowboy boots.

Whatever their sartorial differences, the two got on extremely well, and Kane was inclined to hitch his star to Steinert's. Doing so, however, would be a snub to Wolf Carroll, who, in the fall of 1994, was urging Kane to join the Evil Ones as a first step toward membership in the Hells Angels. Steinert was encouraging Kane to team up with him, to try yet again to establish a Hells Angels puppet gang in the Belleville and Kingston areas. This club would be smaller but more serious than the Demon Keepers, Kane told Lévesque and Verdon, admitting that he was tempted by the idea. It wouldn't happen quickly, though. Steinert would be allowed to sponsor his own puppet gang only when he was a full member of the Hells

Angels, and that wasn't expected to happen until the summer of 1995.

Kane's attraction to Steinert also strained relations with his old friend Pat Lambert. The two had gone back into business together wholesaling drugs, but Lambert was firmly associated with Carroll, who had a significant stake in Agence Aventure. While Kane spent more time with Steinert, the business partnership with Lambert lapsed. But the friendship, he told police, was not affected; it was as solid as ever.

Kane gave the Mounties an update on the gang's progress in expanding into the Toronto area. The eighty-odd members of the Para-Dice Riders were evenly split on the idea of joining the Hells Angels. Similarly, Toronto's Satan's Choice chapters were sympathetic, but those in northern Ontario had loyalties to the Outlaws.

His reports on gang politics allowed his handlers a glimpse into the very different personalities of the two most prominent anglophone members. Walter Stadnick was rich and tight with his money; Wolf Carroll was hard drinking and disorganized, a terrible administrator who, despite his lucrative interests in drugs and prostitution, was chronically broke. The Sorel club had to lend him money to buy a car. As full Hells Angels, the two were cordial but not particularly close. They did little business together and not only because Carroll concentrated on the Atlantic provinces while Stadnick was more interested in Ontario and points west, especially Manitoba. Meanwhile Scott Steinert worked loosely with several full-patch members and without any clearly defined turf. As a prospect, he was lower in rank to Carroll, Stadnick, and other full members, yet as a protegé of Tiny Richard, he had an unofficial influence some full members could only dream about.

At the conclusion of his first formal debriefing, Kane told the Mounties something that should have sounded alarm bells, especially in the months following as an alliance of organized crime groups banded together to resist the Hells Angels' attempts to control Montreal's retail drug market and explosions began to rock the city regularly, setting the beat for Quebec's biker war. Kane described himself as an expert in explosives and claimed that among his duties for the Hells Angels was the preparation of their bombs.

THE ANSWER TO THE MOUNTIES' PRAYERS

In his ten-page, handwritten report of Kane's first debriefing, Corporal Verdon's exhilaration at the prospect of having a source inside the Hells Angels bubbles through every sentence. He clearly understood that Kane could gloriously cap his otherwise unremarkable career. If his man climbed the rungs to full-patch membership, they would make history.

"His potential is unlimited," wrote Verdon. "The goal of the source is to work for us over the long term and he expects to be made a full member of the H.A. in about three to five years. We are all aware of how difficult it is to infiltrate the biker milieu and that such an opportunity has never presented itself before. Such a source could help us not only from the perspective of intelligence on the biker milieu but could also be used in investigations of all illegal activities in which these groups are involved and we know how diverse their activities are."

Verdon's stated goals were laudable but they were focused on the distant future. Absent was any obvious concern for what had been a growing problem in Quebec since July. That month had seen the first undeniable evidence that the province was in the midst of a gang war between the Hells Angels and a loose coalition of independent organized crime groups that called itself the Alliance before coalescing around its main constituent gang, the Rock Machine. For years, these various crime groups had controlled street-level drug sales in Montreal, buying their supplies from disparate sources, including the Hells Angels. By 1994, however, the leaders of the Rock Machine were in jail while the Montreal Hells Angels had fully rebounded from the setback of Lennoxville nine years before. It was time, Mom Boucher and others argued, to expand the gang's turf in the downtown. This prompted the formation of the Alliance, and in July it launched an offensive that its members hoped would derail the Hells' expansionist dreams.

On July 13, a week and a day before Dany Kane was released from prison in Napanee, two men walked into a motorcycle repair shop in east-end Montreal and shot and killed its owner, Pierre Daoust, a longtime Hells Angels associate. The next day, another gang associate, Normand Robitaille, was shot and seriously wounded in an east-end garage, while five Rock Machine members were arrested with three remote-control bombs and twelve sticks of dynamite just as they set out for the Evil Ones' clubhouse on the South Shore. Three days after that, two other heavily armed Rock Machine figures were nabbed as they prowled the streets of the east end hunting, it was said, for Mom Boucher himself. The Hells Angels began a counteroffensive later in the month, and though it suffered an equally spotty success rate, the bodies began piling up. In their questioning of Kane during the first full encounter, the RCMP officers didn't seem much interested in these events.

The debriefing memo's effusive comments about their new source include only one qualifier: "He tells us very clearly that he can help us enormously but that he expects to be remunerated in consequence." No money had yet changed hands, but it would be the last freebie. Kane knew his value, and he wouldn't be bought cheap.

The next meeting was held on Sunday, October 30, this time on Lévesque's turf. Kane made the drive to Ottawa alone. The three men met in the early afternoon in the parking lot of one hotel, then made their way to a room at another, the Welcome Inn in the capital's east end. It was a warm, clear fall day but they weren't going to spend it outside. Just a few days earlier, one of the Pelletier clan brothers and a pillar of the Alliance had been blown to pieces—*déchiqueté,* in the language of the crime tabloids—after his Jeep was booby-trapped with a Hells Angels bomb. The Mounties don't appear to have asked Kane about the incident; rather, they were intent on what might be categorized as deep background.

The main subject of conversation was Wolf Carroll and his myriad business interests and criminal relationships. Along with four other men, one of whom was a fellow Hells Angel, he controlled a string of bars in the suburb of Lasalle but was eager to expand into Montreal's booming Gay Village. One of Carroll's business partners was a gay, though still closeted, former hotel doorman, and they hoped he would help smooth their way into the neighbourhood. "According to the source it's difficult to get established in the gay area," Verdon wrote. "It doesn't work to use violence. Apparently, you must be accepted by them to do business there."

Kane said Carroll was also co-owner of a bar in the resort town of St-Sauveur in the Laurentians, forty-five minutes north of Montreal, along with a Mafioso. His relations with the Italian mob were so cordial that they had given him a drug sale territory in the area. Wolf was tight with the largely anglophone West End crime gang too, as he was with the Loners, a Toronto-based biker gang with close ties to Italian organized crime. (There were three Loners chapters back in the old country.) Carroll's talent for making and keeping good contacts, Verdon noted, made up for his poor business skills.

In the midst of responding to his handlers' inquiries, Kane raised an issue of his own, one that had perhaps occurred to him in the days since their first debriefing session. The RCMP had been battered by scandal in Quebec in recent years: in three separate cases, its officers had been discovered to be on the take from organized crime. In one instance, the officer had killed himself with his service revolver when exposure seemed imminent; in another, the officer had fled to his native Portugal, beyond reach of extradition. Kane may have remembered that the Mounties weren't necessarily as squeaky clean as he had first thought. "The source is worried that a policeman making $55,000 a year could be bought by the other side," Verdon wrote. "According to the source, a Hells Angel like Maurice 'Mom' Boucher, one of the most powerful and rich of the gang, would be ready to pay twice what a policeman makes in salary in return for information." Verdon did his best to reassure Kane, saying the risks of such a leak were minuscule. He likely pointed out that even in the confidential source debriefing reports, Kane was never referred to by name but as C-2994 or "the source." "He left with a feeling of confidence," Verdon noted.

Once again, Verdon enthused about how well he and Lévesque were getting on with Kane but for a single point of contention. "The only cloud on the horizon seems to be the amounts [of money] offered to the source and the amounts demanded." At this meeting Kane was paid $500 "and indicated very clearly that he expects a substantial increase in the near future." Verdon told Kane that if such an increase was to be approved, he'd have to deliver solid, actionable information that could lead to arrests. That seemed to jog Kane's memory. "At this point he maintained that he had seen one kilo of cocaine at the home of Pat Lambert as well as a large quantity of bomb-making materials.... He said he had not alerted us to this discovery at the time it occurred because he hadn't achieved the level of confidence in us that he now has." Kane promised to verify whether Lambert still had the drugs and explosives and to report back.

The Mounties were pleased, and Kane left Ottawa having learned an important lesson: if he wanted to make big money from the force, he would have to give them quality goods. Or at least something that appeared to be quality goods. The information could be past its "best by" date or lacking a crucial detail as long as it looked to be the real thing. The Ottawa interview was the first of many at which Kane gave his handlers tantalizing intelligence a bit too late for them to take any action or without the essential details that would have allowed police to make an arrest.

Over the next two weeks Kane telephoned Verdon three times with more nuggets of information. The officer's subsequent memos reveal the emerging pattern. Kane reported that Pat Lambert had made eight bomb-detonating kits for the Hells Angels but claimed he didn't know where or when they were to be used. He said that two members of the Valleyfield Pirates, another Hells Angels puppet gang, had burned down a bar in Granby but maintained that he couldn't disclose the names of the bikers because he was the only other person to know and so could be easily identified. He revealed that Pat Lambert hid his cocaine and made his bombs at 2289 Rue Hochelaga in east-end Montreal; he neglected, however, to give Verdon the apartment number, and Lambert, of course, was not listed on any lobby directory.

The missing pieces didn't seem to worry Verdon or his RCMP colleagues. It was early in their relationship with Kane, and besides, the intensifying biker war wasn't really their problem. The RCMP's mandate is much more restricted in Quebec, where the Sûreté du Québec is the provincial force, than in those provinces where no provincial police exist. There are some twelve hundred RCMP officers in Quebec, many of whom are specifically assigned to organized crime, but except in cases of national security or large-scale trans-border smuggling, the force's work is limited to a supporting role. The reason is partly political—its covert operations against the sovereignty movement in the 1970s cost it the trust of many Quebeckers, not least of all politicians—and partly practical. But if the RCMP has less of a front-line role in the province, it's also insulated from public outrage at criminal goings-on. Verdon almost certainly appreciated that whatever anger arose at police handling of the biker war, it would be overwhelmingly directed toward the SQ and the Service de la Police de la Communauté urbaine de Montréal, or SPCUM, Montreal's city police force.

Deeply entrenched jealousies and rivalries had long plagued relations among the three forces. The degree to which this impeded smooth cooperation depended on the investigations and the officers involved, though in general the more sensitive and high profile a case, the more guarded were communications. In the case of Kane, very little of his information found its way to the SQ and the Montreal police, especially in the early days, nor was his identity revealed to colleagues outside the RCMP.

Kane's intelligence was most helpful to the RCMP for its illumination of the biker milieu. He said there was no love lost between the Valleyfield Pirates and Laval's Death Riders but that the two gangs tolerated each other because both were affiliated with the Hells. He reported that Wolf Carroll and Mom Boucher had put out contracts on biker associates who were in prison; one had become an informant, the other had crossed over to the Rock Machine and was vowing to whack Boucher when he was released. He noted that Hells Angels from Trois-Rivières and Montreal were moving into the Ottawa area and that the local Outlaws were offering no resistance.

There was one theme Kane returned to frequently in the calls and meetings of November and December: the escalating hostilities between "certain Hells Angels" and the Rock Machine. The Hells were stockpiling explosives in anticipation of a prolonged conflict. Scott Steinert had purchased nine kilos of C4 for bomb-making purposes, and Kane himself had obtained further supplies at Steinert's request.

Kane met Verdon and Lévesque again in mid-November at what would become a familiar venue, the Ramada Inn in Longueuil, just over the Jacques-Cartier Bridge from Montreal. Verdon booked a room for the session, as he would do almost weekly for the next two years. This November meeting, however, would be the last debriefing interview with Lévesque. Handling sources was out of his jurisdiction and so was Montreal. He would be replaced by Verdon's boss, Sgt. Gaetan St. Onge, a twenty-three-year veteran who was interested in meeting the man who had generated such enthusiasm in his subordinate.

At this meeting Kane was again full of fascinating insights into the world of the Hells Angels. The gang had their hands on a large quantity of "extassy," a drug they knew nothing about, apart from the fact that there was demand for it in the Gay Village. They would satisfy and build that market by setting up an unlicensed after-hours club in the area. Wolf Carroll was considering an import/export business with a contact in Russia; the export product was fruit, the imports were girls. Kane let on that he knew two women customs agents—one American, the other Canadian—who worked at border crossings south of St-Jean and who would do favours for Kane when he travelled to and from the United States.

Kane brought up the incident at the Granby bar, the business torched by the Valleyfield Pirates according to his earlier statements. In fact, Kane now admitted, the former owner of the bar had asked Pat Lambert to blow it up after the new owner refused to pay for the bar's inventory. Lambert, Kane said, had made the bomb while Johnny, Carroll's gay doorman, did the dirty work of planting and detonation. The revelation demonstrated that Kane was liable to torque his intelligence from one debriefing session to another, and should have prompted his handlers to ask themselves some serious questions. They might have asked themselves whether Kane's old pal Pat Lambert was really involved in all the crimes Kane attributed to him, or whether he was a convenient scapegoat for the deeds and activities of someone else.

No such doubts appear in any of their debriefing reports. Instead, the documents suggest that Verdon, Lévesque, and later St. Onge accepted all of Kane's information unquestioningly. And there was no shortage of it. In November, Kane telephoned the Mounties at least eight times and met with them on three occasions; in December, Christmas notwithstanding, he called nine times and met with them in Longueuil on four occasions. On one of these, they went for a long sightseeing drive around the South Shore towns of Longueuil, Chambly, Sorel, and Varennes, and through neighbourhoods in Montreal, Kane acting as tour guide. He pointed out the homes of Hells Angels members and sympathizers, as well as the residence of at least one Rock Machine hit man who himself was slated for assassination.

The flow of inside organizational news continued. Kane told of a plan to start a new Hells Angels chapter in Quebec, a sort of uber-chapter not tied to any particular town or city, in late January. Its members would be called the Nomads, he reported, and all other Hells chapters would be obliged to buy their cocaine from them. "This group would have about ten members and their territory would be the whole province of Quebec," Verdon noted. "They would put pressure on clubs which don't work enough as far as drug sales on their turf is concerned. Only a few H.A. are aware of this development. C-2994 learned of it because he was present at the clubhouse."

Mom Boucher would be the Nomads' leader; the chapter would be filled out with long-time Hells and the most promising recruits from the ranks. The Rockers—not to be confused with the enemy Rock Machine—was a Hells Angels puppet club that "belonged" to Boucher, according to Kane. Its members would serve as gofers and underlings to the

Nomads, those who hoped to prove themselves worthy of eventual elevation among the elite. Rockers chapters were proposed for Manitoba, New Brunswick, and London, Ontario, reflecting the Nomads' countrywide ambitions. "They are principally senior and very active members of H.A. Mtl.," Verdon wrote. "According to the information received, the Nomads will be much more 'rock and roll' and will take territory all over Canada."

Still, no amount of organizational retooling could end the feuding and dissension that plagued the larger Hells Angels community, even in the face of serious outside threats. André "Toots" Tousignant, a Rocker who would become one of the gang's top killers, blew up a fellow Rocker from the South Shore because the victim was considered "a rotten apple." The attempted murder of another Rocker in Old Montreal in mid-December was also an inside job, the missed target another *pomme pourrie*. Meanwhile, the Evil Ones were accused of being faint of heart, too rich and too comfortable. Their dedication was questioned when they merely stomped a Rock Machine member instead of following orders to kill him.

There was grumbling too about some of the Hells Angels proper. Several who had recently been promoted to full patch from prospect were seen as duds who "sit on their laurels since they got their colours. They are resented most for not being active in the war against the Alliance and for living a peaceful, nice life." As a result, and because the gang had determined that there were too many members trying to get rich in too little territory, the Montreal chapter decided not to accept any new prospects for two years. This concerned Kane and his handlers. How could C-2994 infiltrate the inner sanctum if there was a moratorium on new members?

Kane suggested to St. Onge that there was a chance he could be made a prospect before the rule came into effect. This was absurdly far-fetched. Officially Kane wasn't even a hangaround or striker at this point, and such a rapid rise in rank was unheard of. The optimism he expressed to St. Onge that he might make such a leap was almost certainly less a real fact and more an attempt to squeeze additional cash out of the Mounties, but there is nothing in their reports to suggest his handlers were on to his game. St. Onge wrote, "To [become a prospect] he would need much more money," a spend-for-success approach designed to impress his biker superiors. "I know that soon enough we will need to make some important decisions in this respect."

Regardless of his low rank, Kane bragged about his acceptance among the Hells and their leadership. He said he had been granted unlimited access to the Hells' new satellite clubhouse in Longueuil and that Mom Boucher himself was "beginning to initiate conversations with him and trust him." The RCMP agents weren't above a bit of chest pounding of their own in their source debriefing reports. After Kane returned from a Hells Angels Christmas party in Sherbrooke full of gossip about who had attended and who hadn't, Verdon gloated that the RCMP had acquired twice as much intelligence on the event as the SQ, which had sent a team of surveillance officers. The Mounties' tab was $250, enough to cover Kane's expenses; the SQ had spent tens of thousands.

A couple of weeks earlier, the RCMP had coughed up $500 for Kane to meet Pat Lambert in Toronto "to negotiate turf for dancers and drugs." Their foray followed that of Lambert, Carroll, and another anglophone Hells Angel, Donald "Pup" Stockford, a week or so previously that had

produced little in the way of results. The three had travelled to Toronto to negotiate an alliance with the Loners,
but they had been rebuffed. Kane and Lambert's trip was
even less fruitful. They were supposed to visit Toronto
and Ottawa, but Kane got no farther than Kingston. He
was telephoned there by Lambert, who had preceded him
to Toronto, and told to turn around—there was too much
heat from the police. Lambert had been stopped by anti-
biker officers who asked questions that suggested to
Lambert that the Ontario police had an informant in the
biker milieu. The episode reinforced Wolf Carroll's theory that "the Ontario bikers are not trustworthy and even
dangerous," Verdon noted. "Also, Lambert said he saw a
policeman shake the hand of several bikers, something
that would be impossible here. The H.A. have lost a lot of
respect for the Ontario biker groups."

In Quebec, the situation was reversed, Kane told his
handlers. It was the police who were selling information
to the bikers. The Evil Ones were tight with certain members of the municipal force in the South Shore suburb of
Brossard, while next door in Greenfield Park a local
officer was in the pay of the bikers. Scott Steinert had his
hands on a photo album of the few remaining Outlaws in
the province. It too came from a crooked cop.

On the subject of explosives, Kane had a great deal to
say. In late November, he reported that the Hells Angels
had ordered a dozen bomb kits from Pat Lambert. They
would be detonated, he said, with a remote-control device
bought at toy stores. A couple of days later he added that
Steinert, who was becoming Mom Boucher's most reliable henchman in the biker war, had planted eight or ten
bombs around Montreal. "The goal was to warn the Rock
Machine and their sympathizers of the seriousness of

the H.A. regarding their taking over entire control of Montreal." The message wasn't delivered, however. None of the bombs exploded because the detonators didn't pack the requisite punch.

That failure did not discourage the Hells Angels. Five days later Kane claimed that another twenty bomb kits had been ordered, and he himself was soon directed to procure aerial photographs of the Montreal neighbourhoods where the Rock Machine and Outlaws clubhouses were located. The objective was to eliminate their rivals "with bombs or machine guns or both. These photos would serve to block off access routes with stolen vehicles to police and firemen and ambulances in the minutes following the attacks. This plan is in its infancy and should not be finalized until mid or late January 1995." No longer would they rely on toy-store devices; instead, they switched to pager-triggered detonators, allowing them to set off the bombs from a greater distance.

In January Kane described an incident that occurred between Christmas and New Year's in which Mom Boucher and several other gang members had worn their Hells Angels colours into a Pelletier-family-run bar in Montreal's east end in a deliberately provocative show of bravado. Nothing happened, though within minutes of their departure about forty Alliance members appeared. This gave the gang an idea: park an Econoline van full of dynamite and nails outside the bar a few nights later and pull the same routine. This time, however, no Alliance members showed up to rumble, and the nightclub was full of regular patrons. The Econoline went undetonated.

There is no indication that the Mounties ever wondered whether their gregarious source might have a hand in the preparation of the bomb kits, the assembling of the bombs themselves, or their placement and detonation. Nonetheless, there is no doubt that Kane was heavily involved in all aspects. During these months, as he would later admit, he participated in countless bombings, some successful, others not, from the purchase and assembly of the components to their actual detonation, including the planned attack on the Pelletier establishment and the torching of the Granby bar.

It's conceivable that Verdon, St. Onge, and Kane had agreed, explicitly or otherwise, to a "don't ask, don't tell" policy. Not only would the Mounties have been contravening the force's regulations but breaking the law themselves had they known that Kane was involved in the bombings or any other serious criminal activity and not taken action. Kane may have known better than to tell them, while they knew better than to inquire. Verdon and St. Onge could hardly have believed that since becoming an informer, Kane had embarked on the straight and narrow. Like Kane, they surely recognized that if he had abruptly ended his criminal activities, he would have raised suspicions among his biker brethren.

If Verdon and St. Onge were aware of Kane's escapades they didn't indicate it in their debriefing reports. It would have made a paper trail, and paper trails are always dangerous. Although the documents were designated "protégé B"—the second-highest level of RCMP classification—the two officers understood that if Kane were ever to testify on behalf of the police, a judge could order the release of their reports. Any evidence that Kane's handlers knew he was committing serious crimes but did nothing about them could torpedo the very cases Kane had helped build.

PLAYING
BOTH SIDES

In early January 1995, Kane reported that Rock Machine member Normand Baker was at the top of the Hells Angels hit list. Baker was suspected in the murder of Pierre Daoust, the motorcycle store owner killed July 13, 1994, and the attempted assassination of the Rocker Normand Robitaille, one of Mom Boucher's closest associates, the next day. The two shootings were considered acts of aggression and a formal declaration of war by the Rock Machine against the Hells Angels.

Steinert had made the Hells' animosity against Baker personal in December when he and a Rocker attended a Rolling Stones concert at the cavernous Olympic Stadium in Montreal's east end. There they ran into Baker and an army of between fifty and seventy Rock Machine members and *sympathisants*. Steinert and Baker had a prolonged, testosterone-charged nose-to-nose showdown. Steinert was armed and may well have flashed his handgun to save himself. The two eventually went their separate ways, though, as St. Onge noted, the incident "can't but poison the situation further."

On January 5, Kane confirmed that another Pelletier brother "is the next on the list of the H.A." Also, "Scott

Steinert is personally after Normand Baker of the R.M. and he also will be among the next to go." Armed with such precise information, the RCMP would usually inform the targets that their lives were in danger and recommend that they take the necessary precautions. There is no indication Verdon or St. Onge contemplated such a step. Even if they had, it was already too late.

Along with other Rock Machine comrades, Baker had taken a New Year's vacation to Acapulco, a favourite getaway of several Montreal Hells Angels too. Mom Boucher, whose criminal record denied him entry into the United States, was said to own a large hotel in the Mexican resort city that he visited regularly.

Whether by coincidence or design, François Hinse, a Hells Angel prospect from the Trois-Rivières chapter, was in Acapulco at the same time as Baker. Late in the evening of January 4, about twelve hours before Kane told his handlers that Baker was a marked man, Hinse walked up to him at the beachside Hard Rock Café, wished him *"Bonne Année"* and, after drawing a handgun from a belt bag, shot him in the head. Other patrons thought it was a stunt. When they saw Baker's spattered blood and then watched Hinse, wearing nothing but a bathing suit, make his escape by plunging through a plate-glass window, they understood otherwise. Despite his Hollywood dramatics, Hinse didn't get far. A friend of Baker's and several waiters gave chase and caught him less than a hundred metres away.

The news of Hinse's hit was not long in reaching Quebec. Kane telephoned Verdon to tell him on January 8, and the Mounties confirmed it the next day. By then Kane was reporting that the Nomads were already working on his release from a Mexican jail. "The H.A. have many contacts in all areas in the Acapulco region and almost everybody can be bought," Verdon wrote after a debriefing meeting with Kane. "It seems that the murder weapon will disappear from the police station today. Also, one of the main witnesses will no longer be a problem." He added, "Our source could not be more specific about how exactly the witnesses' silence will be assured."

A week after the murder and the day after Baker's Montreal funeral (where Steinert was doing routine surveillance and was harassed by police doing the same), Kane gave the Mounties another update. "Two witnesses to the murder in Acapulco will be eliminated," Verdon wrote. And thanks to money spread in the right places, Hinse was being held in the infirmary, not in a prison cell. For a bit extra, he had access to hookers and drugs if he wanted.

The next day Kane had more. He told Verdon that Mom Boucher was taking care of Hinse personally. Indeed, Boucher had been informed by a Mexican policeman of his acquaintance that it would have been cheaper and less bothersome for everyone had the Hells Angels contracted out Baker's execution to a local. It could have been accomplished for a mere $5000, he was told. Boucher flew down to Acapulco on January 14 and got immediate results: Hinse was freed for lack of evidence the next afternoon. St. Onge spoke to the RCMP's man on the ground in Mexico that evening. "The Mexican liaison officer informs us that the liberation of Hinse despite all the proof was a flagrant case of corruption."

Hinse, whose release was rumoured to have cost the Hells Angels a million pesos—$270,000 Canadian— promptly returned to Canada. The affair marked one of the few occasions when the biker war spilled beyond

Quebec's borders. It convinced Verdon and St. Onge of the Hells Angels' reach and reinforced Kane's value. "Our source maintained right from the start that Hinse would not be convicted nor would he be held very long. Events proved him right, which proves to us once again the importance and the reliability of this source in the biker milieu which itself is more and more involved in a broad range of criminal activities."

The RCMP had already been sufficiently persuaded of Kane's worth in early January to offer a three-month informant contract that would pay him $500 a week. It was hoped this would put an end to his relentless demands for more money, but no. Within ten days, the bickering had resumed. By then Kane's $2000 for January had been paid, plus an extra $500. "He says it is not enough," St. Onge wrote on January 12. "I inform him politely that that is all he'll get and that I don't want to have to tell him that the RCMP existed before him and that it would exist without him. He tells me that he under-stands but still insists anyway."

A note from St. Onge's superior, Staff Sgt. Pierre Lemire, that same day was unequivocal. "The agreement with C-2994 will be respected. Only in exceptional circum-stances will a supplementary sum be given him and for spe-cific and justifiable reasons." However firm the RCMP's resolve, it was no match for Kane's wheedling. The next day St. Onge and Verdon met him at the Ramada in Longueuil to hand over another $1000. No specific reasons were provided. Little more than a week later Kane received a further $500.

Kane's carping continued through February and March, until the expiry of the contract. Sometimes he went too far. The Mounties told him it was highly unlikely that the force could give him the $25,000 that would buy him a place in "the Group of Five," a drug importing consortium organized by Wolf Carroll. The group hoped to buy a nightclub in Guadeloupe as a base and cover for a cocaine pipeline they would establish through the Caribbean and into Canada. "The son of a very senior French politician is also involved," St. Onge noted.

Other times Kane did manage to extract additional funds from his handlers, even when the "specific and justifiable reasons" didn't pan out. On February 21, Verdon and St. Onge gave Kane $1500 as pocket money for a road trip to Halifax with Wolf Carroll. "The goal of the trip is to take possession of certain territory in the name of the H.A. Nomads," Verdon wrote. "The source should be able to inform us about many subjects, given that he will be acting as [Carroll's] chauffeur on this trip of sixteen to twenty hours. Furthermore, we should be informed on the precise goals of the H.A. Nomads in Nova Scotia."

Two days later Kane contacted his handlers not from Halifax but from Toronto. There had been a conflicting demand for his services between Carroll and Steinert, Kane explained. Steinert, though still only a prospect, had won because he had Mom Boucher on his side. Kane would have to reimburse the pocket money, St. Onge dutifully noted in a debriefing report, but there is no record that he did so, or that his regular pay was withheld in lieu. On the contrary, Kane was handed another $1500 four days after phoning from Toronto.

Kane's best bonus during this period came as a result of the only tip he was ever to give the RCMP that, according to the debriefing reports, ever resulted in a seizure or arrest. Even then, the money came in the form of a reward from the Montreal police, not the RCMP. The white Econoline van full of dynamite and nails that was to have done so much damage at the Pelletier-run bar in December had been parked in a South Shore garage awaiting another Alliance target. There was a second stolen van in the same garage, possibly full of explosives too, Kane told St. Onge, and at least seven people knew of the hiding place. St. Onge informed the Montreal police on a Friday afternoon, when the SPCUM didn't have the men or the overtime budget to raid the garage. They put off the operation until Monday, hoping that a tempting target wouldn't present itself to the Hells Angels in the meantime and that the vans would not be moved. The police were lucky, the seizure was made, and Kane pocketed a $2000 reward.

It didn't come without risk, however. The Hells called a meeting a day or two after the seizure to discuss how police had learned of the cache. Mom Boucher declared that it was almost certainly due to a telephone wiretap and that everyone had to be more careful. "There were no doubts about the source or any other source," St. Onge wrote with relief. Unfortunately, the next issue of *Photo Police* carried the story of how an Econoline bomb had been aimed at a Pelletier bar but not detonated because there were too many non-bikers on the premises. Thanks to the tabloid, the Hells knew there was an informant in their midst.

Kane's anxiety level rose sharply. Not long before, he had again fretted about the bikers' tentacles into various police forces. Scott Steinert had told him that the Hells had a source in the anti-gang squad of the Montreal police; Mom Boucher knew crooked cops all over from whom "he can obtain pretty much what he needs"; there was another police photo album of bikers, likely put together by the

RCMP's Lévesque, in the gang's hands. "The source is nervous because he is scared that a policeman will talk too much and he'll be found out," Verdon recorded.

During the early months of 1995 the Hells Angels had reason to feel cocky: victory over the Alliance seemed not only guaranteed but imminent. In mid-January, after a Rock Machine member blew himself up while delivering a bomb destined for the Rockers, Wolf Carroll joked that the score was 8–0 in favour of the Hells. That same week, other Rock Machine figures approached Mom Boucher in the hopes of negotiating a peace, but the Hells Angels' top warlord told them it was too late. The Hells were coasting to control of the Montreal drug market, and in early February three Rock Machine members defected, bringing with them details of a plot to assassinate Boucher.

Mom and the gang were convinced that a few solid blows would bring their stumbling adversaries to their knees. He was reported to be supplying weapons to anyone who promised to use them against the Rock Machine, and Kane told the RCMP about a hit list of sixteen Alliance targets prepared by the gang. He took Verdon and St. Onge on another driving tour, showing them the houses of two men already pinpointed by the Hells, one an independent dealer who did too much business with the Rock Machine, the other a member of the rival gang. "The H.A. seem determined to settle the problem once and for all and to show to all concerned their strength and supremacy," Verdon wrote in his debriefing report. But if there was any thought of warning the individuals, Staff Sergeant Lemire put it aside. "With the war that is going on between them, all the members of the various gangs involved are perfectly well aware of the dangers that they face. We will act only in a case of a direct and precise threat against an individual."

The Hells Angels might have been triumphant. They weren't, however, united. Again, Scott Steinert was the cause of much of the friction. It was resented by some gang members that when Steinert was promoted to full patch it would almost certainly be as a member of the Nomads, the all-star chapter where the select few could expect to make a great deal of money. They considered it unjustified leapfrogging, and after much discussion a ruling was rendered at a Hells "mass"—as the gang's regular meetings are known. Steinert was offered two options: either he could become a member of the Montreal chapter of the Hells where he was already a prospect and then perhaps transfer to the Nomads after *"un bon bout de temps,"* an appropriate length of time. Or he could turn in his prospect colours with the Montreal Hells and start from the bottom again as a hangaround on the Nomads' ladder. Steinert chose to stay where he was with the Montreal Hells chapter.

For the Hells Angels, the dispute had an oddly bureaucratic flavour. In reality, these procedural wrangles hid linguistic tensions within the group. Although he had grown up in Sorel and spoke excellent French, Steinert was considered an anglophone, and some of the francophone members felt that *"les blokes"* were taking up too much space in their organization. This was, after all, the early 1990s when the failure of the Meech Lake and Charlottetown accords had polarized English and French Canada. Biker gangs weren't indifferent to the political winds. (During the Charlottetown and sovereignty referendum debates, the Hells Angels adopted a wholly practical position and let it be known that they were on the federalist side. New borders were not in their interests.)

The two solitudes manifested themselves again when Donald "Bam-Bam" Magnussen, a good friend of Steinert's and a former protegé of Stadnick's, was refused hangaround status with the Montreal Hells chapter. It had been thought that the freeze on new members might be waived for him, considering his influence in Winnipeg and Thunder Bay, where he controlled a significant share of the drug market and where the Hells Angels were keen to establish a stronger presence. But the francophone members stood firm, saying they didn't know Magnussen well enough.

Steinert's relations with his fellow anglophones weren't without problems either. He had bigfooted Wolf Carroll when both had called on Kane's services in February, and Carroll felt that Steinert was showing too much interest in areas Carroll considered his—the western part of Montreal's downtown as well as the Laurentians. For similar reasons Walter Stadnick thought Steinert was too pushy and didn't appreciate his obvious appetite for a territory in the West, possibly Winnipeg. Steinert had energy and ambition and could see the potential: a kilo of cocaine that sold for $35,000 in Montreal was worth at least $45,000 just 2400 kilometres west. It was Stadnick who had patiently cultivated contacts in the city, and he would not allow an upstart to shove him aside, even one backed by Mom Boucher. And just as Carroll resented Steinert's poaching Kane, Stadnick resented Steinert's poaching Magnussen.

Steinert was making powerful enemies, but Kane was ever more in his orbit and his confidence. It wasn't only that Steinert was fun to carouse with. He was dynamic and had big business ideas and if he was ruffling feathers, well, wasn't that what fresh winds did? To Kane, Steinert seemed to be the future, whereas Carroll and Stadnick were edging toward retirement. Kane identified with him—but not so much that he wouldn't betray him.

In February Steinert told Kane that he lived in fear of being deported. Despite having resided in Canada almost all his life, he had never taken the trouble to apply for citizenship. A month later, Kane was with Steinert and Magnussen when, high on ecstasy, Steinert confided that Mom Boucher felt that many Hells Angels weren't sufficiently committed to winning the biker war and should be spurred into action. If a Hells Angel were killed in the cause, that might do the trick. And if the Rock Machine couldn't manage the hit, well, maybe Mom would have to do it himself, ensuring that the Rock Machine took the blame. Boucher, Steinert told Kane, was the most dangerous man he'd ever met.

However dangerous he might be, Boucher would soon be out of the action for a while. On Friday, March 24, ten days after returning from a Mexican vacation, Boucher got into a car driven by Toots Tousignant to attend to some errands before both headed to a Hells Angels–sponsored bike show in Sherbrooke. It was one of the gang's annual public-relations initiatives and a way to dupe regular folks into contributing to their legal defence fund. Stupidly, Boucher was carrying a 9 mm revolver, its serial number filed off, in his belt when the car was pulled over by the police even before they'd left the city. During his interrogation an SQ investigator told Boucher that police had a "coded informant" inside his gang whose tip had led to the Econoline seizure. After ruminating awhile, Boucher concluded that the source had to be one of six people, among them Tousignant, Steinert, and Kane. Kane was told by Marc Sigman, a low-level player also on Boucher's list, that of the six Boucher suspected Kane the most because he knew him the least.

On April Fool's Day 1995, Kane received a call in the early afternoon with a succinct order to make his way to the clubhouse in Sorel to meet "certain members." It was a year to the day after the Belleville bust, and Kane thought he had been nailed again, this time by a much less forgiving crew than the OPP. He phoned Verdon in a panic, afraid he had been found out. They agreed he had to show up in Sorel; failure to appear would be as good as a confession.

Kane arrived at the meeting to be told that because of the leak only full-patch members and prospects would henceforth be allowed into the Sorel clubhouse. He dropped in on Steinert while in Sorel, who told him that talk of a leak was all "blah-blah"—nonsense. At the same time Kane found his friend to be cooler than usual. "For the time being no one trusts anyone," Kane told Verdon. Mom Boucher, he said, "would move land and sea to find the informant, whatever the cost."

Kane was reprieved but couldn't relax. Then, serendipitously, Serge Quesnel, a hit man on a $500-a-week salary (plus bonuses for each successful job) from the Trois-Rivières chapter, was arrested and quickly agreed to a deal with authorities. Based on his information, thirteen members and associates of the Trois-Rivières Hells were apprehended on April 3. With attention diverted to elsewhere, the Montreal leak was temporarily forgotten and the heat came off. Suddenly life was looking up.

And to top it off, Dany Kane had fallen in love.

9

LOVE AND BOMBS

After his release from Quinte Detention Centre in July 1994, Kane spent even less time at home with his family than he had before. His absence didn't trouble Josée. The couple fought regularly, with Kane's brand of violence escalating from the psychological and verbal to the physical. Consumed by furies, he would smash anything within reach—plates of macaroni and cheese, radios, even their microwave oven. Two or three times he hit Josée, but if he regretted his outbursts, he never asked forgiveness.

The untidy state of the household, upstairs in the duplex they shared with his parents, often set him off. With three youngsters under five and Josée effectively the sole caregiver, she sometimes let order and cleanliness fall by the wayside. She felt that taking good care of the children—playing with them at home, excursions to the park—was more important than taking good care of the house. But Kane wouldn't listen. It was as if he needed an outlet for his anger, some excuse to let fly. Josée understood this, once asking what could possibly wind him up so much that he had to explode. He said only, "Someday you'll find out."

Josée attributed part of Kane's anger and aggression to his consumption of steroids and other muscle-building products. After his stint at Napanee, Kane began taking what Josée describes as an *"hormone des morts,"* human growth hormone, which Kane said came from cadavers. He would inject himself in the bathroom out of sight of the children, and whatever the substance's impact on his biceps it had a sour effect on his moods.

Kane's narcissistic obsession with appearances occasionally extended beyond his own physique and wardrobe to Josée. As she was his common-law wife, her looks reflected on him, even if they rarely stepped out together. Kane pushed Josée to have breast enlargement surgery and a nose job, but she wasn't interested, saying she was happy as she was, slimmed down from the days of her first pregnancy. Instead she asked for money to buy new clothes, a few items to replace the maternity garb now several sizes too large. Kane refused, even though by this time he was on the RCMP payroll. "I'm the one who has to look good because I'm the one who goes out," Josée remembers him saying. "You just stay at home, so it doesn't matter."

As the children emerged from diapers, his interest in them increased, and when he was home, he fell easily into the role of father. Once he took Benjamin, the eldest, to the barber for a haircut that matched his own *coupe Longueuil*. With Josée, however, he grew more emotionally distant. She would encourage him to open up a bit about what he was feeling—not what he was doing; she knew that was territory she couldn't broach—but he resisted. She tried to book time with him for conversation, but he wasn't having any of it. After a while, she stopped making the effort.

That Kane was seeing other women would not have been a surprise to Josée. While they had sex as frequently as ever, Josée knew that Kane was hardly monogamous. It just wasn't the biker way, especially those bikers who spent as much time in the company of escorts and strippers as Kane did through his association with Pat Lambert and Agence Aventure. One woman who was no secret was an exotic dancer with the stage name of Stevie Wheels. She was *"un feature,"* a headline act whose appearances were promoted by the bars who booked her. True to her stage name, Stevie Wheels incorporated roller skates into her show.

Whether she was the source or not, Kane came home with a sexually transmitted disease around this time. He didn't own up to Josée right away. Only after he refused her advances one evening did she suspect something was wrong; she couldn't remember his ever saying no to sex. After some questioning, he came clean, so to speak. The incident subsequently drove Kane to schedule regular checkups for STDs; it didn't, however, dull his interest in extramarital dalliances or in strippers.

Patricia was enjoying a rare night out on the town in the spring of 1995 when she met Dany Kane. As a twenty-one-year-old single mother, she didn't have many such opportunities.

The third of four daughters, Patricia was born in Haiti to parents who were both teachers. The early 1970s was an especially horrific time in Haiti: the brutal reign of the dictator François "Papa Doc" Duvalier came to an end in 1971, only to be followed by more of the same under his son, Jean-Claude. Patricia's father made his way to Montreal, and once established, he sent for his wife and children. They had barely arrived when he was diagnosed with cancer, and soon Patricia's mother was left to fend for herself and her girls. Patricia's studies were sidetracked when she got pregnant at sixteen, but after a few years she was back at school, studying office management and supporting herself and her son, Steve, as a stripper.

Her world and Kane's overlapped on a weekday night in April in a bar on Ste-Catherine Street. Someone at another table sent her a drink. She sent it back. A second drink arrived, and this one she accepted. A friend who had joined her was able to vouch for the fellow who was trying to get her attention. Bar protocol and basic politesse dictated that she at least thank him, and eventually Patricia approached Kane's table. They clicked. She found him charming and full of energy, muscular and fit, and obviously attentive to his appearance. He could keep up with Patricia's sharp, no-nonsense mind, although that night it was gradually dulled by alcohol: "I was very drunk," she remembers.

Patricia would not bring a strange man home to the apartment she shared with her young son. After a call to her sitter, they headed to a motel in Joliette, about fifty kilometres northeast of Montreal. Kane had to make a court appearance there the next day, for traffic tickets, he told her. The next morning, Patricia awoke to find herself alone. She first checked her purse, but her money and credit cards were untouched. She had a shower, got dressed, and was about to make her way back to Montreal when Kane reappeared with a broad smile on his face, ready to take her home. "You thought I'd leave you here, didn't you?" he asked.

"It was supposed to be a one-night stand and I was never going to see him again," Patricia recalled. But he phoned her later the same day.

Kane didn't yet have the biker tattoos he would eventually sport, and Patricia had only vague suspicions of what he was involved in. These were partly corroborated by her friend at the bar when she asked how Kane earned his living. If he knew, he didn't tell her, saying only, "You wouldn't bring him to church on Sunday." Patricia understood this didn't mean Kane wasn't Catholic. Organized crime was a reasonable guess: there was no shortage of cash and he didn't work a nine-to-five job, not to mention the company he kept.

Patricia was completely unaware of the other facts of Kane's life, that he was still living with Josée, that he had three children, that he had exhibited a shameless racism not long before. He was never short of conversation yet rarely spoke about himself. Patricia did learn of Benjamin's existence, but took Kane at his word when he said that Benjamin was an only child, the result of a brief relationship. He promptly ended his affair with Stevie Wheels, and Patricia believed he had no others.

Still, Patricia did not regard their relationship as a long-term commitment. "He was just a guy I would hang around with until one of us got fed up," she says. For this reason, whenever Kane slept over she would bundle him out of the house early before Steve awoke. When the three did spend time together, Steve and Kane were comfortable and happy in each other's company, but Patricia didn't want her son becoming attached to a man she didn't expect to have in her life very long.

The RCMP's debriefing report for April 13, 1995, included a note that "the new concubine of C-2994 is of the black race" and mentioned the name of a previous boyfriend. But the Mounties were not as interested in

Kane's romantic liaisons as they were in the Hells Angels' business affairs.

In the spring and summer of 1995, the biker war was reaching a peak. Bombings seemed a weekly, sometimes daily, occurrence in the Montreal region, with occasional explosions in Quebec City and elsewhere. As often as not, the blasts blew out the windows of neighbouring houses and storefronts. It was evident to everyone that sooner or later innocent bystanders would be seriously injured or killed. Public outrage was mounting toward the Hells Angels in particular, and the gang's leaders were shrewd enough to know they should pay attention. Enough public pressure would result in more police pressure.

In mid-April the edict went out: "The milieu will settle its accounts with revolvers from now on and not with explosives," Kane told his handlers. "Explosives disturb public opinion too much." But biker gangs don't have the cohesion or discipline of other institutions, and their leaders are prone to making decisions on a whim and changing their minds almost as quickly. Before they'd fully ceased using bombs, gang members were planting them again.

Other initiatives in the Hells' public-relations campaign were better executed, though with no more beneficial effect on popular opinion. These included unsigned press releases that accused the SQ of "flooding the milieu with falsehoods" in an effort to pit gang against gang. One claimed the SQ was responsible for one of the bar bombings.

The Hells Angels also lodged a complaint with the Conseil de Presse du Québec, the province's media watchdog, after the *Journal de Montréal* published a group photograph of gang members. They claimed the photo endangered their lives by providing their enemies with the means to identify them. Pierre Panaccio, the lawyer who laid the complaint, told the Conseil that the next step could be the publication of the members' home addresses or the names of the schools their children attended. The Conseil's decision was nuanced: it ruled that the *Journal* was justified in printing a photo of the gang and alleging that it was a criminal organization, but the paper should not have identified the people in the photo if they didn't figure in the accompanying story.

Mom Boucher, still languishing in jail, was as concerned with spin as any of his colleagues. He was caught on a wiretap speculating that perhaps the Hells and their lawyers weren't up to the task of handling their own PR, that a professional communications firm ought to be hired. Boucher floated this idea to Gaétan Rivest, one of several disgraced former policemen he did business with over the course of the biker war. Two years later Boucher and Rivest would go further than simply hiring specialists: they started their own crime tabloid called *Le Juste Milieu—A Fair Shake* or *The Happy Medium*. It was dedicated almost exclusively to bashing the police and justice system, especially the SQ, for whom Rivest had worked.

A public-relations strategy the Hells Angels did not seriously consider in the first half of 1995 was laying down their weapons or slowing their expansion. Kane found himself on the front line of their drive for control of more territory. In February and March he spent time in southern Ontario with Pat Lambert on the Hells' version of a goodwill diplomatic tour. The pair had been received, he told Verdon, "with the greatest consideration" at the Loners clubhouse in Toronto; in Hamilton they had visited a Mafia-controlled nightclub where they "were treated like kings." The owner took care of them personally, refusing their money like a generous host.

In mid-April, he did another tour of southern Ontario on his own, through Ottawa, Kingston, Toronto, and Niagara Falls, to build on the contacts made earlier. Almost immediately afterwards he spent a week in Winnipeg with Walter Stadnick. The Hells had captured the drug market in Thunder Bay from the Satan's Choice, and Stadnick was in Winnipeg to set up a regular drug run between Winnipeg and the northwestern Ontario city. Bam-Bam Magnussen facilitated introductions to other major dealers and local crime figures. All were given the same message by Stadnick: get onside with the Hells Angels while there is still time.

Kane had been offered the job of administering the day-to-day business of the Winnipeg–Thunder Bay corridor by Stadnick, a sign of acceptance that his handlers used in their arguments for a more lucrative contract from RCMP brass. "The source can inform us almost daily on the takeover of Ontario and Prairies by the Hells Angels. No police squad however good could give us such precise and rapid information."

Kane's $500-a-week contract had expired, and Verdon and St. Onge knew they would have to offer a lot more money to keep their source happy and talkative. They offered $1000 a week, but Kane wanted at least twice that amount. Ever the hard bargainer, he grew tightlipped in late April, and he used the Winnipeg trip as proof that he needed substantial walking-around money if only to cover his expenses. The week-long excursion had cost him $4000, he told Verdon, much of it spent keeping up appearances with the millionaire crime figures with whom he was consorting.

Verdon buttressed his case by pointing out that Jean-Pierre Lévesque at CISC telephoned him at least twice a week from Ottawa, requesting updates on biker activities in Quebec and elsewhere in Canada. "Ninety per cent of the information transmitted to S/Sgt. Lévesque comes from source C-2994.... He depends greatly on the information transmitted by C-2994 and it is very important for the force to keep this source." In early May RCMP management buckled, and at a meeting in a downtown Montreal hotel Kane was offered a three-month contract at $2000 a week. Kane signed happily, pocketed his first fortnightly payment of $4000 cash, and was off again.

This time he travelled east to Halifax, by Harley rather than by car or plane, and for pleasure rather than business. It was the spring run, one of the annual rituals of all self-respecting motorcycle clubs, criminal or not, in North America. Most clubs levied fines or otherwise penalized members who missed these rites without a good excuse. But as Quebec's Hells Angels became more business oriented and with the biker war demanding ongoing vigilance, such traditions were allowed to lapse. It was also true that these runs offered police not-to-be-missed opportunities for low-level harassment: pulling over the bikers en masse to verify their papers, ensuring that their customized bikes conformed to all regulations, checking for any outstanding warrants, or otherwise delaying their trip and spoiling their fun.

That year's spring run to Halifax attracted an impressive but far from full turnout. Missing was the national president, Tiny Richard, who was having health problems, and his eventual successor, Richard Mayrand. Mayrand had seen his brother executed in the Lennoxville massacre but stuck by the gang nonetheless. Nomads Normand "Biff" Hamel, one of Mom Boucher's oldest comrades, and Wolf Carroll, the godfather of the Halifax Hells Angels chapter and the liaison between the gang's East Coast and Quebec members, were among the other notable absentees. Mom Boucher sent his regrets from prison.

Even so, Kane was impressed by the show of force as about sixty bikers made their way through Quebec and New Brunswick to Nova Scotia, accompanied by a half-dozen escort vehicles. Onlookers were even more awestruck. This, after all, was the world's most notorious biker gang fulfilling the raison d'être of all motorcycle clubs, and reinforcing their status as icons of freedom, violence, and power. Frequently, Kane reported, the Hells were asked to pose for photographs. At one gas station, a Pepsi-Cola delivery man offered them cases of pop free of charge.

Once in Halifax, the partying started at a restaurant booked for the occasion, then continued at the Halifax clubhouse. Between the festivities, there was some business conducted, but not a great deal. Scott Steinert told Kane he was selling ten kilos of cocaine a month to a client in Thunder Bay at $45,000 a kilo, netting him a monthly profit of roughly $100,000. He revealed he was working on a large import project that could go ahead only when Boucher was out of prison. And he told Kane that he and an associate were planning a trip to Jamaica. There they would recruit candidates for a street gang they hoped to set up in Montreal to challenge Master 13, an existing Caribbean street gang associated with the Alliance. Steinert's Jamaican gang never materialized, and little wonder, considering how many other enterprises the prospect had on the go. Kane's debriefing reports suggest Steinert's involvement in countless schemes in every region, though his prominence is probably related to the fact that he was C-2994's primary source of information.

After the Quesnel affair and the careless SQ revelation to Boucher that there was an informant in the Montreal network, the gang's leaders became more cautious. The signs were that Kane was trusted, but he, like others in relatively low-level positions, was increasingly out of the loop. Meetings became closed-door affairs with efforts taken to escape monitoring by police and underlings. One gathering was announced for Sherbrooke but held secretly in Quebec City. Several others were convened on a pontoon boat in the middle of the St. Lawrence. Furthermore, "they make more and more use of handwritten messages that are burned after being read," Kane told the Mounties.

In Halifax, however, Steinert was as voluble as ever, and Kane was an undoubted sidekick. The RCMP learned of a major cocaine and hash shortage that had plagued the gang through the spring due, it was felt, to Mom Boucher's imprisonment. The drought had allowed the Rock Machine to recover lost ground, especially in the Gay Village where they had taken back several clubs, stomping a few Hells Angels–affiliated dealers in the process. Steinert himself was having trouble filling his orders in Thunder Bay and elsewhere and was worried his reputation was suffering.

Another Steinert scheme was a monopoly of the stripper supply business in Quebec and beyond through his Sensations agency. This placed him in direct conflict with Carroll, Lambert, and Agence Aventure, a brash move not looked on approvingly by the gang in general. But Steinert didn't appear cowed, perhaps because of his powerful patrons, national president Tiny Richard and chief warlord Mom Boucher. He threw his weight around recklessly as if he answered to no one. In early July he severely beat a doorman who had refused him entry to a downtown Montreal nightclub even after he flashed his Hells Angels colours. Unknown to Steinert, the doorman worked for a full-patch Hells Angel named Michel "The Animal" Lavoie-Smith, who was himself notorious for arbitrary violence and unprovoked assaults. Steinert had alienated at least one more influential member of the gang.

On a second trip to the Maritimes that season, Steinert participated in the East Coast Run in Prince Edward Island, an event not restricted to Hells Angels chapters. There he intended to pick a fight with several Satan's Choice members, simply because they wore the colours of a different gang. Before he could find an opportunity his bike broke down with serious mechanical problems. Into the breach stepped the Choice, who restored his machine to better condition than before, and with their compliments.

Steinert's unpredictability and violent temper were issues enough among the more level-headed Hells Angels that he thought it advisable to move out of his Sorel home for several weeks that summer. The gang quite regularly rid themselves of problematic members, so as a precaution Steinert and Magnussen took up residence in a Longueuil motel while the climate cooled. Steinert relinquished none of his warrior duties during these weeks. He was put in charge of paying the $10,000 bounty placed on the head of every enemy gang member. In mid-July he led a dozen Hells Angels supporters to a club where Rock Machine members had been showing their faces. The Hells' plan was straightforward—crack some heads—but none of their adversaries showed up.

Then, on Tuesday, August 8, Kane informed his handlers that Steinert had ordered three more bomb kits from Pat Lambert. Steinert was excited and impatient, insisting that the kits be delivered that evening. The rush request came two weeks after the gang's leadership had once again banned bombings without express instruction from senior members. The directive followed the narrow escape of a couple and their two young children when a bomb blew up their house in the Laurentian bedroom community of St-Lin. Wolf Carroll described it as a "dirty job"; not only were the kids almost killed but their father wasn't the intended target. It was his brother the bikers were after. Carroll hinted that whoever had planted the bomb might be eliminated for his mistake. "According to the Hells Angel philosophy, you can't kill the children of even your worst enemy," Kane reported.

If Steinert heard the leadership's message, he chose not to heed it. He was a law unto himself that summer. Too soon, he and the rest of the gang would learn that quite apart from the Hells' questionable code of conduct, there were very practical reasons not to kill children.

10

KANE
THE KILLER

In the early afternoon of Wednesday, August 9, 1995, Kane got a call from Gaetan St. Onge: did he know anything about the bombing in Montreal's east end? At half-past noon that day, a remote-control bomb had detonated under the driver's seat of a Jeep in the Hochelaga-Maisonneuve district, just a few blocks from the Olympic Stadium. The explosion was powerful enough to lift the Jeep clear off the street and blow the man at the wheel out of the vehicle and three metres into the air. Both legs were ripped off, and he died almost instantly. Pieces of debris were scattered as far as fifty metres away, but it was a single shard of metal that had prompted St. Onge's call to Kane.

The piece of metal, about the size of a child's thumb, shot like a bullet across Rue Adam and hit an eleven-year-old boy in the back of the head, boring through his skull and into his brain. Daniel Desrochers had been playing on the grass in front of the Saint-Nom-de-Jésus school with his best friend when he was struck. He was rushed to hospital, where he lay for four days in critical condition, severely brain damaged, before dying.

Kane claimed he didn't know anything about the bombing when St. Onge contacted him. But he called back that evening to say that Marc Dubé, the owner of the Jeep and the man killed in the blast, was a small-time dealer for Mom Boucher. The next day, Kane called again to confirm that, yes, it was the Hells Angels who had been targeted by the attack. He added that Dubé wasn't one of their drug dealers but only a delivery man; no one could understand why the Alliance would go after a mere courier. Kane was asked by his handlers to find out everything he could about the incident, but he appears to have offered nothing more on the subject until almost two weeks later.

For no reason made clear in RCMP documents, Kane travelled to Ottawa on August 22 for a long evening meeting with Verdon and Lévesque of the CISC. Accepting his fortnightly $4000, he began the debriefing with all sorts of unrelated intelligence. National president Tiny Richard had undergone abdominal surgery at the Sorel hospital and was being guarded at night by a protegé of Steinert's. Steinert himself was in touch with a gunsmith for the tune-up and maintenance of about twenty prohibited firearms belonging to the gang. Mom Boucher, released from jail at last, had a new right-hand man who had no criminal record and *du style clean cut,* the better to escape police attention when he served as Boucher's cocaine courier.

Halfway through the meeting, Kane almost casually addressed the Jeep bombing himself, without apparent prodding from St. Onge or Lévesque. The timing was odd, to say the least. By this time, Daniel Desrochers' death had galvanized public attention in a way no other incident in the biker war would. The outrage against the bikers had been turned in the direction of the police and their apparent indifference to ending the conflict. It was widely believed that the authorities were quite happy to stand back and cheer as two criminal groups went after each other with whatever weapons were available. The police tried to deflect the criticism by saying the deck was stacked against them, that they didn't have the resources to take on sophisticated and violent criminal organizations. Two days after the bombing, one of Montreal's top cops had appealed publicly for stiff anti-gang legislation that would enable more severe crackdowns on criminal motorcycle gangs and organized crime in general. His call was quickly taken up by Mayor Pierre Bourque, various provincial and opposition politicians, and any number of columnists and editorialists. Eventually, Josée-Anne Desrochers, Daniel's grieving and angry mother, became the movement's figurehead.

In the shorter term, the police knew they would have to come up with initiatives of their own, and at that time their best idea was a special multi-force squad dedicated exclusively to ending the biker war. This squad, named Carcajou—Wolverine—wouldn't be formally announced until September 23. At the outset, it would be confined to investigators from the SQ and Montreal police. The RCMP weren't invited to join until the force itself put pressure on Quebec's sovereignist public security minister, Serge Ménard. Nonetheless, by mid-August federal authorities knew some joint effort was in the offing. That might explain why Kane was meeting again with Lévesque: to be reassured that the RCMP's involvement in Carcajou wouldn't compromise his security or reveal his identity to the SQ and the SPCUM.

Why the Desrochers bombing didn't receive more attention in the sessions with Kane is difficult to divine. An arrest in the case, even on the slimmest evidence, would have been a coup for the police in the immediate aftermath of the tragedy. Kane may not have had any more information about the case than he had already supplied to Verdon and St. Onge, but nothing in their debriefing reports suggests they were even asking for new details.

Contrary to the details Kane had offered weeks earlier, he suggested very strongly on August 22 that Scott Steinert was behind the bombing. He reminded them of Steinert's urgent order for three bomb kits the night before the event. "Since that day," Kane reported, "Steinert has never again spoken of the bombs which he ordered and never spoken of using them for one thing or another. Also, Steinert asked certain people he's close to what they thought of the incident and also whether they thought the perpetrator of the bombing deserves to be liquidated. After his friends answered that the perpetrator of this act of violence should indeed be liquidated, Steinert didn't answer and became very pensive." In his report of the meeting, Verdon concludes the obvious: Kane's information "makes us think that [Steinert] might be involved in the incident." He adds, however, that more evidence would be required before any action might be taken.

Kane then moved on to other biker news. The drug drought was abating but business recovery was slow. Steinert wanted to start up a gang in Kingston, with Kane and others dispatched to "clean things up" and take over eastern Ontario completely. Wolf Carroll thought it best to leave the province be. All gang members remained cautious and careful in what they said and did. In conclusion, Kane told Verdon and St. Onge that Pat Lambert had a new associate who was teaching him how to detonate bombs using a pager activated by a car alarm system. The man was a former member of the armed forces, the debriefing memo noted. "His first name is Roland."

Roland Lebrasseur's father had been a heavy-equipment operator in the mining industry near Sept-Îles before being crippled in an accident when Roland was eight years old. With four children and a quadriplegic husband who needed constant care, Roland's mother found herself overwhelmed. She made the wrenching decision to send her children to live with relatives. Just as Dany Kane had been relocated to an aunt and uncle in Lemoyne, Roland Lebrasseur moved in with his aunt, her husband, and their three children in Baie-Comeau. Lebrasseur's aunt was also a teacher, but unlike Kane he excelled under his aunt's strict guidance and did well enough in school to be selected for a *Reach for the Top*–type competition known as *Génies en herbe*— "Geniuses in the Grass."

Lebrasseur's ambition was to follow his father and become a heavy-equipment operator. The armed forces could teach him the skills for such a career and show him a bit of the world besides, so Lebrasseur signed up for basic training a few days after his eighteenth birthday. Over the next seven years he did two tours of duty as a United Nations peacekeeper in Cyprus and was based for a time in Germany. It was there that he married a fellow Quebecker, also in the military; in 1988 the couple had a daughter. They wanted their child to grow up in Quebec near family, and with the Canadian military winding down its operations in Germany, they left the forces soon after the birth. They settled in Sept-Îles, where Lebrasseur held a variety of jobs over the next few years. He worked as an armoured car driver and taught electronics at a community college. But nothing worked out, and gradually his marriage dissolved. On occasion he hit the bottle heavily. His mother, who had remarried, remembers searching the Sept-Îles bars and taverns looking for him after getting a call from her furious daughter-in-law.

Eventually the couple divorced, and Lebrasseur moved to the lower Laurentians, about fifty kilometres north of Montreal, to make a clean start. For several months he lived with his mother and her new husband in St-Jerôme, where his mother had taken an administrative job with the local police force. For Lebrasseur, however, employment opportunities were scarce. He had no connections in the area, his years with the military didn't seem to count for much, and he wasn't especially outgoing or assertive. In the summer of 1995 his mother returned to Sept-Îles after the Bloc Québécois MP for the riding offered her a job as a political attaché. Lebrasseur packed his things and moved to Montreal.

Shortly thereafter a chance meeting in a restaurant or pool hall led Lebrasseur to apply for a job as a driver for Agence Aventure. He had his own car and, having handled tanks and other vehicles in the army, was more than capable behind the wheel. The tip that got him the job may have come from Daniel Bouchard, another native of the Sept-Îles area, who had worked for several years on the Quebec North Shore and Labrador Railway before landing in Montreal. Or Lebrasseur may have started work at Agence Aventure only to discover that an acquaintance from back home also worked for Wolf Carroll. One way or another, the two men made the connection.

Bouchard came from the working-class elite. His father had been a full-time employee of the Confédération des syndicats nationaux, the labour federation that exercised enormous influence in a hard-hat, steel-toe union town like Sept-Îles. He had married young and fathered a daughter; when he and his wife later divorced, he had insisted on custody. Around Sept-Îles, Bouchard was well liked, admired for his friendly personality, handsome good looks, and above all for his devotion to his daughter. Somehow, though, he became involved with biker gangs and eventually the Hells Angels, either while in Sept-Îles or after he moved to Montreal. His participation wasn't a full-time commitment; once in Montreal, Bouchard parlayed his work on the NS & L Railway into a job with VIA Rail. His two lives may have been complementary: according to police documents Bouchard was suspected of using his frequent travels on the trains to transport drugs across the country.

Thanks to Bouchard and Agence Aventure, Lebrasseur also found himself involved with the Hells Angels. His apprenticeship began quickly: a week after his first mention in the Mounties' debriefing reports in connection with Pat Lambert's bomb-making operation, Lebrasseur was driving Carroll to Nova Scotia where the veteran Hells Angel had gone to "shake things up." He was inside Kane's network, and it was inevitable they would meet.

The day after Daniel Desrochers was fatally wounded, Montreal's police brass had warned all the gangs to drop explosives from their arsenals. Still the bombing continued, and with greater frequency. On August 22, three bombs went off in Laval and the lower Laurentians. In the most serious incident, a large bomb—police estimated it contained between ten and fifteen kilograms of dynamite—levelled the bungalow clubhouse of a Hells Angels puppet gang, the Rowdy Crew, in Le Gardeur, off the eastern tip of the island of Montreal. No one was killed in the explosion, although the gang's dog wasn't so lucky.

Four days later another bomb, only slightly smaller, destroyed the back of a prominent Hells Angels landmark, the Bob Chopper motorcycle shop in Longueuil. A dud grenade had been thrown at the front window the week before, but this attack was more successful: once again, there were no fatalities, but windows were blown out on houses sixty metres away. When police arrived at the scene, Hells Angels lawyers were already in place, denying them access to the site until they produced a search warrant. The next night, in what police took as a tit-for-tat attack, a Rock Machine–linked tattoo parlour in Montreal's north end was firebombed.

Kane told Verdon that the bombing strikes against the Hells had aroused considerable paranoid speculation— that the Bob Chopper bomb had actually been planted by police as part of their campaign for an anti-gang law— and not a little debate as to the best counterstrategy. Retaliatory attacks were expected, Kane said, but some senior members were "impatient" with the scattered, unfocused campaign to date. Tossing Molotov cocktails into empty tattoo parlours didn't cut it, was the argument. "They envisage limiting their ripostes to actions which count," Verdon wrote. "We can expect that some leading figures of the Alliance will be targeted soon."

Before the Hells Angels could strike, however, the Alliance scored its biggest coup of the hostilities. On September 15, a hit man tracked down Richard "Crow" Émond, a former Missile, a founder of the Trois-Rivières Hells Angel chapter, and an elder among outlaw bikers in the province, to a north-end Montreal mall where he was doing some Friday-afternoon shopping with his girlfriend.

There in the parking lot, the hit man put three bullets into Émond as he was stepping into his Pontiac Bonneville. He was the first full-patch Hells Angel to die in the biker war, and his murder both enraged and disheartened the gang. Two weeks earlier the Pelletier clan, one of the mainstays of the Alliance, had defected to the Hells, encouraging some to think that victory was theirs. The assassination of Émond suggested quite the opposite.

The day after the killing, Kane told Verdon that Mom Boucher was upset by Émond's death but hoped it would "wake up the other Hells Angels and so serve his cause." Two days later he reported that calls for retaliation were increasing, especially from Mom and Wolf Carroll. But the explosions that followed were mostly the work of the Alliance. The morning of Émond's funeral the Alliance successfully blew up another bar associated with the Hells. That night they made an attempt on the clubhouse of the Jokers, the St-Luc puppet gang that Émond had controlled.

At about 2 a.m. an unlit van approached the clubhouse. One Rock Machine associate got out and crept toward the clubhouse, presumably to scout a spot for the bomb. Two others unloaded the explosive device. The driver stayed in the van. All the while they were being monitored by two Jokers on the gang's elaborate video-camera security system. When their intentions became clear, one of the Jokers emerged from the building and sprayed the van with machine-gun fire. Either a bullet hit the device or it was accidentally detonated in the ensuing panic; in the event, only the scout survived.

A journalist who arrived at dawn found a bucolic early autumn scene of sunlight and morning mist, disturbed somewhat by the sounds of police dogs sniffing out and occasionally scarfing down bits of human remains spread over a hundred-metre radius. It would take police three weeks to gather up what the dogs and other scavengers left behind. It would be more than two months before they came across the various body parts, including a thirty-centimetre-long section of a spine that members of the Jokers had grabbed and preserved in formaldehyde and in their freezer.

The Hells Angels were being attacked from without; within, they were racked by familiar problems. The day after Labour Day, Kane was able to confirm to his handlers that the bomb that killed Daniel Desrochers was definitely a Hells Angels job. He gave no explanation why Dubé had been targeted. Was it Mom Boucher's attempt to rile up passive gang members? Or another case of mistaken identity? A Rock Machine dealer drove a Jeep almost identical to Dubé's, and the two men had apparently traded custom hubcaps not long before the bombing. Kane did, however, point the finger more squarely, if circumstantially, at Scott Steinert.

Without saying whether others in the Hells Angels network suspected Steinert, Kane told his handlers that his friend had been somewhat depressed of late and was devoting more time to his escort agency. Steinert "was losing credibility among many members of the Montreal chapter ... who don't appreciate his methods or his way of acting in general." Steinert was far from assured of winning his full colours in early December, as had been expected.

Around this time, Kane, at Steinert's behest, torched the house of a neighbour of Mom Boucher's in the South Shore municipality of Contrecoeur. Boucher had had a dispute with the neighbour over the purchase of a piece of land. It wasn't the only time the home of one of Boucher's antagonists went up in flames. In early October the residence of the deputy warden of the Sorel prison was firebombed, six months after that of the warden. Boucher had served most of his firearms stint in the prison, and he hadn't been happy with his treatment or the food.

The Hells hadn't taken the Carcajou squad seriously after its official inauguration in late September. Mom Boucher told his colleagues that the special task force would just make his life easier: the crooked cops on his payroll would now enjoy access to information from all police forces, not just the ones they worked for. Likewise, Toots Tousignant claimed that his source in the Greenfield Park force was a fount of new intelligence.

Before long, however, the bikers felt quite differently about the new squad. No expense was spared by the Quebec government to ensure that Carcajou made an impact, and quickly. Dominated by the SQ, it brought together many of the force's top officers and agents. The police seconded from the SPCUM and eventually the RCMP—including Verdon and St. Onge—were a more mixed bag of experienced investigators, green-horns, and officers whose respective forces didn't know what else to do with them. The rivalries that existed among the three forces followed them to Carcajou, where they were only amplified. The Mounties and the SPCUM cops believed the SQ investigators saw Carcajou's generous budget as an opportunity to go wild with their expense accounts; the SQ staff felt the RCMP and Montreal police kept too much intelligence to themselves and took more information away from the squad's meetings than they contributed.

Still, many veterans of the squad say it was the best experience of their careers, the one occasion when they had the freedom and the budget to police as they had always wanted to. Even in September, the month Carcajou was created, the bikers noticed that the SQ was monitoring them more closely. By November senior Hells were singing a different tune about the squad. "They see them everywhere," Kane told Verdon. "The bikers are aware they are being watched constantly."

Boucher, understandably, was the prime target for surveillance and harassment. When they caught him on a wiretap counselling one of his lieutenants to take a baseball bat to a man who had given the lieutenant a thumping in a bar fight, they had enough to go after him. The advice constituted breach of parole, the Crown argued, and in the course of apprehending Boucher, police took the opportunity to raid several clubhouses and homes. Boucher surrendered himself in short order. Other police raids on Hells Angels hangouts were less frivolous. A series in late October led to drugs and weapons charges against fifteen associates. Worse for the gang, one of the charged bikers turned under police interrogation and provided information that led to the arrest of ten more gang associates.

These setbacks provoked two distinctly different reactions from senior Hells Angels. Some wanted to pull out all the stops. The Nomads, Kane told his handlers in October, "are pissed off with the ongoing war which is costing them a lot of money and want to get it over with as quickly as possible. They are ready for anything ... even attacking the families of their enemies, which goes against their old ways. It is also planned to go after the families of informants used against the H.A." That reflex response prompted consideration of a diesel-fuel-and-fertilizer-type bomb similar to the one that had caused such devastation in Oklahoma City six months earlier. A computer-savvy roommate of Pat Lambert's was downloading recipes for such explosives from the net, Kane reported. The ingredients were kept in an apartment in Longueuil.

Wolf Carroll seemed especially intent on an iron-fisted approach. He was taking the war personally and had decided that any negotiated resolution was out of the question. Remarkable for a full-patch member, he was spending a lot of time actively gathering intelligence on Rock Machine and other Alliance targets, surreptitiously observing their haunts to identify members, tailing them to find out where they lived, noting the makes of their vehicles and licence plate numbers.

The other response to these hard times was less expected. After yet another witch hunt of suspected informants in early December, Mom Boucher toyed with the idea of hanging up his Harley. "[He] is thinking very seriously about retiring to Mexico within a year, which explains his frequent trips to Mexico," Kane told St. Onge in a phone call. "He explains his decision by the fact that the police have become too strong and are everywhere and that he can't move. Several other Nomads are thinking in the same direction."

Another source of discouragement was the slump in the drug market. The summer drought was long past, but with the threat of deadly fireworks, not to mention the stepped-up police raids in Montreal's drug bars, the customers were staying away. Happily, the growing popularity of ecstasy was proving very lucrative. Mom Boucher alone was said to make $1 on every pill or capsule of the drug sold by anyone connected to the gang. With his approval, junior members were given specific territories where they controlled the drug's sales. Some of the more enterprising went into the rave business to create demand

and marshal the market. They rented enormous industrial spaces, hired DJs, lighting crews, and security, and then put out the word. Even if the drug sales at these events were sometimes disappointing—some partiers brought their own—the profits from obscenely overpriced bottled water made the ventures attractive.

Shortly after the Desrochers bombing, Mom Boucher had suggested that Kane and Marc Sigman, another Steinert protegé, sign on formally with the Rockers. The two were among the very few *non-patchés* who were allowed back into the Sorel and Longueuil clubhouses when the blanket ban of the previous spring had been relaxed. Mom flattered them by saying that with their experience and contacts, they could contribute a lot to the Rockers. In late October Kane and Sigman and one other biker were officially brought into the fold as strikers. The honour was not without its price: each had to pay a one-time initiation fee of $1500 plus 10 percent of their monthly incomes, that amount to be no less than $300 a month. The perks were less tangible but no less real: the fear-inspired respect of others and a chance to build a network of criminal contacts, one that became increasingly lucrative the higher a man rose in the gang's hierarchy.

Kane's new status didn't affect his working relationships. He remained a close associate of Steinert's and travelled to Thunder Bay on several occasions to tend to the details of Steinert's business there. Whether he was transporting drugs isn't mentioned in the debriefing reports. There can be no doubt, however, that St. Onge and Verdon knew he was actively involved in large-quantity cocaine deals. They weren't overly concerned about it. "I asked him to phone me halfway through his trip," St. Onge wrote on November 9. "The reason for his trip involves cocaine since the price in Thunder Bay is now $50,000 the kilo and $32,000 in Montreal." There was no suggestion that Kane keep his hands clean or any warning that if he was arrested he was on his own.

Another omission that raises questions about how much of what Kane told the Mounties was reported in their memos concerns the gang's response to the creation of the Carcajou squad. In mid-October, Staff Sergeant Lemire, St. Onge's superior, put one of his occasional notes into Kane's file. He wrote that Kane's revelation of Rocker plots to threaten police officers and Montreal's mayor, Pierre Bourque, was "worthy of being taken seriously." Yet there was no mention of such scheming in the debriefing reports of Verdon or St. Onge, and Lemire was never in direct contact with Kane.

The reports were also silent on some of the RCMP's more questionable financial accommodations with Kane. Not long after Kane was made a striker for the Rockers, St. Onge put in a request for an additional $1200 a month for his prize source. The funds would provide Kane with *"un véhicule sécuritaire,"* a safe car. And for that money, presumably a very fancy one. "Being very active as a biker he is becoming a potential target for the enemies of the H.A.," St. Onge wrote in a funding request. "Travelling around in his personal car makes him easy prey." The request was authorized but Kane's new car was never mentioned in the debriefing reports.

Kane's relationships with the women in his life were no less complicated during these months than those with his fellow bikers or his handlers. Patricia remained unaware of Josée and two of Kane's kids and the fact that he maintained the semblance of a family life with them.

Josée had no idea that Kane was in love with Patricia or that he spent most nights with her. She could have no expectation of complete fidelity, but she did believe that while he might sometimes look elsewhere for fun, his family came first.

There were signs that supported the notion that Kane still valued some aspects of family life. In December 1995 he took Josée and the children to the gang's Christmas party at the *cabane à sucre* of Pierre Provencher, a senior member of the Rockers. There was a Santa in a sleigh, rides for the kids, and food and drink in abundance. Josée enjoyed mingling with other bikers' wives, even if she spent much of the party chasing after the children, a chore Kane didn't bother himself with. By this time, they had moved out of the apartment above Kane's parents. Josée insisted on it, she says, after she found herself turning into Dany's mother, peering out from behind the curtains to spy on the neighbours.

Meanwhile, Patricia wasn't simply ignorant of Josée; she claims she still didn't know Kane was affiliated with the Hells Angels or any biker gang. Part of this, she concedes, might have been wilful blindness; she didn't see what she didn't want to see. The fact that he had so wholeheartedly fallen for her made her feel special, as did his frequent phone calls just to ask about her day or how she was doing. Steve obviously adored this fun-loving man. Perhaps it was then that she began thinking there might be a future with Dany Kane.

That rosy prospect was short-lived. In early February, at the end of an evening out with a crowd that included Roland Lebrasseur as well as Patricia and Kane, Lebrasseur steered Patricia aside and made a play for her. He had been drinking heavily and dipping liberally into his bag of cocaine, a practice that had become a habit in recent months.

"Why don't you hook up with me?" he asked her.

"How can I hook up with you when I'm with Dany," she replied.

He looked at her coolly. "How can you be with Dany when he's married with three kids?"

Patricia was speechless, but not for long. Cornering Dany alone, she let loose. At the end of the tirade, she called it quits, telling Kane she never wanted to see or hear from him again. Knowing him to be persistent and not likely to leave her alone, she soon left her apartment and moved out of the city.

On the evening of March 4, 1996, a month after the rupture with Patricia, Kane met with Verdon and St. Onge for a payment and debriefing meeting at the Ramada in Longueuil. He gave them a typical laundry list of updates. Scott Steinert had been made a full-patch Hells Angel in spite of the mixed feelings he inspired among other gang members and the fact that barely a month earlier there had been talk of expelling him and Donald Magnussen. The promotion was a way of honouring the memory of Steinert's first patron in the gang, national president Tiny Richard, who had died suddenly of a heart attack on February 23. Some five hundred kilograms of cocaine had come into Montreal the week previously and was selling for $34,500 a kilo. The Matticks brothers, kingpins of the West End Gang and power-brokers at the port of Montreal, were awaiting a big shipment of hash. And Roland Lebrasseur, Wolf Carroll's increasingly troublesome driver, was waiting for a space to open at a cocaine detoxification centre. "It seems that Wolf is not too happy with this situation because Lebrasseur was entrusted certain tasks by him and he has shown signs of weakness," Verdon wrote in his debriefing report.

Kane neglected to tell his handlers that a couple of nights earlier he had been over at Josée's with Lebrasseur. When the pair was leaving, Lebrasseur went out into the winter night first and Josée told Dany that she found Lebrasseur to be very pleasant and considerate, quite different from most of his friends. Kane could bring him around anytime, Josée said. "That's too bad," he said cryptically, as if to wound her, "because it's the last time you'll be seeing him."

Just before midnight on March 4, a few hours after leaving the Ramada, Kane telephoned Verdon with an update: Lebrasseur had been killed and his body found on the outskirts of the South Shore community of Brossard. Verdon noted no other details from Kane, simply that the Brossard police would be notified.

RCMP documents indicate few contacts between Kane and his handlers over the next two weeks and only one short phone call from Verdon to Kane during which Lebrasseur's murder apparently wasn't mentioned. Only on March 20, at the conclusion of another Ramada Inn payment and debriefing session, was Lebrasseur's death discussed. Kane reported that "a man of Wolf Carroll's"— the name is blacked out in the debriefing report—had heard Daniel Bouchard admit to the murder. According to this source, who Kane claimed had himself been threatened by Bouchard, Lebrasseur's old acquaintance from Sept-Îles had killed him for personal reasons; Wolf Carroll had nothing to do with it. Muddying the waters still further, Kane cast doubt on Bouchard's involvement. Lebrasseur was a cokehead, Kane said, "who led a secret

life and had compromised different groups, which makes
the list of suspects pretty long."

If he knew it, Kane made no reference to the fact that
Bouchard and Lebrasseur knew each other from Sept-
Îles; at least there is no mention of it in the debriefing
reports. The RCMP in Sept-Îles, however, already suspected Bouchard of large-scale drug trafficking. Within
a week St. Onge and four other RCMP officers chartered a plane and flew to the North Shore on what
amounted to a wild-goose chase set in motion by Kane.
Bouchard wasn't even in Sept-Îles at the time. As Kane
told St. Onge on his return, Bouchard was in either
Toronto or Ottawa working his VIA day job.

Kane now produced a raft of other intriguing details.
He said that the formal ownership of Carroll's bar, Les
Boys in the Gay Village, had been registered first in
Lebrasseur's name, then Bouchard's, and had probably
been transferred again to someone else. He gave St. Onge
no fewer than six telephone numbers for Bouchard, two
addresses, the make and colour of his car, plus the names
of three brothers and his daughter. He said Bouchard
wasn't entirely trusted by the Hells Angels because it was
known that he'd had business dealings with the Rock
Machine. Finally, he claimed that Lebrasseur had lived
with Bouchard in Pointe-St-Charles for a time, along with
a third man by the name of Stéphane Boire. Boire had
disappeared, Kane said. Was it possible he too had been
murdered and that Bouchard had a penchant for killing
his roommates?

Sure enough, as police would discover three months
later, Boire was dead and had been since the fall of 1995.
A beekeeper had stumbled across a marijuana patch in a
field near his hives. Among the plants was a shallow grave,

and in the grave, stuffed into a cheap sleeping bag, was Boire's decomposing body. His links, if any, to Bouchard were more difficult to confirm. Boire was a St-Jean-sur-Richelieu native; Josée and Boire had been in the same kindergarten class. He'd had many run-ins with police as a youth and by his early twenties had compiled a long string of convictions for theft, dealing in stolen goods, assault, firearms offences, and drug trafficking, an enterprise that would have led him to cross paths with Kane.

It's doubtful Boire ever lived with Bouchard. Those who knew Bouchard say he wouldn't have introduced his gang associates to his daughter, let alone allowed them to live under the same roof. And it's almost certain that Lebrasseur didn't live with him, at least not in the spring of 1995, as Kane claimed. That was when Lebrasseur was packing up his life in Sept-Îles and relocating to the lower Laurentians to start anew. His mother is not aware of his living anywhere during this period other than at his home on the North Shore or with her in St-Jerôme.

These facts weren't known to his Mountie handlers when Kane spun his speculations about the fates of Lebrasseur and Boire in late March. Nor did they know the truth of Kane's activities just hours before he reported Lebrasseur's worrisome unreliability in a routine debriefing session.

In the early-morning darkness of March 3, he had driven with Lebrasseur to a secluded spot on Montée Gobeil, an unpaved, unlit road on the outskirts of Brossard. There he had stopped the car—or told Lebrasseur to—and pulled out a gun. He ordered Lebrasseur out of the vehicle. Beside a field where model-plane enthusiasts gathered on weekends and the only buildings in sight were sleeping greenhouses, Kane shot Lebrasseur three times in the head and chest.

The body, left with no identification, was discovered at
about 6:45 a.m. by a factory worker taking a shortcut home
after the night shift. It wouldn't be confirmed as
Lebrasseur's until March 5, by which time Kane had help-
fully informed St. Onge of its identity.

11

IN THE CENTRE
OF THE STORM

If the briefing reports filed by Corporal Verdon and
Sergeant St. Onge are an accurate record, they never again
spoke to Kane about Roland Lebrasseur. Finding his
killer, or Stéphane Boire's, was low on the RCMP's list of
priorities; these were investigations that fell more directly
into the laps of the SQ or local authorities. Nonetheless,
both deaths were added to the tally of biker war victims,
a total that was climbing toward fifty by March 1996,
the overwhelming majority unsolved.

Patricia was more preoccupied than the Mounties with
Lebrasseur's murder. When he wasn't fuelled up on booze
or cocaine, she too had enjoyed his company and found
him a refreshing change from most of Kane's cohorts. His
death, reported in *Allô Police,* was disturbing, and so too
were her suspicions. Patricia's immediate assumption was
that Kane had murdered Lebrasseur for spilling the beans
to her about his other life. It convinced her that she had
made the right decision to end the relationship and move
out of town.

Not more than two months later, however, she bumped
into Kane at Pat Lambert's office. She believed Kane had
engineered this chance encounter, and she was cold and

curt, pointedly inquiring after Josée and his children. Kane protested that he and Josée were finished. Patricia gave him a doubting look. Kane pulled out his phone and called Josée on the spot, asking her to confirm it. As Patricia remembers it, Josée told her, "He's your problem now."

Kane worked hard to charm his way back into Patricia's affections. She confronted him about Lebrasseur. Had Kane killed him? "Are you nuts?" was Kane's reply, and his protestations of innocence, his incredulity that she would even ask such a question, were persuasive. Their relationship picked up where it had left off. Kane adored her, it was springtime, and the two were soon a couple again. On July 1, the traditional province-wide moving day for apartment dwellers, they signed for a tiny flat together on Montreal's Rue St-Christophe, below Sherbrooke Street.

The space was known in Quebec as a three and a half—a bedroom, a kitchen, a living room, and a bathroom. It was cramped enough that Steve continued to live with his grandmother. But it wasn't so small that Kane didn't bring over his three children. The first time they visited, he stuck around to take care of them. The next time, he told Patricia he had to dash out to the store for something. Kane was gone the whole evening, making Patricia their babysitter by default. Subsequent evenings were different only insofar as Kane didn't bother with the pretext of shopping errands.

If it was small, the apartment was also central, steps away from the buzzing Gay Village where the Rockers had a strong presence and met regularly in bars and restaurants. It was close to the offices of Agence Aventure, as well as Scott Steinert's competing business, Agence Sensation. Given its location and Kane's natural gregariousness, his criminal associates were frequent visitors. Steinert and Magnussen often dropped in, as did others whose names Patricia never knew but whose faces she would one day recognize in newspaper photographs.

Although she knew Kane was involved in shady and sometimes odious dealings, Patricia maintains that she hadn't yet realized he was a member of the Rockers and thus a willing soldier in the violence that was racking the city. That changed when a package of photos arrived from a film-processing outfit. Instead of snapshots from a roll they had taken together, the pictures were of Kane and several of his cronies, decked out in their biker colours. The revelation didn't provoke another tirade, nor did she quietly pack her things and move again. Deep down, she had suspected as much all along. Thereafter, whenever they were to travel in Kane's car, Patricia simply made him drive around the block before she would get in. "I figured if he went around twice they would have time to blow up the car if they were planning to." She also knew better than to press for details when he made vague comments about a rough day or a deal gone awry.

There were irritations between them—the constant, uninvited guests, the collect calls from pals in prison, Kane's insistence that Patricia take her cigarettes outside even in winter while allowing Steinert to smoke as much hash in their apartment as he wanted—but Kane always managed to smooth them over. Patricia says the Dany Kane she knew was an utterly different person from the man Josée had come to dread.

Josée doesn't recall the telephone exchange in which she allegedly told Patricia that Kane was her problem. For Josée, the definitive break came one day in the fall of 1996 when she was registering for a course at the

Université du Québec à Montréal and needed a downtown parking spot. She knew that Kane had rented the St-Christophe Street apartment; it was close to his work and saved him the forty-five-minute drive to and from St-Jean. Besides, he said, the dog he had bought Josée to keep her company—as if the kids weren't enough—gave him respiratory problems.

Kane had told Josée that he was sharing the apartment with a woman who was trying to get out of the stripping racket, that she was staying there as a friend and sleeping on the sofa. That fall day Josée decided to stop in to ask if the parking space that came with the apartment was available for a few hours. Patricia answered the door, and Josée could read the scene well enough to know that she and Kane weren't just roommates. After that awkward encounter, Josée accepted that Kane had found someone else and felt that she was free to do likewise. Kane didn't see things in the same light.

For much of 1996 the Hells Angels fraternity in Quebec was riven with suspicion and internal ill will. Kane reported that "the Nomads, especially Carroll and Boucher, see the Evil Ones and the majority of the [Montreal Hells Angels] as old and chicken and think they use their colours to profit in business but do nothing when the heat is on." The Montreal Hells weren't contributing enough to the war effort, according to Wolf and Mom, and spats inevitably erupted over the spoils when former Rock Machine territory came up for grabs.

Scott Steinert, a pre-eminent if controversial figure among the Montreal Hells, deeply resented the Nomads' charges of cowardice in the biker war. In April relations between the Montreal chapter and the Nomads were so strained that Steinert warned Kane that it might be dangerous for him if he didn't cut his ties to Wolf Carroll. By forcing him to choose sides, Steinert was perhaps hoping to lure Kane entirely into his camp and away from the Rockers and their Nomad masters. It's possible Kane was receptive just at that moment. Earlier that spring he had lost his striker patch with the Rockers after a violent altercation with a more senior member of the gang. He was knocked down a rung, a demotion that frustrated him and greatly disappointed his handlers.

Concerns about informants were as high as ever, and around this time suspicion fell on Donald Magnussen, Steinert's closest lieutenant and a friend of Kane's. Kane realized that if Magnussen's loyalty was under scrutiny, his could easily be next.

Thanks to his regular RCMP pay packets and his various criminal enterprises, Kane was living large. As Patricia remembers, "He had to have the big car and the nice clothes and the bling-bling. His attitude was that it was no use having money if it didn't show." But his fellow bikers must have wondered how, even when the gang's business was slow, Kane generated a steady, abundant cash flow. Sooner or later, someone would figure out where the money really came from.

Kane needed a legitimate business to serve as his cover, and in the early summer of 1996, he became the unlikely proprietor of a weekly newspaper. He had no intention of competing with the established community newspaper chains by sending reporters to cover town council meetings, ringette tournaments, or the birthdays of local octogenarians. Instead, with the RCMP's financial backing, Kane founded *Rencontres Sélectes* (Special encounters) for an audience of gay male and female readers who were looking for new sexual partners. It would be full of ads for bars, escort agencies, and phone sex services, Kane and the Mounties imagined, as well as tantalizing "personals." But the serious money would be made through a gay telephone dating service that the paper would launch and promote in every issue.

The enterprise required seed money, of course, and on June 10, St. Onge composed a six-page request to his superiors for the necessary investment capital. He began with the back story. In the biker world, he said, direct questions about a person's source of revenue weren't acceptable. Nonetheless, "speculation runs rife" about associates who don't have a known business. "The leaders of the Hells Angels know that the police, especially the RCMP, have informers in their ranks and are trying to find out who they are by all means available," St. Onge wrote.

Kane had been searching for a cover business concept when he met a psychologist—a woman—who owned "a serious dating service" and who was interested in launching a spinoff venture through some sort of publication. Inspired by the successful free publications he saw as he wandered the Gay Village, Kane decided a gay sex magazine was a good bet. He went into partnership with the psychologist who, St. Onge noted, was not in a position to support the enterprise financially. She was going through a divorce and "didn't want anything to show up."

A list of expenses was duly itemized and attached: phone lines $600, ads in other papers $2200, office furniture $1500, a photocopier $3118, a fax machine $500, layout, printing, and distribution $5150, metal display stands $6300. Along with other expenses such as rent and staff, the total came to $30,325. Kane had already paid $5500 of that amount, a clear sign of his commitment,

St. Onge pointed out. "I frankly believe that this enterprise will generate profits. At very least, as long as it covers its costs, our goal will have been achieved."

After weeks of deliberation, Supt. Rowland Sugrue, one of the top Mounties in Quebec, gave his blessing to the scheme. The funds were deposited in an account at a branch of the Laurentian Bank conveniently located at the corner of Sherbrooke and St-Hubert, one street over from Kane's apartment and half a block from the *Rencontres Sélectes* offices. Pat Lambert's establishment was almost directly across the street. "This location for the business is ideal since it will be very visible to the bikers and the strippers who hang around Agence Aventure," St. Onge enthused.

On the weekend of May 11 and 12, the Halifax chapter of the Hells Angels invited bikers from across Canada and the northeastern United States to their annual bash, a celebration of their twelfth anniversary. The milestone was not especially noteworthy, but it was a good excuse for a party. For most, it meant an unbridled good time, but for Walter Stadnick, it was an opportunity to network, to build alliances, and to politic.

Just as he had made efforts to establish the Hells Angels in Ontario, Stadnick had diligently pursued a foothold in Manitoba and especially in Winnipeg, a central transit point for drug shipments across the country. Since the early 1990s he had been engaged in an elaborate courtship dance with two long-time motorcycle gangs in the city, the Spartans and Los Brovos (frequently misspelled Los Bravos). The gangs were ambivalent: they enjoyed their independence yet were attracted by the big-league status of the Hells Angels patch. At the same time, the Hells wanted to recruit the best of their members, the most dedicated and hardened, who would do what was necessary to dominate the city and the province. At one point Stadnick, in a Machiavellian stroke, started a puppet gang called the Redliners in Winnipeg to stir the pot and put pressure on the existing gangs.

By May 1996, however, Los Brovos had emerged as the stronger force, and Stadnick was eager to seal an agreement that would see them patch over to the Hells Angels. To this end Mike McCrea of the Hells' Halifax chapter urged David Boyko, one of the most senior and influential among Los Brovos, to fly east for the May event. Boyko was reluctant, but McCrea insisted, and the Winnipeg biker eventually joined the festivities.

Donald Magnussen also attended, though his presence was less welcome. Like his patron Steinert, Magnussen was a good money-maker for the gang, but pushy and troublesome. Once based in Winnipeg, he had a history with Boyko, a grudge that stemmed from an occasion when he'd been stiffed by the Los Brovos veteran in a drug deal. When Magnussen saw Boyko at the party, he decided it was time to settle accounts. That weekend Boyko was shot in the head and his body dumped on a gravel road in Dartmouth. The killing cast a pall over the event—even Hells Angels party planners don't like murders in their midst. More significantly, it threatened to torpedo the gang's expansion into Manitoba and the Prairie provinces.

To Los Brovos, Boyko's killing looked like the worst sort of Hells Angels treachery. They believed he had been first asked and then coerced by senior members of the gang to the Halifax party for the express purpose of being eliminated by Magnussen. Members of other western gangs took it as proof of what they had long suspected:

the Hells Angels, in particular Quebec's Hells, couldn't be trusted.

Mike McCrea travelled to Winnipeg for Boyko's funeral, hoping to demonstrate to the Manitoba bikers and their allies that there was no set-up, that Boyko's killer had acted alone. The event was a classic biker send-off, with representatives from Ontario's Satan's Choice, Alberta's Grim Reapers, and even the rival Spartans showing their colours in respect. McCrea was given the coldest of receptions. No one spoke to him, and the members of Los Brovos turned their backs every time he approached.

The chill was such that five weeks later Kane reported concerns that Stadnick might be murdered in retaliation. Several of the anglophone Nomads, including Carroll and Stadnick, had decided that the Hells themselves should eliminate Magnussen. "This, in effect, would be the only way to prove to other biker groups in western Canada that the assassination of Boyko wasn't ordered by the Hells Angels," Kane told St. Onge and Verdon.

On this occasion, the RCMP decided that the target should be warned of the threat against his life; why is unclear. It wasn't that the information the force had was any more "direct and precise"—Lemire's criteria—than for other men on the gang's hit list. Instead, it may have been part of a larger RCMP strategy to thwart Hells Angels expansion: keep Magnussen alive and keep the gang out of Manitoba. It may have been because Magnussen was one of their source's best contacts and friends in the organization. Whatever the reason, Verdon and St. Onge decided to share the information with their closest ally in Carcajou, Benoît Roberge, a Montreal police detective whose desk adjoined Verdon's at the squad's headquarters. When the two Mounties had information from Kane to pass on to

other Carcajou members, it almost invariably went to
Roberge. In fact, there are some SQ members of Carcajou
who suspect that just as Kane was a coded source for
Verdon, Verdon was a coded source for Roberge, relaying
much of what Kane told the RCMP. This was the case
with the news that the Hells were gunning for Magnussen.

Roberge's was a familiar face to many of Montreal's
bikers. They had been his beat for a decade, long before
Carcajou was created. Tipped off by Verdon and St. Onge,
the tall, blond detective with a reputation for claiming
more overtime than any of his colleagues, tracked down
Magnussen to tell him that members of his own gang were
after him. Although Magnussen later bragged to Kane that
he had laughed in Roberge's face, he seems to have taken
the warning seriously and likely stayed alive because of it.
Thereafter he rarely ventured out without company. But
his conduct hardly changed. In late July Kane described an
incident at a Hells Angels–controlled after-hours club
where Magnussen got into an altercation with a dealer
who he felt had insulted him. True to his nickname, Bam-
Bam became violent and beat the man into a coma.

Magnussen and Scott Steinert, cocky and pigheaded by
nature, were also reckless and greedy consumers of
steroids. With little or no control on their steroid intake,
both were prime candidates for the aggressive "'roid rage"
that afflicts abusers. In the spring and summer of 1996 their
use was heavier than ever and the impact on their behaviour
more pronounced. As a whole, the role of steroids in the
biker war was significant; in the convulsive careers of
Magnussen and Steinert it was a determining factor.

The summer of 1996 brought a lull in hostilities, with the
Alliance and the Hells Angels and their acolytes applying

themselves to existing enterprises while keeping their eyes open to new ones.

Pat Lambert returned to Guadeloupe to investigate opportunities with a pair of French crooks working in the Caribbean, one of whom, according to Kane, had been an associate of Jacques Mesrine, the legendary French bank robber and escape artist of the 1960s and '70s. The other was a French secret policeman who, Kane reported nervously, boasted about having crooked contacts in the RCMP. Lambert, like Mom Boucher, may have been contemplating an exit. Kane reported that Lambert was "very unsatisfied with the way [drug] sales are done and is losing his illusions about the Hells Angels." Lambert held dual Spanish-Canadian citizenship and was thinking of moving to Europe to begin a new life.

His travels paled in comparison with those of Guillaume "Mimo" Serra, a fast-rising member of the gang and another favourite of Mom Boucher's who was a major cocaine importer and distributor, well connected to Italian and Colombian organized crime, as well as the Hells Angels and Rock Machine. In May Kane had him off to the Dominican Republic to set up a coke deal; in July he was on his way to Costa Rica to look into hotel construction in partnership with Boucher. In August he went first to Cuba and then to Brazil, again organizing drug shipments.

Locally, $3 million in two-dollar coins were stolen from the port of Montreal in early August. The haul presented something of a laundering problem: how to, say, buy a car or deposit a small fortune with nothing but coins? So "Moune"—as the crony of Carroll's who was handling the fencing operation was known—was offering a 25 percent premium to anyone willing to take at least

$10,000 of the coins off his hands: $20,000 in bills netted a buyer $25,000 in toonies.

Steinert, described by Kane as one of the few Hells Angels who did his own dirty work, was also very active. Over the summer he made a move into the sprawling northern suburb of Laval, forming his own circle of thugs to take over its bars and other points of sale. He travelled west with Magnussen on drug and dancer business. Then in late August Steinert, who for all his failings never shied from pulling his weight in the war, organized an attack against the Rock Machine in their stronghold of Verdun.

He and several others, almost certainly including Kane, got their hands on two stolen grey vans and affixed yellow stickers to them to make them look like the ubiquitous service vehicles of the provincial electrical utility, Hydro-Québec. They loaded one of the vans with ninety kilograms of dynamite and the necessary detonators and headed to Verdun. The plan was to crash the van into the industrial building that housed the Rock Machine's informal clubhouse and motorcycle storage area. Once through the doors, the explosives would be detonated. But the driver jumped out too soon, and after hitting a detour sign, the van drifted harmlessly through an intersection and up a side street. The essential last step in the wiring of the explosive charge hadn't been completed. Police later estimated that the truck bomb would have levelled everything within a thirty-metre radius and caused significant damage over an area many times that size.

Even by the low standards of the biker war, the botched job seemed particularly amateurish and must have irked Steinert. Yet he remained determined to take over Verdun and any other Montreal territory still in the hands of the Rock Machine. To that end, he established another clique

with five key members—some Hells Angels, some not—
and a larger pool of *exécuteurs,* or enforcers, among them
Magnussen and Marc Sigman. Part of Steinert's motivation was to defend the honour of the Montreal chapter. He
had been denied membership in the Nomads when they
were first created and instead consigned to extensive
service with the Montreal Hells. Since then he had "heard
enough from the Nomads about the Montreal chapter
being a bunch of goofs who were scared of taking action,"
Kane recounted. His new squad wasn't an idle undertak-
ing. Although not a puppet gang per se—all members
retained their existing affiliations—it was a parallel organization, complete with identifying ring and separate clubhouse. Given Steinert's grandiose ambitions, no industrial
or residential stronghold would do. Instead, he had his
eyes on the Lavigueur mansion, a seventeen-room *faux
château* on its own island in the Mille-Îles River and one
of the most famous private houses in the Montreal area.

A decade earlier, in March 1986, a man named William
Murphy had stumbled across a wallet in downtown
Montreal. Inside was a man's identification and a half-
dozen lottery tickets. From the driver's licence, Murphy
located the owner's address and dropped the wallet into
his mailbox. He kept the lottery tickets. A welfare recipient with 56 cents in his bank account, he hoped they
might provide a modest reward for his good deed.

But when he checked the winning numbers he discovered that one of the tickets was worth $7.6 million—the
Lotto 6/49 jackpot. After some hours of soul-searching,
Murphy returned to the apartment in Montreal's east end
to turn over the ticket. The man's son, however, slammed
the door in Murphy's face: Murphy spoke only English
while the Lavigueur family were unilingual francophones.

"It's a tough neighbourhood, and we were all asleep," the son explained.

The next night Murphy returned with a friend who spoke French and explained the situation. The wallet's owner, Jean-Guy Lavigueur, had been pooling his cash with that of his children and a brother-in-law to buy their Lotto tickets. On the spot they offered Murphy a one-sixth share of the prize. The story captivated Montrealers. Lavigueur, a widower, was like Murphy dependent on welfare: he'd been laid off from the mattress company where he had worked for thirty-two years, and his UI benefits had run out.

Murphy dropped out of sight, but the Lavigueur family, flush with their millions, made like the Beverly Hillbillies and paid $850,000 for the island château. They soon discovered that luxurious surroundings couldn't buy them happiness, and within two years they were ready to sell and head home.

The next person to occupy the château was Scott Steinert. By October 1996 he had worked out a deal to purchase the building for $550,000, of which $300,000 cash would be paid under the table to the real-estate agent. In order that it not be traced to Steinert, Kane told his handlers, the house's ownership would be registered to several *prêt-noms*—literally "lent-names," those indispensable bit players in organized crime who shield criminal assets from proceeds-of-crime legislation.

Steinert told Kane he could be a *prêt-nom* on the house if he agreed to become one of the leaders of the new clique. That privilege was expensive: it would cost $100,000 to be one of the five. Still, if the squad was successful in wrenching territory from the Rock Machine, the payoff would make it well worth the investment. Steinert dangled another carrot: the $100,000 would also win him living accommodations in one of the outbuildings on the grounds of the mansion. Given his spending habits, Kane didn't have that kind of money and the RCMP didn't consider contributing. Their $30,000 capitalization of *Rencontres Sélectes* was already looking precarious.

Nonetheless, Kane spent considerable time at the Lavigueur mansion, often performing watch duty, a routine chore for gang underlings and a not infrequent one even for ranking Hells Angels. Steinert had fortified the mansion with new fencing and gates and a video surveillance system worth tens of thousands, but monitoring the grounds was not only biker tradition, it was a prudent precaution while the war with the Rock Machine still raged.

Time spent at the mansion wasn't all work. On at least one occasion, Kane took along Benjamin, then six, for some father-son quality time. He allowed the boy to do watch—or at least pretend to—and handle a few of the firearms on the premises, much to Josée's alarm. There were amusements of a more adult nature when the picturesque mansion was used as a backdrop for pornographic films.

There is a long history of vanity porn among the Hells Angels: members of chapters across North America have produced and starred in their own hardcore productions, along with girlfriends, strippers, and prostitutes of their acquaintance. Few if any have been released commercially, but a number enjoy wide underground and curio distribution.

Steinert's introduction to the film business literally came knocking at his door. According to accepted lore, Steinert and several of the squad were at the mansion when a man named Stéphane Chouinard came calling without an invitation. Chouinard, aged twenty-six, was an irrepressible entrepreneur who had sold vacuum cleaners, waterbeds, bread, and cars. But it was in the production of porn films that he found his niche. His first film, 1995's *Quebec Sexy Girls #1,* was made on a shoe-string; it garnered attention for its strikingly familiar locales—public places in and around Quebec City, including the front lawn of the Quebec Legislature. His second film, *Quebec Sexy Girls #2,* created even more buzz through a stroke of casting genius: the male lead was Cpl. Patrick Cloutier, the armed forces soldier who became famous during the Oka Crisis of 1991 for his nose-to-nose standoff with a Mohawk Warrior, only to fall from military grace because of cocaine problems.

In late 1996 Chouinard was searching for a set for his next film, and his instinct for publicity led him to the Lavigueur mansion. Steinert was captivated by the notion. Whether it was his stipulation or Chouinard's flattery, it was agreed that Steinert and his cohorts could star in the productions. *Babe's Angels* was made that winter and released the summer following. Chouinard's marketing sense again proved impeccable: the Montreal media loved the story of a Hells Angels porn film shot at the Lavigueur mansion. But such flamboyant exposure disturbed others in the Hells' higher echelons. Steinert would have to be cut down to size.

12

UNE RENCONTRE
SÉLECTE

Were it not for *Rencontres Sélectes*, Aimé Simard might still be a small-time fraud artist, drifting from one low-paying job to the next, hungry for the big break that would raise him above the pack.

In November 1996 Simard was a twenty-eight-year-old night clerk at a hotel at the foot of Mont-Ste-Anne, one of Quebec's largest ski resorts. He hoped to move to Montreal, where he could start a new life, perhaps complete a university degree, maybe find companionship. He was looking for a friend, or a boyfriend, in the city when he placed a personal ad with Kane's telephone dating service, the business that was meant to be the money-spinning adjunct to *Rencontres Sélectes*.

Simard was making yet another attempt to mend his ways. For most of the previous decade he had bounced in and out of jail, each short sentence followed by an apparently earnest but even shorter period of good behaviour before he passed another bad cheque, pretended to be someone he wasn't, or committed some minor fraud or property crime. It was a pattern he couldn't seem to escape, though hardly one he'd been compelled to follow.

Simard's mother, Elisa, had grown up in wartorn Italy, where food was frequently in short supply and school was a luxury her family couldn't afford. She didn't attend past Grade 3 and got used to hard work very young. In the mid-1960s she found herself doing menial labour on the French Riviera with a young daughter from one man and pregnant by another. Her mother and sister had emigrated several years before to Quebec City, and it was time to join them and start a new life in the New World, she decided. Money, always in short supply in Elisa's world, was no more abundant during her first months and years in Canada, and shortly after arriving she was obliged to place her children in foster care as she worked various jobs and tried to build a life for herself. By 1967 things were looking up. She had met Georges Simard, an unsophisticated labourer with the city of Quebec. Although he was neither educated nor ambitious and drank to excess as often as possible, he at least wasn't physically violent. When he asked her to marry him she accepted.

Elisa soon had another child, a boy they called Aimé, "beloved." Georges Simard was a very indulgent father to Aimé, though largely indifferent to the young girl and boy—five and three years older than Aimé—whom Elisa retrieved from foster care when circumstances permitted. The quick-witted Aimé soon realized the sway he held over his father. Whenever he broke something or otherwise found himself on the verge of trouble, he was quick to blame his half sister or half brother. Seeing others suffer for his sins didn't seem to trouble Aimé; his sister remembers him as a chronic liar and manipulator from his earliest years.

Aimé was ten when his doting father died suddenly, and the family was once again in financial peril. His mother fell into a two-year depression, so her daughter, by then in early teens, was obliged to sustain the household both financially and emotionally. Eventually, however, Elisa's depression lifted when she was offered a job managing a tailor shop. She had wanted to work when she was married to Simard, but he had forbidden it; now she thrived. In time she acquired the tailoring business, bought a small detached house in the Quebec City suburbs, and accumulated enough cash to establish another business, one she hoped her children would eventually take over. The lunch-counter-style restaurant would employ her eldest son as cook and her daughter as personnel and general manager, Elisa hoped. Aimé, who excelled in school without doing a stitch of homework, was expected to become its bookkeeper.

By this time Aimé's half siblings had left the nest and he was living alone with his mother. As the youngest, he was her coddled *"chou-chou."* He didn't stray far from the restaurant. "He was always there," recalls Elisa. "He drank soft drinks constantly and he ate junk food constantly. He ate away his sadness." At age fifteen, Aimé was hugely overweight and plagued with acne. "When he was big, people rejected him. For him to have friends he had to pay for everything."

And to pay for everything Aimé began to commit minor crimes, usually frauds, which came easily to an experienced liar and manipulator. Often too petty to warrant reporting or prosecuting, these misdemeanours didn't prevent Simard from graduating high school or studying police technology at a CEGEP in Alma, Quebec, in the fall of 1985. After dropping out—he was told that at five foot seven and well over 250 pounds he was too short and fat to be hired as a policeman—he returned to the Quebec

City region, where he pursued studies in administration and resumed his errant ways. In April 1986 he passed a bad cheque at a stereo store; in May he hit a Miracle Mart, a sports store, and a garden centre twice; in June he bilked another sports store. The spree ended later that month when he was arrested and the fake identification he'd used to back up the bum cheques was found in his wallet.

Simard pleaded guilty and spent a short time in jail. After his release he applied himself to his classes and living on the right side of the law. Then between February and May of 1987 he went on another bad-cheque tear. His victims this time included Sears, Eaton's, Kmart, a tool-rental business, and a maternity boutique. Once again, he pleaded guilty to a list of charges, almost all of which were for fraud of under $1000, and served a slightly longer prison sentence before being released. He dodged yet another fraud charge a few months later by relocating to Hamilton, then to Edmonton. He hoped improving his English might enhance his career prospects, but neither city helped break the cycle of his criminal habits.

In mid-1990 Simard moved back to his mother's house in the Charlesbourg neighbourhood of Quebec City, where he was well known by the prosecutors at the city's courthouse. They considered him something of an oddity and a largely harmless one. Unlike other young perpetrators, he wasn't advancing from petty offences to more serious crimes; indeed, so far there was a naive quality to his criminal career. Simard was obviously intelligent and an excellent talker, but he seemed incapable of either going straight or eluding capture. Even in 1994, after Simard had grandiosely taken to carrying a gun for "protection," it was clear that however he might pretend and posture to the contrary, he was a long way from being a hard case.

Simard had decided he needed a weapon when he briefly served as an informant for the Quebec City police. During one of his innumerable stints in prison he had learned certain details about the cocaine trade in the city, and when he was released he offered to share them with a Charlesbourg cop of his acquaintance. Simard claimed he did it as part of his rehabilitation therapy; others suggest he had a grudge against a dealer. Either way, it's evident he still harboured fantasies about becoming a policeman: he asked neither for money nor for a suspension of the charges against him. Simard made a couple of buys of small quantities of cocaine on behalf of the police. When he tried to purchase a larger volume, however, the dealer recognized the man accompanying him as a cop. Word soon circulated that Simard was a snitch, and he acquired the gun.

A more legitimate element of Simard's rehabilitation was a night course in nursing at a local high school. One evening a classmate saw Simard transfer the weapon from one jacket pocket to another. When the man asked Simard what he was doing with a handgun, Simard pointed it at him. Simard claimed he was just showing it to his fellow student, adding that the gun wasn't loaded anyway. The man maintained Simard had threatened him with it. Soon he was facing more serious charges than before: illegal possession of a restricted firearm and pointing a firearm. In the end he pleaded guilty to these offences as well as a charge of attempting to intimidate a witness and he received his severest prison sentence to that point—eighteen months.

Before his incarceration Simard had decided that Montreal was where he belonged, though it would be many months before he could hope to establish himself there. When he was not in prison he was on probation and under strict conditions as to where and in what circumstances he could live.

Simard also wanted to reinvent himself physically. His obesity was a continuing source of embarrassment to him and, in his mind, one of the reasons he had never managed to finish a degree, hang on to a job, or stay on the straight and narrow. He tried steroids, but without any more discipline in the gym than in the classroom, he was not encouraged by the results. He looked into surgical options, such as liposuction, and learned that the Québec health care system would pay for stomach stapling and intestine shortening for people who were at least twice their optimal weight. Simard hadn't quite reached that heft, but after a few months of binge eating he made the grade, tipping the scales at 355 pounds. The operation was performed, and he began to slim down considerably.

His surgery afforded Simard an unanticipated benefit once he was in prison. Now that he had a dramatically reduced stomach capacity, the breakfast-lunch-supper routine was both too much and not enough. He couldn't handle full-size meals but needed frequent snacks. There were also certain foods he couldn't eat. This won him a perk that was the envy of many of his fellow prisoners: a mini-kitchen in his cell, complete with personal bar fridge.

For Simard 1995 began and ended in jail, but he wasn't inside the entire twelve months. He had been scheduled for release on full parole during the course of the year, but on a weekend pass just before it took effect, he made a typically unwise decision to retrieve the gun that had put him behind bars in the first place. The friend who had kept it for him wanted to be rid of it, so Simard picked it up on his way to a night of dancing at a club. After parking his Jeep he thought to transfer the gun to the floor under the driver's seat, a manoeuvre that was observed by a passing police officer. Simard's parole and dance plans were cancelled for several more months.

When he finally did get out, he moved back into his mother's house and took the night clerk job at the Château Mont-Ste-Anne. As part of his parole he was to see a psychiatrist regularly, as well as his probation officer. Still he found time to make regular trips to Montreal where his bad behaviour resurfaced. Between October and December 1996 he wrote at least $1200 worth of cheques to Marks and Spencer on an empty account.

When he placed his ad in the *Rencontres Sélectes* telephone personals, Simard listed himself in the Montreal section, even though he was still living in Quebec City. His latest plan was to study criminology at the Université de Montréal, and he was keen to make some friends before the move. Whatever his sexual experience or his fantasies, Simard maintained to his family that he had an interest in women, if only to placate his very traditional mother. In this spirit he advertised in the bisexual category and before long received a phone call from Dany Kane. Kane was calling not as the proprietor of the publication to confirm the listing but in answer to the ad, as a potential partner for Simard.

Apart from the possibility of prison initiation, there is little to suggest that Kane had much sexual experience with men before he began seeing Aimé Simard. Indeed, those who knew him well wonder where he might have found the time or the energy. Kane was by all accounts, including his own, a vigorous chaser of women who didn't hesitate to boast of his multiple exploits, even to his RCMP handlers. But he was sexually adventurous, and he was capable of living at least one shadow life. Whether he was seeking a novel thrill or another in a string of homosexual lovers, Kane responded to Simard's ad.

The two men talked on the phone several times, sharing carefully selected biographical details. During one of those chats Simard admitted that he lived in Quebec City, a fact that didn't trouble Kane. He said he would soon be passing through the provincial capital. In late November or early December they met in the parking lot of a McDonald's between two strip malls in the Quebec City suburb of Sainte-Foy. Simard, coming from the other side of town, arrived a few minutes after Kane and identified him by his car, a dark blue 1996 Cadillac with tinted windows. They spent the afternoon together, talking and driving around before going out for supper. Midway through the meal Kane asked if Simard knew a half-decent hotel where he could spend the night. Simard invited him to bunk down at his mother's. Elisa had gone to Florida to spend the winter in her trailer, and Simard had the run of the place.

Back at the house, Simard showed Kane to one of the spare rooms and gave him a tour of the modest single-storey home. One of the few luxuries Elisa had allowed herself was a whirlpool bath in the basement. Kane asked if he could use it. "No problem—make yourself at home," Simard said.

After his soak, Kane came upstairs in his pyjamas and broached the question that had been hanging in the air, unasked but insistent, since their first greeting in the McDonald's parking lot: did Simard want to sleep with him? Simard said yes.

When Kane removed his pyjama top, Simard saw the tattoo on Kane's arm: "SS 81," the *S*'s shaped like light-ning bolts. From his prison education, Simard instantly recognized the tattoo as that of a Hells Angel. The gang's fascination with numerology was reflected in the potent number 81, *H* being the eighth letter of the alphabet and *A* the first. The *SS* was both an echo of Nazism with all its shock value and, to some, a signal of membership in the so-called Filthy Few, the sub-sect of Hells Angels members who have killed in the service of the gang.

Earlier Kane had described himself as a businessman who "invested money in bars and agencies" and managed a bulging stock portfolio. He had told Simard he was on his way to Halifax to look into a bar as a potential business opportunity. Simard had also edited his CV, simply telling Kane that he was studying criminology and working at the ski resort. Staring at the tattoo Simard knew there was more to Kane's story.

Kane responded to Simard's curiosity with a question of his own. "How come you know this type of tattoo?" he asked. At that point Simard told Kane that he had spent time in prison, embellishing his criminal past to make it sound more impressive. He glossed over his convictions for petty fraud and claimed the firearms charges were laid after he had shot at a cop. Simard's exaggerations on the table, Kane reciprocated in kind, claiming that he was a prospect of the Hells Angels, one step below full member.

The two men then had sex in Simard's mother's bed.

The next day Kane continued on to Halifax. Despite what he may have told Simard, the main purpose of his trip concerned much more than an investment opportunity.

By late 1996 the Hells Angels chapter in Halifax had fallen into disarray. Whether its members were more relaxed and laissez-faire than their brothers elsewhere or not as ambitious and acquisitive, the Halifax chapter resembled the Hells Angels of yore—more a gaggle of hard-partying thugs than a cadre of cutthroat business-men. As a result the Halifax drug market was controlled not by a multinational organized crime group—the Hells Angels—but by a cast of "independents" who, Kane told his handlers, had the Hells at their mercy.

Financially the gang was also a disaster. The chapter was hundreds of thousands of dollars in debt, and its members personally owed much more. Wolf Carroll, who wholesaled supplies of cocaine and hashish to Halifax, was a major creditor as well as an informal god-father to the chapter. He had lost all patience, referring to the chapter's members as "a bunch of Boy Scouts" for their reluctance to use violence to further their interests. But even his exhortations hadn't spurred them to action. By December the situation was dire enough that the Halifax chapter was placed under the Hells' equivalent of trusteeship. Their lavish clubhouse was sold to help pay off debts, and Carroll decided to take over the local drug market himself. Kane told Verdon and St. Onge that Wolf was dispatching *éclaireurs*—shock troops—to the city to shake things up and grab control. The shock troops would be black for the most part, although their leader was white and a long-time associate of Carroll's, a Halifax bar owner by the name of Paul Wilson.

Kane had met Wilson on several occasions in Halifax and in Montreal. As a gofer for Carroll, Kane had chauf-feured Wilson to and from Dorval airport, and he'd spent time with him socially. If Kane was serious about invest-ing in a Halifax drinking establishment, it might have been Wilson's Reflections, a gay bar that was nonetheless one of the local Hells Angels' favourite hangouts. It's more likely, however, that Kane was actually one of Carroll's shock troops, sent to show the Hells colours in advance of taking over the city's drug trade. This would inevitably entail some nastiness, including the elimination of those parties who proved annoying to Carroll and his old friend Paul Wilson.

Kane didn't stop in Quebec City on his return trip home, but he did call Simard as he passed by, inviting him to spend the following weekend in Montreal. Kane gave him his pager number—like those of many bikers, an 800 number—and when Simard arrived in the city they arranged to meet at a designated street corner. From there Kane gave Simard a crash course in his life.

He introduced him to Patricia and to Pat Lambert and to another aspiring biker by the name of Claude-Grégoire McCarter. He took him to St-Jean, where he met Josée and Kane's parents. They collected the children and brought them back to Montreal for the weekend, everyone crammed into the tiny apartment on Rue St-Christophe. Kane was his usual gregarious self, eager to please a new best friend, however peculiar the circumstances.

Within a few weeks, Simard was spending almost as much time in Montreal as Quebec City, despite his job at the Château Mont-Ste-Anne. He had met a number of full-patch Hells Angels, among them Carroll and Steinert. He'd hung out at the Lavigueur mansion and exercised at the Pro-Gym, joining the group workout that was the Rockers' daily fitness ritual and business meeting. He'd served as muscle when gang members wanted to make their presence felt at bars and on the street.

Kane introduced Simard as a close friend, someone he'd known for six, seven years, in order to reassure the wary bikers and their associates. But that was not to say Kane and Simard were to be regarded as equals. In a culture where hierarchy was strictly observed and prestige measured in the number of flunkies in tow, Kane made it very clear that Simard was his junior. When Simard was in town he served as Kane's driver, the message being that even if Kane had to do the bidding of Steinert or Carroll, he had an underling of his own to serve him in turn.

Not every chore was easily delegated, however. Kane was still expected to prove himself, and in the fall of 1996, he was assigned a critical test: the murder of Donald Magnussen. The job had been given to one of the Rockers' more prolific killers, Toots Tousignant, the previous summer but the careful Magnussen was an elusive target. In late October Wolf Carroll, Walter Stadnick, and Donald "Pup" Stockford told Kane the gig was now his. The fact that he was Magnussen's friend would make the job easier to accomplish, they reasoned. Kane would have ample opportunity to be alone with Magnussen, a moment when he could pull out his handgun, say, "Sorry about this," and pull the trigger. The Nomads promised Kane $10,000 for the hit.

The contract put Kane in an impossible position and not only because as an RCMP informant he was supposed to keep his hands clean. The Montreal chapter of the Hells Angels felt quite differently about Magnussen than the Nomads; as far as the Montreal Hells were concerned, Magnussen redeemed himself every time he went after a member of the Rock Machine. Furthermore, Magnussen was Scott Steinert's best friend. Kane's competing loyalties to Carroll and Steinert, to the Nomads and to the Montreal Hells, were about to be brought to a head.

Kane delayed taking any action for two weeks, by which time providence intervened in the person of Mom Boucher. Mom decided that if Magnussen had to die, his killer should be a full-patch Hells Angel. The hit was no longer Kane's to execute. "According to Boucher, Dick Mayrand [now Montreal chapter and national president] and Scott Steinert would never accept that a *non-patché* eliminate a close friend of the Montreal chapter," Kane reported to his handlers. "Since it is Walter Stadnick who will benefit most by the death of Magnussen, it seems that he will do the job himself."

Despite the heightened activity on several fronts—the tensions between the Nomads and the Montreal Hells, the problems in Halifax, and Kane's recruitment of Simard— the RCMP file for informant C-2994 was strangely thin in December. Only one meeting is recorded between November 26 and December 23, that of December 4, and the account of the session is oddly cursory. Whereas details from the debriefings regularly ran to ten pages or more, this report is a single page. It was filled out by St. Onge and signed off by him, in effect making him his own supervisor, more than three weeks later, after the Christmas holidays.

For Patricia those holidays proved to be something of an eye-opener: it was the first time she met Kane's family. Christmas dinner was being held at Gisèle's house in St-Jean, and the rest of the clan was there by the time she and Dany arrived. Although the party was in full swing, the room went silent when they made their entrance. Apparently Kane hadn't told them his new girlfriend was black. The awkwardness passed, and dinner, a buffet-style affair with people eating off their laps in the basement, resumed. Patricia, however, had been put off her food. She found the family loud and boorish, almost a caricature of small-town values and attitudes.

Kane picked up on her discomfort, and as soon as they were on their way back to Montreal he apologized for his family.

His friendly intentions went awry again a month later when Simard's probation expired and he was free to move to Montreal. Kane suggested he stay with them on Rue St-Christophe, an offer that enraged Patricia, who hadn't been fond of Simard from the start. But Simard at least was sensitive to the situation. Thanks to his lunch-counter experience, he was an excellent cook and would ingratiate himself with Patricia by preparing lavish gourmet meals. "It would come to a point that I was about to explode and then Simard would cook us a really nice meal," Patricia remembers. "Then I'd think, Maybe he's not such a bad guy." Indeed, with Simard around, Kane and Patricia found themselves eating together at home much more often than before. Even on Valentine's Day, they stayed in to eat an especially exquisite dinner that Simard had created for them.

Early on, Patricia had suggested to Kane that his new friend might be gay. Kane said he didn't think so. "Anyway, what difference would it make?" he asked. None, she replied. A week or two later, Kane put the question to Simard out of the blue when the three of them were together. No, Simard replied, he wasn't gay, just well mannered, the result of a private school education. It was a mistake people often made, confusing his sophistication with homosexuality, he claimed. It might have been a nose stretcher, but Patricia bought it.

The cramped living quarters were made endurable by the fact that none of them spent much time at the apartment. Patricia was working as a secretary at an office in the northeast end of the city, and with commuting time she was out of the apartment almost all day. Kane and Simard, meanwhile, were often gone most of the night. Patricia and Kane communicated through an endless stream of notes. Sometimes it felt as if they really were roommates, as Kane had told Josée. "The only time I'd see Dany was in the morning before he left or when he came home. We lived in the same place and had sex, but we weren't really *living* together."

Kane and Simard were busy attending to Kane's regular business, dealing drugs and doing the chores assigned him by the gang. On occasion Simard unknowingly chauffeured him to meetings with his Mountie handlers. *Rencontres Sélectes* was more or less moribund after its second issue, and the two concocted myriad money-making schemes. One of these was a brazen, or perhaps harebrained, plan for a robbery at the Montreal casino. Not surprisingly, it never happened.

The pair's usual routine took them first to the Hells' and Rockers' morning get-together at the Pro-Gym, then in and out of the apartment depending on the day's demands, not returning until the wee hours. Sometimes Simard didn't come back at all. When things got too close in the apartment or when he and Kane wanted to have sex, Simard would rent a room in a cheap hotel near the bus terminal.

Occasionally Simard had to return to Quebec City. He was still nominally employed at the Château Mont-Ste-Anne, although a minor on-the-job injury had allowed him to go weeks without doing a shift. On one of these trips he bragged to his brother about having become a "somebody with power." He said that he had finally fallen in with people who appreciated him and that he'd found his niche. He revealed that his new friends were bikers, the notorious Nomads. His brother read the crime pages and knew what

Aimé was talking about. He and his sister were appalled
and alarmed, but Simard was unmoved by sibling disap-
proval. On the contrary he was determined to demonstrate
to his Nomad acquaintances that their acceptance of him
was more than justified.

On the evening of February 12 Simard was driving
around Quebec City with Steve Leclerc, a friend from one
of his stints in prison. They headed to a bar in the Lower
Town that was known as a Rock Machine point of sale.
Their plans were vague. Perhaps they'd start a fight or
otherwise cause trouble. They found the establishment
closed down by a police raid, and so made for another. At
the second bar, Leclerc recognized a man to whom he
owed money. The fellow was a dealer for the Rock
Machine, he told Simard; they should leave.

"I'll take care of this," Simard replied. They went outside to sit in Simard's car and wait for the dealer to
emerge. Tucked in his belt, Simard carried a .44-calibre
Magnum semi-automatic pistol that Kane had given him
as payment for a debt. He decided the time had come to
use it.

Eventually the man appeared, accompanied by a
woman and swaying from too much drink. Simard noted
which way they were walking and drove around the block
so he could come up behind them. As he drew alongside
he lowered the passenger window, using the driver's con-
trols, and told Leclerc to recline his seat. Then he leaned
over and shouted, "Hey, you pig!" at the man. As the
dealer turned toward him, Simard shot five times. The
woman made the mistake of looking into the car instead
of fleeing. Simard shot her twice. He had learned quickly
and well from his new friends; in such situations, the
important thing was to leave no witnesses.

Assuming, incorrectly, that their victims were dead, Simard and Leclerc sped off. The next day Simard hurried back to Montreal to cook that Valentine's Day feast for Kane and Patricia. To Kane alone he recounted his Quebec City escapade, with considerable elaboration. There had been a white car, possibly a Ford Taurus, with five people in it, all associated with the Rock Machine. Someone in the car recognized Simard and began firing at him. Word on the streets of Quebec, Simard implied, was that he was now known to be consorting with the Hells. Then two people got out of the car and Simard let them have it.

Kane was impressed. Even if Simard had succeeded only in seriously wounding the pair, the shooting proved that Simard had the right stuff. He was ready, Kane concluded, for his first big job for the Hells Angels—a job out in Halifax, perhaps as early as the next week.

But first Kane relayed all the details of Simard's exploits to St. Onge by telephone. He provided the Mounties not only with Simard's cellphone number but also his mother's address.

The move could have torpedoed Kane's own plans to use Simard as the trigger man in Halifax. After all, the police might have arrested or at least interrogated Simard for the shootings in Quebec City, saying they had tracked him down through his licence plate or some other witness identification. Kane's role as their source need not have been exposed. But apparently Kane was sure that the force would not take action on the information he provided. He was confident that he could tell his handlers who was behind the shooting and not risk Simard's arrest. His faith wasn't misplaced.

13

THE HIT
IN HALIFAX

Robert MacFarlane wasn't a native Haligonian, but he was a man who swaggered about the city as if he owned it. He came from a tough family on Prince Edward Island, one whose members were no strangers to bar brawls and jail cells. At six foot four and well over two hundred pounds, Robert was built to carry on the tradition.

While in his teens he left PEI for Halifax and was soon moving in its seedier circles. For a time he was a bouncer at the Misty Moon, one of the port city's rowdiest bars. But MacFarlane was too smart and ambitious for a life as hired brawn, and soon his flare for entrepreneurial sidelines, legitimate or otherwise, meant that he didn't have to accept such humble employment.

One business interest was cocaine, a drug for which he also had a large personal appetite. This brought him into contact with Halifax's Hells Angels and other organized crime groups in the city. At the same time he managed to impress a more respectable crowd with the opportune launch of a successful cellphone business. Cellular Connection may have been conceived as a cover to launder drug money, but it prospered during the mobile phone explosion of the early 1990s. MacFarlane, the dynamic young businessman, was invited to accompany the Nova Scotia premier, John Savage, on a trade mission to Cuba. In 1995 MacFarlane sold the business for a reported $1 million, enough to make him a rich man. By his early thirties he had already accumulated the assets that many men only dream about. He owned several properties, including a spacious lakefront home just outside Halifax. He kept a fleet of luxury cars and a boat for cruising the harbour and south shore waterways. And he had married a woman who was considered to be among the most beautiful in Nova Scotia.

But not long after MacFarlane sold the business his drug use and alcohol consumption got out of hand. Increasingly belligerent and bellicose, he was constantly spoiling for a fight, looking for any excuse to prove his toughness and virility. "A total animal" is how a Halifax defence lawyer described him.

One man he regularly provoked was Paul Wilson, the owner of the Reflections bar. For years MacFarlane and Wilson had been close friends and for a spell roommates, but they'd had a falling-out, Wilson later told police, over MacFarlane's substance abuse. The rupture had left MacFarlane embittered. On several occasions in the summer and fall of 1996 he took friends out on his boat and afterwards treated them to several hours of drinking at Reflections. MacFarlane then left without paying, challenging Wilson to do something about it. Other times he simply went to the bar, became drunk, and aggravated Wilson's employees and customers. Frequently his presence attracted the unwanted attendance of police; once he arrived carrying a gas can and threatened to burn down the building; another time he was charged with sexually assaulting a waitress.

MacFarlane wasn't just a headache for Wilson. The Hells Angels Halifax chapter also found him troublesome. He was considered a mid-level independent dealer, one who occasionally did business through the gang but all too often did not. It was lone operators like MacFarlane whom Wolf Carroll had in mind when he exhorted the Halifax Hells to exercise greater control over the region's drug market. The independents had to fall into line or leave the scene, Wolf admonished them.

In 1996 the gang had approached MacFarlane to become a more closely integrated associate, an invitation the braggart MacFarlane lorded over those he hoped to intimidate. But he resisted the gang's overture and refused to show its members the appropriate respect. During one visit to the chapter's clubhouse he got into a dispute with a member and proceeded to beat him severely on his own turf. Still, the Halifax Hells Angels were a barely cohesive group, and MacFarlane remained on good terms with at least one influential member.

That man was with MacFarlane when he finally went a step too far with Paul Wilson. After yet another drunken ejection from Reflections, MacFarlane made threats against not only Wilson but also his wife, his children, and his mother, the nominal owner of the bar and a manager there. Patrons and staff who witnessed the scene were reportedly afraid to testify against MacFarlane. Wilson believed his erstwhile friend might be true to his word and began carrying a handgun. He also contacted Wolf Carroll, contracting with him for a pre-emptive hit on MacFarlane. Carroll, a senior Nomad, wouldn't dream of carrying out the job himself. Instead he passed on the $25,000 assignment to a favourite lieutenant,

Dany Kane. And Kane gave the nod to his new lover and flunky, Aimé Simard.

It was shortly after the shoot-up in Quebec City when Kane informed Simard that the gang had a hit for him to do. At first Kane didn't give many details: the job would be out of town, and he would accompany Simard to see how he performed. He said that while it was "a very, very delicate assignment," there wouldn't be much cash in it—"pocket money" was all Simard should expect. Over the next week or so Kane let slip a few more details. The location was Halifax, and the target was "a well-liked guy, a guy on our side." That's why the hit was being given to out-of-towners. Although it was a "housekeeping" matter, an "inside elimination" commissioned by someone Kane described as a Hells Angel, other members of the gang couldn't know who was behind it.

On the evening of February 23, 1997, Kane told Simard they would leave the next day, and that night they began their preparations. At one of their regular bars on a trendy strip of St-Laurent Boulevard, Kane obtained a .38-calibre handgun, which he presented to Simard as the weapon to be used. But the next morning, just before their departure, Simard told Kane he found the .38 too heavy and awkward; couldn't he find him something smaller, maybe a semi-automatic 9 mm? Kane said he'd look into it.

Then there was the issue of a vehicle. In early January Simard had written off his Jeep in a crash. With the insurance money he'd bought a Chrysler Intrepid and promptly wrecked it. A couple of days before the Halifax trip he'd tried to overtake a van in a snowstorm on the highway between Quebec City and Montreal, again lost control, and run into the ditch. While the Intrepid was back in the

shop the insurance company provided a Buick LeSabre,
which they had to pick up on the morning of February 24.
Transportation secured, they stopped at a downtown tav-
ern to buy a 9 mm that Kane had located with the help of
the Rocker René Charlebois. Simard had to pay the $900
for the gun himself, although Kane promised he'd be
reimbursed.

They were on their way to Halifax by early afternoon,
making a stop at Quebec City where Simard had a rendezvous with Jimmy Miller, a friend who had stored the
.44 Magnum that Simard used in the Lower Town shooting. Kane had instructed Simard to throw the gun away
and Simard claimed to have done so. But he thought it a
waste to discard it and he'd asked Miller to hang on to it
for him. Miller, however, was getting nervous. Steve
Leclerc, Simard's companion the night of the shooting,
was starting to talk, and Miller worried that the police
might get wind of it and draw a link to him.

Simard met up with Miller at the zoo near his mother's
home in Charlesbourg. Asking Kane to stay in the car he
surreptitiously took possession of the gun and kept it hidden when he got back into the Buick. Later, at a brief stop
to collect clothes at his mother's, Simard cut a hole in the
back seat and stashed the .44 there while Kane was in the
house. There was one more stop at Château Mont-Ste-
Anne, where Simard picked up his last paycheque.

By then it was too late to drive straight through to
Halifax, so after about two hundred kilometres they
checked into a roadside motel for the night. There they
took some professional precautions, including the
removal of the batteries from their pagers and cellphones
so that the devices couldn't later be used to prove that
they had travelled to Halifax.

The next day's sunny drive through eastern Quebec, New Brunswick, and across Nova Scotia was uneventful, but for an incident just before 3 p.m. About fifteen kilometres short of Fredericton, Kane and Simard passed an RCMP cruiser travelling in the opposite direction. The officer at the wheel, Const. Gilles Blinn, an earnest, ten-year veteran of the force, had long experience and extensive training in "highway interdiction" and considered himself an expert in reading the subtle signals unconsciously conveyed by motorists, by their cars, and by the way they drove them. With him was Dale Hutley, a building contractor and auxiliary RCMP constable, an unarmed, volunteer Mountie. Blinn's curiosity was aroused by the two young men in the "classy" late-model Buick, and he did a quick U-turn, following Kane and Simard for about four kilometres. He thought the pair were playing it too cool, chatting and apparently carefree, even though it was obvious they were being followed by a police car. He decided to pull them over.

Blinn approached the driver's side to talk to Simard while Hutley handled Kane. After a brief exchange, they took their names and birthdates, and Blinn and Hutley returned to their cruiser to run checks through the Canadian Police Information Centre network via an on-board computer. The information that came back was extensive: the complete criminal records of both men, along with a note that Kane was involved with Quebec's outlaw biker gangs.

Simard's crimes were small time, and having deduced that he would be the more garrulous of the pair Blinn sent Hutley back to the Buick to fetch him. In the back seat of the cruiser, the 9 mm in his waistband and concealed under a jacket, Simard was chatty and apparently candid.

He said he had known Kane only a couple of months and wasn't aware of his lengthy criminal record. He explained they were on their way to Fredericton to spend the weekend with some strippers, and he indicated Kane was in the stripper agency business. No, he didn't know where in Fredericton these women worked.

Blinn had decided that Kane and Simard probably weren't drug couriers, but his suspicions were nonetheless aroused. Simard was talking about a quick weekend trip but this was Tuesday. Blinn accompanied Simard back to the Buick and approached Kane, who, beyond giving his name and date of birth, had been utterly unforthcoming with Hutley. He was no more cooperative with Blinn, to the point that the Mountie asked him whether he was "anti-police." Kane responded that he just didn't like talking to cops.

Blinn asked if he could look in the trunk, and Simard opened it, revealing a considerable amount of luggage for what was described as a short visit. Then Hutley lifted out a plastic grocery bag. Inside were a pair of walkie-talkies, a police scanner, and a pager. Blinn asked Kane what they were for, but Kane clammed up even tighter. "He just sat in his seat with a bull-moose look on his face," Blinn said later. "There was something wrong, something not right."

Because of his menacing silence, Kane made a much deeper impression on Blinn than did the chirpy Simard. Months later he would remember Kane's earrings and chunky, expensive-looking jewellery, his smart clothes and close-cropped goatee, his short stature and the pumped-up biceps. "A typical Montrealer," Blinn remarked. "If there is such a thing."

When the CPIC network confirmed that neither of the two was actively sought by any police force, Blinn let them go. He had no other choice, even though he was quite sure they were up to no good. Burglars, Blinn thought. Stick-up men, maybe. He never imagined their true mission.

Blinn's check of Kane triggered a "silent hit" with St. Onge's computer back in Montreal. Thus notified of his source's far-flung travels, St. Onge promptly contacted the New Brunswick Mountie to ask why he had stopped Kane. Blinn gave him a complete rundown: who Kane was with, what kind of car they were driving, the walkie-talkies and police scanner found in the trunk. St. Onge offered no explanation for the inquiry, saying only that he was investigating biker gangs.

Kane and Simard arrived in Halifax that evening not long after nine and went straight to the Halifax Shopping Centre. MacFarlane had recently opened a retail business there called the Spy Shop. Perhaps reflecting his growing paranoia, it specialized in electronic surveillance equipment.

The stores in the mall were either closed or closing for the day; the Spy Shop was dark and locked. Kane clearly knew the layout of the mall and the city; he revealed to Simard that he had made a visit three weeks earlier to find and follow MacFarlane and to scout the best locations for the hit. Fortunately MacFarlane's routines were predictable: he always closed up the shop himself, left the mall by the same exit, and parked in the same spot. The corridor leading to the exit door would be the ideal site, but that night they had arrived too late. Kane and Simard got back into their car and drove to MacFarlane's house on Hatchet Lake. There was no sign of his vehicle, a black Jeep Grand Cherokee with gold trim and the licence plate

2 BAD 4U, so they called it a day and found a motel, a Days Inn near the highway.

MacFarlane had returned that very day from more than two weeks away, during which he had visited British Columbia and Cuba and made a fresh batch of enemies. He'd flown first to Vancouver, where he was met at the airport by a Halifax friend, Mike Miller. According to police intelligence, Miller had left the East Coast a few months earlier, after he had been fronted a kilogram of cocaine—$40,000 worth—by Paul Wilson. Miller had never paid up, and MacFarlane had publicly mocked Wilson about it. Wilson was out a key of coke but was too much of a wimp to do anything about it.

The purpose of MacFarlane's trip west was unclear. It might have been purely for pleasure, though there was speculation that he was ferrying as much as $250,000 in cash for a B.C. Hells Angel with Halifax roots. Others wondered if he was out to collect on Miller's obligation to Wilson, given that muscular debt collection had long been one of MacFarlane's money-making sidelines. He was known to buy bad debts in the criminal community for, say, 25 cents on the dollar, then use his fists and feet to maximize his investment. Given relations between Wilson and MacFarlane at the time, it's unlikely they had made such a deal, but it is possible that MacFarlane bought Wilson's debt from a third party. Or, indeed, that MacFarlane figured that if Wilson wasn't going to collect what was his, he might as well help himself to it.

But business of any kind wasn't at the top of MacFarlane's and Miller's minds. The two hit the bars as soon as they drove into town from the airport and were at it again the next day. They settled into an establishment where, in the words of one guidebook, "women shower for men who don't": the No. 5 Orange, a strip bar in the Downtown Eastside co-owned by a senior Hells Angel. Its stage had hosted the likes of Courtney Love and Pamela Anderson, but the dancer MacFarlane and Miller were to meet used the stage name Red Sonya, and was considerably less famous.

While there MacFarlane loudly dropped the names of East Coast Hells Angels he knew. If the B.C. bikers were impressed it didn't show; several members of Vancouver's East End Hells chapter approached to tell him to keep quiet. MacFarlane promised to do so, but after the bikers left he started acting up again. When a bouncer finally asked him to leave, MacFarlane had the opening he was looking for. In the ensuing melee he broke one employee's nose, another's arm, and bit deeply into the forearm of a third before he and Miller hightailed it out of the rear exit of the club. Police arrived shortly thereafter, followed by ten "very agitated" East End Hells Angels, according to a police report.

MacFarlane kept a lower profile in the days following, seeing the sights with Miller, visiting a tanning salon, and buying inventory for the Spy Shop. Eventually he felt it politic to make amends with the co-owner of the No. 5 Orange, and he offered to send the East End Hells one hundred pounds of lobster as reparation—an apology he thought the proprietor accepted. But as soon as he was out the door the Hells Angel took the unusual step of phoning the police. MacFarlane and Miller spent that night in jail.

The two men were released separately the next day, and for the rest of MacFarlane's week in Vancouver, Miller steered clear of him, standing him up on at least two occasions. MacFarlane went to Miller's home to track him down, leading to another run-in with the police when

a neighbour reported him as a prowler. On his last afternoon on the West Coast MacFarlane lunched with an
employee of Spy vs. Spy, the store where he bought stock,
during which he complained about his buddy Mike stiffing him on the $40,000 he owed him for a kilo of cocaine.

MacFarlane's next destination was a resort near
Camaguey, Cuba. Heavy drinking there led to predictable
results: outrageous boasting, broken furniture, an assault
on a female employee, and another brief sojourn in a jail
cell, this time one with mosquitoes.

During the stopover in Toronto between Vancouver and
Cuba, MacFarlane had phoned his wife to have her send
the promised lobster—or at least 50 pounds of it—to the
East End Hells Angels chapter. By the time he returned to
Halifax on February 25, she was off on a southern vacation of her own, to the Dominican Republic, with some
women friends. He was picked up at the airport by one of
his employees with whom he made plans to go out on the
town the following evening.

On Wednesday, February 26, Kane and Simard headed
back to the mall soon after rising. They hung out in the
food court in front of the Spy Shop drinking juice, eating
doughnuts and waiting for MacFarlane to arrive so that
Kane could identify him to Simard. Once Simard had
seen his target he and Kane cased the surrounding neighbourhood, finding a discreet place to park the Buick and
plotting their escape route back to the motel. They tested
the walkie-talkies and reviewed the plan. Simard would
shoot MacFarlane as he left the mall at closing time. First,
though, they had to kill the day.

Kane and Simard decided they should develop a Plan
B, and in the afternoon they revisited MacFarlane's house

to settle on a suitable hiding place for Simard should they miss him at the shop. Then it was back to the mall, where Simard bought an all-black ensemble—gloves, shoes, and jacket—to wear for the occasion. While he shopped Kane stole a Nova Scotia licence plate off a car in the underground parking garage to disguise the origins of the Buick. Their chores done, the pair felt like a rest and returned to the Days Inn.

Around 8 p.m., they arrived at the shopping centre for what they hoped would be the last time. Simard was dressed in his new duds, a balaclava rolled up on his head. The 9 mm was tucked into his waistband at the small of his back, the .38 in the front. While Kane waited in the car Simard made his way to a washroom entrance from which he could see MacFarlane lock up and walk down the corridor. After a few minutes MacFarlane came out of the Spy Shop and made for the corridor, but he wasn't alone. There were three other men with him and too many witnesses.

Simard consulted Kane on his walkie-talkie, and they agreed to implement Plan B. At MacFarlane's house they saw no sign of his car, so Simard snuck across a neighbour's property and through some undergrowth to what he hoped would be a good ambush spot. But as he came alongside the house he set off MacFarlane's bull mastiffs, and their prolonged barking unnerved him. They scrapped Plan B and returned to the motel for another early evening.

MacFarlane, meanwhile, had a long night of coke and alcohol ahead of him. He and Paul Macphail, the employee who picked him up at the airport, intended to stay up all night belatedly celebrating MacFarlane's thirty-fourth birthday, an occasion that had passed in lonely fashion while he was in Cuba. On this night, since

MacFarlane would be laying out the lines, there was no shortage of company. Over the course of the party MacFarlane mentioned several times that since returning from Cuba, he sensed he was being followed, maybe by the cops, maybe by members of the Outlaws biker gang, about whom he claimed to have incriminating documents. Someone was staking out his residence, and if the Outlaws were after him, he intended to stay away from the house as much as possible.

MacFarlane did return home that night, but not until near dawn and then in the company of Macphail. There he eventually fell asleep for what would be the last time.

On Thursday, February 27, Kane and Simard woke up hungry for lobster. Simard picked up ten at a seafood stand near the motel and persuaded a desk clerk to cook them up in the kitchenette behind the office for a fee of $10. After their feast the two men drove into downtown Halifax for a full day of leisure activities. They did a bit of sightseeing, Kane pointing out the Reflections bar, worked out in the gym of a hotel where Kane had stayed previously, ate a pizza near the ferry dock, and took in a movie. By the time the film was over, the mall's closing hour was approaching, so they hurried back to the Days Inn, collected the guns and returned to the Halifax Shopping Centre. They took up their positions, Kane waiting in the car on a residential side street, Simard in the mall's washroom, checking periodically for MacFarlane.

Once more their plan was foiled. First a restaurant employee taking out garbage studied Simard suspiciously when she saw him loitering at the washroom door. Then, when MacFarlane finally left his store, he was again accompanied by others. Simard called Kane on the walkie-talkie to say he couldn't do the hit. Back at the Buick he noticed MacFarlane pulling out of the parking lot. Kane and Simard gave chase.

MacFarlane's two companions on this evening were out-of-town visitors: David Roberts, a cousin from P.E.I. with whom he was close, and an old prison friend of Roberts's from Moncton, Claude Blanchard. Roberts had persuaded Blanchard to drive to Halifax, where they could hook up with his rich, party-loving cousin. They had dropped Blanchard's girlfriend at a friend's house, then arrived at the Spy Shop about half an hour before closing. As MacFarlane did the cash and dealt with the last customers of the day, Roberts told Blanchard about MacFarlane's string of luxury cars, in particular his 1957 Corvette.

"The fuck you got one of those," said Blanchard. "I'd like to see it."

MacFarlane offered to show it to him, and it was agreed that MacFarlane and Roberts would go in his Jeep Cherokee while Blanchard followed in his girlfriend's car. Instead of driving at normal speed to MacFarlane's home, as he expected, Blanchard found himself racing to keep up with the Jeep as it sped toward a warehouse area and onto an unpaved, heavily potholed road. It led to a muddy lot in the Lakeside Industrial Park on which sat a handful of tractor-trailers and two rows of warehouse buildings. In one of these MacFarlane rented space to house his auto-mobile collection, including two BMWs, a Mercedes, and the Corvette.

As Blanchard pulled into the lot near the Jeep, MacFarlane was standing beside it urinating on the ground and complaining to Roberts about the white car that had been following them. Must be the police, MacFarlane said. Blanchard's medium-size mutt, Jazz, had waited patiently for him in the car at the shopping centre, so he opened his door to let her have a run around the lot. After MacFarlane zipped up, he had a few seconds to play with the dog before the white car appeared around the corner.

"The fucking cops, man," MacFarlane muttered as the Buick drove by slowly, perhaps three metres from where they were standing. The three of them watched as the car did a large loop and passed in front of them again. This time it pulled to a stop and the passenger side window was lowered. Jazz ran playfully toward the Buick and put her paws on the door to greet the strangers. MacFarlane, still expecting the police, shouted at them, "What the fuck you want?"

Simard asked if they knew where they could find the Tire Shack. Both MacFarlane and Blanchard approached the car, MacFarlane to confront the men he knew had been following him, Blanchard to pull Jazz off the car. It was a bad habit of hers that had caused problems before.

"There's no fuckin' Tire Shack around here," MacFarlane said as Blanchard reached for the dog. He'd no sooner taken hold of her collar than Simard started shooting. "I just fucking ran, man. Ran for my fucking life," Blanchard remembers. In his panic he ripped the collar right over Jazz's head and never looked back, scrambling under one semi-trailer, then another until he was around the back of the warehouse. Blanchard later told RCMP investigators that he had never run so fast in his life, even when being chased by police. By fleeing he missed witnessing a murder that was as much Keystone as gangland in its execution.

Kane and Simard had bought the handguns fully loaded and hadn't bothered testing them, nor had they purchased extra ammunition. They realized their mistake when Simard pulled the trigger on the .38 and it misfired. He tried again. Another misfire. And a third time. Finally the gun went off. By then MacFarlane was running too, but Simard was either a good shot or lucky: he hit MacFarlane in the upper body.

MacFarlane continued running, screaming all the while, and Simard got out of the car to pursue him. He fired off another round or two from the .38, before throwing it aside in frustration and yanking the 9 mm from his waistband. The sudden jerk probably popped the waistband of Simard's black overpants, which started slipping down his legs as he ran, tripping him up. They were at his ankles when he fired off another round, and MacFarlane fell face first into the mud. Once free of the pants Simard walked over to MacFarlane and put two bullets into the back of his neck.

By this time Kane had got out of the Buick and picked up the .38. While Simard ran back to the car he approached the prone MacFarlane and fired off two more rounds. To anyone looking on, it appeared Kane was making sure the job was done. In fact, the two bullets he fired went into the dirt beside MacFarlane's head. Kane then got back behind the wheel, passed the .38 to Simard with orders to wipe it down, and roared off in the direction they had come.

Blanchard didn't stop running until he saw the white car racing away. At that point he concluded the killers wouldn't be coming after him, so he returned to his girlfriend's car, bundled the shaking Jazz into the back seat, and made to leave the scene as quickly as possible. His headlights picked up MacFarlane's body, however, and he stopped.

MacFarlane was twitching and seemed to be breathing. Blanchard turned him over but couldn't find a pulse on his neck or at his wrist. He tried CPR, as he'd seen on television, shouting to Roberts for help. "You fucking idiot! Your fucking cousin—look at him, he's fucking dead!"

Roberts emerged from his hiding place and, at the sight of MacFarlane's body, began crying hysterically. He ripped open MacFarlane's shirt to see where he had been shot, but realized there was nothing to be done. He called Paul Macphail from the cellphone in Blanchard's car. As Roberts talked Blanchard considered leaving again. He didn't want to be there when police arrived. "I was fucking standing there, fucking wondering what the fuck to do, man," he told police a week later. "Buddy's dead. You know what I mean? Nothing you can do except get the fuck outta there."

That's what he did, leaving Roberts to wait for Macphail and deal with the police. Blanchard, who didn't know Halifax well, spent an hour looking for the house where his girlfriend was visiting. Then he hit the Dome bar and got "right fucking drunk."

Kane and Simard tore back to the Days Inn, stopping for mere seconds on the curving ramp leading to a highway and the motel. There, with no other vehicles in sight, Simard threw the two firearms as far as he could into a wooded area. As the 9 mm landed, it discharged a final round. Then he ripped off the Nova Scotia licence plate and whipped it like a Frisbee in the same direction. Back in the car Simard stripped off his remaining top layer of clothing, Kane jettisoning the articles through the window like so much ballast from a sinking ship. Out went Simard's gloves, shoes, jacket, and sweater—anything that might have been contaminated by gunpowder residue or could otherwise connect them to the murder. Kane removed the rubber boots he'd been wearing and threw them toward the ditch.

Back at the motel they ran sock-footed into their room and hastily collected their belongings, tossing everything into the trunk of the Buick. The weather was changing as they found the Trans-Canada out of town, transforming a dank and chilly evening into a raging winter storm. Simard proposed they stop for the night, but Kane was eager to get home. Taking turns behind the wheel, they drove sixteen hours non-stop through snow and ice, arriving back in Montreal in the afternoon of the last day of February.

PSYCHOPATH ON THE SOFA

After a single night in Montreal, Kane and Simard were once again on the highway, heading east this time, back toward Quebec City. Simard had promised a free weekend of skiing and snowmobiling at Mont-Ste-Anne, and perhaps Kane felt they'd earned a bit of R and R. On Saturday, March 1, 1997, various cars carrying Kane, Patricia and assorted children, the Rocker associate Claude Grégoire McCarter and his girlfriend, as well as Josée's brother Dominique (now serving as Kane's occasional driver) and Simard headed out on Autoroute 20.

Pretending that he still worked at the resort, Simard had managed to finagle three suites with no deposit or credit card up front. Soon the group split up to pursue their favourite activities in the remaining light of late afternoon. For Kane this meant skiing and in particular introducing Patricia to the sport. He had learned as a child living with his aunt and uncle; she, however, had never been close to a ski hill and didn't know a T-bar from a step-in binding. Kane was unfazed. He got her outfitted and took her straight up the slopes; there was no time to waste on snow-plowing the bunny hill. And he wasn't going to wait until morning; if he could night-ski, so could she.

Disembarking from the chairlift at the top, Patricia fell and had to scramble on her hands and knees to avoid being struck by other skiers behind her. She refused to go any farther. Kane tried to cajole her into continuing down the hill. "Any dummy can learn to ski," he said.

Patricia was no dummy, but that was enough skiing for her.

"Fuck off and grab a phone," she told Kane. A ski patrol snowmobile eventually transported her to the bottom at a cost to Kane of $200.

While his guests amused themselves, Simard attended to old business. When a nervous Jimmy Miller had told him that Steve Leclerc was spreading talk about the Lower Town shooting, Simard had wondered what to do about his gossipy prison buddy. It gnawed at him for most of the trip to Halifax, but he knew what to do after shooting MacFarlane and discovering how easy it was to kill.

After settling Kane and the others into their suites, Simard telephoned Leclerc in Quebec City and told him he needed a backup for a drug transaction scheduled for that night at a remote location just off the highway between Montreal and Quebec City. All he asked was that Leclerc hide in the nearby woods with a gun and come out firing if the situation turned sour. Leclerc agreed, Simard picked him up, and the two were soon on Autoroute 20 heading back toward Montreal.

Roughly halfway through the 240-kilometre journey, Simard pulled off the highway at a dark exit. He drove to the end of a rural cul-de-sac and told Leclerc to head for a stand of trees a few metres off. As Leclerc waded into waist-deep snow, Simard pulled his gun from his waistband, loaded a bullet into the chamber, and called out to his friend.

Simard was a quick study in the code of the criminal milieu. He knew that shooting a person in the back was cowardly. The shooter had to look into the eyes of his victim and still pull the trigger; the victim had to understand, at least for a split second, that he was about to die. Simard wanted to ensure Leclerc's silence, but he wanted even more the gang's respect. So he waited while Leclerc turned to face him, then shot him in the head four, perhaps five, times. He chose to ignore the code's injunction against stripping a corpse of its clothes when he removed Leclerc's coat. He had lent it to his friend several months earlier and decided he wanted it back. Simard tossed it into his Chrysler Intrepid and drove back toward the highway.

In the days before his Halifax trip, Kane had been in frequent contact with his Mountie handlers, passing on a catalogue of updates, rumours, and hard information from the biker netherworld.

Donald Magnussen had laid a beating on the son of Montreal's top Mafioso outside a Boulevard St-Laurent nightclub. Magnussen hadn't known his victim's identity, and Leonardo Rizzutto may well have deserved the thrashing, but that didn't alter the consequences. The word was that Vito Rizzutto had dispatched two thugs to exact revenge. As a result Magnussen wasn't leaving the Lavigueur estate unaccompanied.

Kane reported that Wolf Carroll had teamed up with a local businessman to buy a substantial piece of real estate at the foot of Mont-St-Sauveur, the closest ski hill of decent size north of Montreal. The two planned to build condos on the site and a cinema in the booming resort town. "Everything will be legal but the name of Carroll won't appear anywhere," Verdon noted in the debriefing report. "A nice opportunity to launder a bit of money!"

The most important piece of news Kane offered concerned the creation of a shock squad of about forty Hells Angels wannabes and underlings whose assignment was to overrun the last remaining Rock Machine strongholds, the southwest Montreal neighbourhoods of Pointe-St-Charles, St-Henri, Verdun, Lasalle, Lachine, Ville-Émard, and Côte-St-Paul. In these areas the Rock Machine was wholesaling its drugs at discount prices, undercutting the Hells and frustrating their attempts to corner the entire Montreal market. "The group in question is formed of commando-like subgroups," Verdon wrote. "These will have the task of executing strong-arm jobs where initial attempts at intimidation haven't worked."

The subgroups would receive 30 percent of the drug revenue generated from the conquered territory, Verdon added, recording the names of five men in the Rockers organization involved in the shock squad. Along with Pierre Provencher and Stephen Falls were Normand Robitaille, the rising star and Mom Boucher favourite who would marry one of the gang's lawyers; Gregory Wooley, a former member of a Haitian street gang who would come as close to full-fledged Hells Angel status as any black man; and Stéphane "Godasse" Gagné, a weaselly Hochelaga-Maisonneuve dealer who, having been given little choice, had thrown in his lot with the Hells.

On February 24, just before his departure for Halifax, Kane had received a telephone call from Verdon. No mention of the trip appears in the report of the call, but the timing suggests that the Mounties were aware Kane would be out of contact for a while. The call came minutes before he was to leave town, and in the "purpose of contact" field Verdon wrote "to ask certain information." Yet the only item Verdon noted concerned one of the shock squad's first *"jobs de bras."*

A small-time dealer by the name of Gros Mo—Big Mo—was severely beaten in a St-Henri bar when it was suspected that contrary to his claims of fealty to the Hells, he was procuring some of his drug supply from other sources. The squad had engineered a sting, sending a buyer to make a purchase. The buyer was charged less than the Hells' wholesale price to Gros Mo, making him either a very bad businessman or a double-dealer. Either way, he had to be taught a lesson.

In his account of the assault Verdon makes no reference to the fact that Aimé Simard went along on the job and was the only member of the squad carrying a firearm. His role was to ensure that no one left the bar while Gros Mo was being thrashed. When a patron did flee, Simard chased after him and would have taken a shot had he not been stopped by another member of the squad who declared the fellow "okay."

After Halifax Simard returned to the shock squad with much buttressed bona fides. He'd done a hit for the gang and rubbed out a friend who was talking too much. Though such things weren't spoken about openly, there were whispers and veiled references, all of which elevated his reputation and won him increased acceptance into the circle of hangers-on who revolved around the Rockers and the Nomads.

At a meeting on the South Shore in early March, two Rockers formally invited Simard to join the subgroup known as the "football team," the deadliest of the squad's units. When an adversary needed a beating, the "baseball team" went into action. But if a kill was required, the football team got the job. To join, Simard had to give one of the Rockers his social insurance number as well as his driver's licence details. If he were ever to cross the squad, they would know how to find him.

The gang's confidence in Simard may have been growing, but Kane's faith was wavering. After Halifax, and particularly after the killing of Leclerc, Kane began to view him as a loose cannon who could become a dangerous liability to the gang and certainly to Kane himself. Although there is no report of Leclerc's murder in their briefing notes, Kane told his handlers on March 11 that Simard "is very unpredictable and dangerous.... He is capable of anything." The physical description he gave of Simard on that date was hardly necessary, considering the voluminous file available to the Mounties, and it was also misleading. He was right about Simard's five-foot-seven height and thick black eyebrows, but when he suggested (or Verdon recorded) that Simard weighed only 150 pounds, either Kane was of half a mind to protect his lover or someone was confusing pounds with kilograms.

Kane had good reason for mixed feelings. On the one hand, Simard had done him many small services and made him good money. None of the $25,000 Wilson paid for the hit on MacFarlane ever found its way into Simard's wallet, despite Kane's promise. Simard wasn't even reimbursed the $900 he spent on the 9 mm semi-automatic or the miscellaneous expenses he accumulated on the trip.

On the other hand Simard was an undeniably irritating loudmouth who was only becoming more so as he convinced himself he was a truly hardened criminal. Patricia had an especially low tolerance for his bluster, and after their return from Mont-Ste-Anne, she urged Kane to evict

Simard from the Rue St-Christophe apartment. Kane didn't argue. He and Simard bickered frequently, and at one point he confided to Patricia that Simard was "a real psychopath." "Don't tell me that the guy sleeping on the sofa is a psychopath," she told Kane, insisting Simard leave.

The timing was propitious for everyone involved. Kane and Patricia were discussing a move out of the downtown, to a place with enough room that the kids didn't have to sleep on the couch or the floor, or share the bed with them. Simard was spending more time with other Hells and Rockers associates, people such as Pierre Provencher, Stephen Falls, and Daniel St-Pierre, to whom he had been assigned as driver and underling in the sale of drugs in the Verdun and Montreal North neighbourhoods. Indeed, when Simard was ushered out of the Rue St-Christophe apartment, he went to live in the basement of a house rented by St-Pierre. The house was the base of operations for the shock squad and its lower level a sort of crash pad for a revolving cast of members.

But the relationship between Kane and Simard was nothing if not complicated, and while the cramped quarters of the St-Christophe apartment may have led to sore feelings and arguments, it didn't end their association. After the accumulated frustrations of a long fall and winter, Kane was eager for a holiday in the sun and keen to spend some time with his children, at least the two who were out of diapers. Patricia excused herself, unwilling to serve as babysitter for a whole week, and Kane took Simard along instead.

The March 15–22 trip to Jamaica's all-inclusive Trelawny Beach Resort, not far from Montego Bay, was largely uneventful. The real drama occurred the day before they were to leave. On an excursion to a downtown

Montreal pharmacy to get a special sunscreen for one of the children, Kane, Patricia, and Dominique were pulled over. As driver, Dominique handed his licence and the car's registration to the officer. Kane and Patricia knew that as passengers they were within their rights to refuse to provide identification and did so. A standoff ensued, during which the police closed down a busy four-block stretch of Ste-Catherine Street. One of the officers finally lost his patience, smashed the back window of Kane's Cadillac with his baton, and pepper-sprayed the occupants. Kane, Patricia, and Dominique spent the rest of the day in a jail cell and were released just in time for Kane to make his early-morning flight. No one was charged, but Patricia got a ticket for not wearing her seat belt.

In Jamaica Kane, Simard, and the children had a cottage and were among the quieter guests. The two men didn't, however, hide the fact from other Quebeckers they met that they were bikers involved with the Hells Angels and the horrific gang war raging back home. Simard, who spent more time than Kane consorting with his fellow guests, revealed his youthful ambitions to be a policeman and that his weight problems had kept him out of law enforcement. He said that when he returned to Canada he was going to get out of the biker underworld and change his life "180 degrees." The guest took this as an indication that Simard intended to try to work for the police. Simard might have known something he wasn't telling, or had a premonition, or it may simply have been a coincidence. In any case, within a month he would indeed be working for the police.

Kane, Simard, and the kids had flown out of Mirabel airport, about an hour north of Montreal. They had driven there in Simard's Intrepid and left the car in one of the airport's parking lots. Simard had forgotten or simply ignored the fact that the lease on the car had expired a few days before their departure. When the Intrepid wasn't returned, the leasing company reported it stolen.

On March 20 a Mirabel policeman did a routine check of the licence plates in the airport lots. He came across the Intrepid, and bells went off. A search of the vehicle turned up .44-calibre ammunition of the same sort used in the Quebec City Lower Town shooting. That and the stolen car report were enough to notify Canada Customs. When Kane and Simard stepped off the plane they and the children were taken aside and whisked through a separate gate. They were not detained for long, possibly because authorities were alerted to the fact that Kane was an RCMP informant and Simard was his companion. Kane and Simard were freed to go about their business.

Their Caribbean holiday together notwithstanding, Kane didn't have anything good to say about Simard at a March 26 debriefing and payment session with the Mounties. He reported that almost everyone in the Hells organization was tiring of him and that senior Nomads and Rockers were worried by his conduct. "They find him too unpredictable, [think] that he has a big mouth, always brags about his exploits and he is dangerous for the organization," Kane said.

Simard also had it in for the police. "Simard hates police as much as is possible and dreams of killing one," Verdon recorded. "He has said he will never go back to prison and will take every step possible not to do so." It was again noted that Kane considered Simard "very dangerous."

Simard's open hostility toward cops may have been another routine designed to impress his peers at a moment when the authorities had stepped up their harassment of

Montreal's gangs and the Hells Angels in particular. In the winter of 1997 Montreal police had launched Operation Respect, increasing the number of raids on gang-controlled bars and arrests of small-time dealers, and beefing up surveillance patrols. The gang was sufficiently irritated that the Rockers considered retaliatory measures. One idea was to lure the police into illegal acts of their own, perhaps goading them into an assault during an arrest or a routine traffic stop. The bikers would secretly videotape the act and then use it in criminal or civil proceedings. Some Rockers proposed that they engage in direct intimidation of police at their homes. It could be easily done: thanks to a source in the police union, the gang had the addresses of some of SPCUM's elite officers, members of the tactical squad included. But Kane told his handlers that "the authorities"—in this case the Nomads—kiboshed the suggestion.

The Nomads were more supportive of the ongoing offensive against the Rock Machine in the city's south-west. The football team's plan was as simple as it was brutal. They would kidnap street-level Rock Machine dealers one by one. If necessary they would torture them into revealing who they bought their drugs from, where these people operated, and where they stashed their drugs, guns, and money. Then they would kill or convert the kidnapped dealers and move on to the next people in the chain. In this way they would either knock off the major players or scare them out of the game.

The football team had a preliminary list of at least four Rock Machine dealers it planned to go after, a roster Kane had transmitted to his handlers on March 5. One of the names on it belonged to a small-time dealer named Jean-Marc Caissy. Over the next three weeks Simard, Kane, and others stalked these men in anticipation of their kidnappings, but as was so often the case in the biker war, events didn't unfold as planned.

On March 28 the football team learned that the Rock Machine had beaten one of their own dealers. They considered their response at the morning get-together at the Pro-Gym, deciding they should strike back immediately. The football team's leader, Pierre Provencher, asked Simard, "Is there someone on the list you can kill right away?"

Caissy was scheduled to play floor hockey at a recreation centre in Côte-St-Paul that night and would be an easy target. Simard, Kane, Claude Grégoire McCarter, and another Rockers associate had cased the rec centre in the weeks previous and saw no difficulties. "That's your territory," Provencher told Simard, according to his subsequent testimony in court. "They have to be sent a message." Stephen Falls chimed in, "It's not just a question of killing him. It has to be horrible, disgusting. You have to mess up his face."

That evening, toward ten-thirty, Simard and his backup man arrived at the rec centre just as the hockey game was ending. Absurdly, one team was made up of young, small-time Rock Machine dealers, Caissy among them, while the other comprised low-level Hells associates. Simard slipped on black overclothes and pocketed the .357 handgun he had been given for the job. He stood at the entrance to the rec centre and held the door open for Caissy as he came out. Caissy thanked him with a nod of the head. He was a few steps past when Simard drew his gun and shouted after him, "Hey, Caissy!"

Caissy looked back and Simard, as instructed, shot him in the face, five times. Simard then drove away and, after stashing the .357 in a locker at the Pro-Gym, went to the Rockers' fifth birthday bash.

This celebration at the gang's clubhouse in the Rosemont district of north central Montreal was a major event, attracting not only the cream of the Quebec Hells Angels but also the province's top biker cops, Verdon included. Plainclothes police officers stood about outside, not bothering to conceal their presence. Kane didn't attend, but Simard wasn't going to miss it. He expected to be congratulated on another kill for the gang. It was odd, then, that no one seemed overjoyed to see him and that they kept him waiting several minutes under the observant gaze of any number of police officers before they opened the door to let him in.

The hit was a relatively clean one that might have joined scores of others on the list of unsolved biker war murders. But Kane was looking for a way to get Simard out of his life with the least trouble or risk. Killing him was one option; certainly, Simard wouldn't have been the first trigger man who, having outlived his usefulness to the Hells organization, was himself dispatched. But Kane preferred another solution, one that could benefit his Mountie handlers as well.

St. Onge and Verdon were under fresh pressure from above to show real results—arrests and seizures—from C-2994's information. The demand for actionable, rather than simply "nice to know," intelligence had increased substantially with the recent retirement of Staff Sgt. Pierre Lemire, St. Onge's immediate boss. Lemire was considered an easygoing taskmaster, a man putting in time until his departure. Despite the substantial sums paid to C-2994, he had allowed St. Onge and Verdon a largely free hand in the management of their source. His successor was Staff Sgt. J.H.P. Bolduc, a stocky, long-time organized crime investigator whose good nature didn't prevent him from being exacting and rigorous. He felt that Kane's pay should be commensurate with the number of arrests and seizures that resulted from his information. In that light Kane had so far been a serious underachiever. Bolduc meant to change that.

Kane—perhaps in consultation with his handlers—decided to give up Simard for the Caissy murder. Though there is strong reason to believe the information was transmitted earlier, Kane's RCMP file indicates that just over twenty-four hours after Caissy's death, Kane paged St. Onge with the details of the murder. By 11 a.m. the next day, March 30, Easter Sunday, St. Onge had informed Montreal detective and Carcajou member Benoît Roberge that Simard was the shooter. "Neither [Carcajou] nor the Montreal police had any suspect."

St. Onge noted Kane's message that Simard was planning another hit that evening. That detail was also transmitted to Carcajou who put a tail on Simard at about 6 p.m. By then, however, Simard and seven other Hells associates had beaten the man they were after into a coma with a baseball bat.

"Unfortunately," St. Onge noted, "the attack was pushed forward to the afternoon rather than the evening."

Kane pinpointed the location of the Caissy murder weapon—a locker at the Pro-Gym—as well as the van used as Simard's getaway vehicle. He knew who the van belonged to and reported that it would be disposed of in the traditional biker manner, set aflame in a remote location.

By this time the SQ members of the Carcajou squad were beginning to suspect that the RCMP's source must be intimately involved in Caissy's hit and that his RCMP handlers were protecting him. That evening an SQ corporal telephoned St. Onge at home and accused the Mounties of withholding information from their Carcajou colleagues. In his notes about the call St. Onge expressed a perhaps exaggerated indignation. "Had it not been for C-2994, a murder, an attempted murder, and an arson would have remained unexplained despite all the evidence which was gathered."

St. Onge's protestations that he and Verdon were passing on all relevant information to other investigators within Carcajou didn't wash, even with his own bosses. On April 1 St. Onge had to fend off suggestions from one of the RCMP's top brass in Montreal that Kane had had a hand in the Caissy killing. "Many believe that C-2994 is involved in these crimes and this false belief even went as high as Supt. [Henri] Dion," St. Onge wrote in his handler's notes. He added a defensive addendum: "C-2994 is intelligent, quick and well-directed but it is above all thanks to Simard himself, he has a 'big mouth' and tells anyone who will listen—'or almost'—of his crimes. If Simard had closed his trap, we would have only circumstantial evidence. There are strong rumours that he is now too dangerous and might harm the club."

The days following were tense for everyone concerned. Simard knew he was being followed and was liable to be arrested at any moment. His gang brothers were aware that Simard was highly toxic and sought to avoid him. St. Onge and Verdon were under intense scrutiny for their handling of C-2994 and for their particular neglect to warn Caissy his life was in danger when they knew weeks before that he was a shock squad target. The two Mounties attempted to defuse some of Carcajou's mistrust by meeting with

Kane on the last day of March and reviewing with him a list of questions about the Caissy murder put forward by other investigators.

Verdon phoned Kane again the next day with more questions and Kane called him back on April 2 with another update. Simard, Kane reported, had been told to take a vacation by the gang "because he is too 'hot.' The shock squad and other Rockers no longer want anything to do with him." Simard tried repeatedly to reach members of the group, but his calls and pages were ignored. On April 3 St. Onge advised Kane to do the same: he was not to hang around with Simard. The exact details of the conversation are unknown: the debriefing report from the meeting has gone missing from the RCMP files.

Then on April 8 Kane met with his handlers to answer another round of queries from Carcajou investigators and to match biker photos with nicknames. By then the sap was running in Quebec's maple trees, and Kane told St. Onge and Verdon that there had been a meeting at Provencher's sugar shack where the Simard problem had been discussed at length. No conclusion was reached but everyone agreed something had to be done. "The group is somewhat disorganized and sees police everywhere," Kane reported. "Nonetheless, even if they are going to be more careful, the shock squad and their associates plan to remain active."

By this time the bikers might well have concluded that they would be better off with Simard dead. His arrest appeared inevitable—it was hard to understand why it hadn't yet happened—and Simard, of all people, might be expected to squeal under pressure from police. He was a prime candidate for the role of *délateur,* a term for which no precise English translation exists but that means a criminal informant who agrees to testify for the prosecution in return for a lighter sentence. Sending in the football team was problematic, however, given the near constant police surveillance on Simard.

At the same time there was a precedent to suggest that if Simard did turn, the gang could weather the storm. Destroying the credibility of Serge Quesnel, the last high-profile Hells killer to turn *délateur,* had proven to be child's play for the gang's high-priced lawyers. While a verdict in the main case in which Quesnel was testifying had yet to be rendered, everyone was confident that the Angels on trial would be acquitted, as indeed they were on April 9.

Kane had more reason to fear Simard's revelations than anyone else. There was the MacFarlane murder and any number of other crimes, including whatever advance knowledge or planning role Kane might have had in the Caissy killing. But Kane no doubt felt a degree of confidence that others in the gang did not. He was, after all, prized informant C-2994, a man whose rise within the Hells Angels had been supported by the RCMP to the tune of well over $200,000. They wouldn't flush that investment, Kane was convinced. The Mounties would protect him.

If he counted on this, he underestimated the complexities, not to mention the antipathies, in the relationships between the RCMP, the Sûreté du Québec, and the Montreal police. And he didn't fully appreciate that the RCMP in Nova Scotia had different priorities from the RCMP in Montreal.

15

AN INFORMANT
INFORMED ON

Montreal police finally moved on Simard at 8:35 p.m. on April 11, 1997, while he was chauffeuring Daniel St-Pierre on his rounds. The official version of Simard's apprehension soon followed: the Pro-Gym didn't allow their lockers to be occupied overnight; a janitor, assiduously applying the rule, had discovered the stashed handgun and dutifully contacted police. The gym's security video, police claimed, later allowed them to identify Simard.

Given that the Pro-Gym served as a second clubhouse for Mom Boucher, his Nomads, and the Rockers, the notion that a janitor might cut a member's lock is highly questionable. To think that he would call in the police after uncovering a gun is absurd. The truth is much simpler. The Montreal police, thanks to C-2994 and the RCMP, knew the identity of the shooter and the whereabouts of the murder weapon. They seized the gun and then obtained warrants for the supporting evidence of security videos from the gym and the recreation centre. Thus armed, and their source's existence and identity still more or less secure, they arrested Simard.

Simard's interrogation by officers of the Montreal force began at 11:20 p.m., and if he played the silent tough guy as bikers were expected to, it wasn't for long. Although police reports of his questioning are contradictory, Simard seems to have started cooperating almost immediately. By six-twenty the next morning he had confessed to the Caissy killing and agreed to testify against his Rockers colleagues in return for lenient sentencing. As in all *délateur* contracts, part of the deal was that he own up to all the crimes he had committed but had never been charged with. In return, provincial justice officials agreed not to prosecute him for such crimes, including those committed outside their jurisdiction. The arrangement promised him the chance of parole after twelve years, $2000 for cosmetic surgery while in prison, a new identity, and relocation expenses when he was freed. Thereafter, he would receive $400 a week for up to two years.

According to police Simard folded quickly after they convinced him that the case against him was sufficiently solid to sway any jury and that his purported pals among the Rockers and the shock squad intended to kill him. There are those in the milieu, however, who believe Simard's deal may have been struck back at Mirabel airport. It's speculated that at the time police had enough evidence to charge him with the Quebec City shootings and the Leclerc murder. Simard was willing to cooperate, but he had nothing incriminating to offer on anyone in the gang other than Kane. He was allowed to return to his outlaw life in order to collect information on various Rockers and their associates and then turn *délateur* for them.

Whatever prompted his flip, over a long weekend of tell-all, Simard admitted to the Leclerc killing, the shoot-up in Quebec City's Lower Town, and the baseball bat assault, as well as a host of other offences. He also revealed that barely six weeks earlier he and his friend and lover, Dany Kane, had killed a man named Robert MacFarlane in Halifax. It wasn't a case that was familiar to the Montreal investigators.

On Monday, April 14, a senior SPCUM officer, Det. Sgt. Roger Agnessi, contacted Det. Sgt. Gordon Barnett of the Halifax RCMP General Investigation Section to solicit the details of the MacFarlane hit. He explained that he and his colleagues wanted to verify the story of a man they had in custody, one whose name he did not divulge. Barnett was forthcoming, stipulating only that if the man was telling the truth, he would be sending investigators to Montreal to question him. MacFarlane's murder was squarely in Barnett's jurisdiction; as the force that provided police services to the province of Nova Scotia and that held a mandate to fight organized crime nationwide, the RCMP was responsible for bringing MacFarlane's killer to justice.

Up to this point, the Halifax RCMP had been concentrating on the likelihood that MacFarlane was killed for his transgressions in Vancouver. He had seriously offended the wrong people and perhaps they had retaliated two weeks later. A second theory was that his cousin David Roberts and Claude Blanchard had killed him in an argument over a coke deal. Or perhaps MacFarlane's wife, Denise, had something to do with his murder. There was more than enough motive: Denise was in line for all of her husband's assets in the event of his death but, according to their prenuptial agreement, very little if they divorced. And there were signs of a strained relationship: apart from their recent separate southern vacations, police heard abundant reports of MacFarlane and Denise pawing and being pawed by others at various Halifax nightclubs.

Another flag: just weeks before his demise, MacFarlane had taken out a life insurance policy worth $500,000, in which Denise was named the sole beneficiary. At least two of these theories had room for the involvement of out-of-town hit men. Barnett thought the Montreal lead might be the break he needed.

The next day Det. Sgt. Agnessi called back to say he was satisfied that Simard's account of MacFarlane's death was accurate and that Simard had implicated another person in the episode. He added that Simard had confessed to a litany of crimes and was due to be handed over to the Carcajou squad for more interrogation. The Halifax Mounties would have to deal with Carcajou if they wanted access to him.

This set off a flurry of phone calls between competing authorities and much jockeying for position. By this time St. Onge and Verdon knew that Simard had been turned by his Montreal police interrogators. Indeed, the news was buzzing around the biker community as well, since Pierre Panaccio, the lawyer engaged by the Rockers to defend Simard, had been rebuffed by his client with a full explanation. St. Onge was determined that the Halifax Mounties should meet with their Montreal counterparts before dealing with the Carcajou brass. There was more to the case than met the eye, St. Onge told Barnett.

Two rival welcoming committees were on hand to greet Barnett and the main investigator in the MacFarlane case, Cst. Tom Townsend, when they arrived from Halifax the next day. Carcajou's officials went so far as to have the Mounties paged before they disembarked from their flight, but Barnett and Townsend travelled into town with their RCMP colleagues. At the force's Westmount headquarters they were told that Kane, the man fingered by Simard as the organizer of and accessory to the MacFarlane killing, was the RCMP's cherished mole inside the Hells Angels.

There is no indication in RCMP documents whether the Montreal Mounties tried to persuade their Halifax colleagues to overlook Kane's involvement in the MacFarlane murder. It is hard to imagine that the subject wasn't discussed. St. Onge and Verdon would almost certainly have argued strenuously for this tack: Kane's arrest and prosecution would put an end to the promise he held out both as an informant and as a boon to the career fortunes of his handlers.

Barnett and Townsend would not have been receptive to the idea of giving Kane a pass. In the first place, the MacFarlane murder was a high-profile case in a part of the country that saw relatively few fatal crimes in any given year. Furthermore, Barnett was not happy that the Montreal police and justice officials had already promised Simard immunity for the MacFarlane murder in exchange for his confession to the Caissy killing. (The SQ felt similarly about the Leclerc murder.) He and his Halifax colleagues wanted to nail at least one person for the MacFarlane hit.

Kane's career as an RCMP informant was in jeopardy even without the Halifax RCMP's intervention. Simard's confessions to police would be among the first documents examined by the defence lawyers of anyone he might testify against. If these lawyers saw that he had implicated Kane in the MacFarlane murder but Kane hadn't been charged, suspicions about his relationship with police would immediately arise.

In fact Sgt. James Lauzon, the senior Carcajou officer assigned as liaison with Barnett and Townsend, informed them shortly after their arrival of rumours that members of the Hells Angels organization were looking for Kane. He, along with other SQ and SPCUM members of Carcajou, suspected that Kane was the valuable informant that the RCMP had been keeping to themselves for so long. The penny had dropped for one investigator in the group when he studied the details of the MacFarlane murder: why, after Simard had returned to the car, had Kane pretended to fire two bullets point-blank into MacFarlane's head but instead shot into the mud? The only explanation the investigator could come up with was that Kane was walking a tightrope between the bikers and the police and hoped that firing into the ground might diminish his role in the murder and provide him a measure of deniability.

Lauzon confronted Townsend with the SQ's suspicions about Kane, but Townsend brushed them off, saying that the RCMP would never employ a murderer as an informant. He maintained with sufficient conviction that such a scenario was impossible, that Lauzon, according to sources, was satisfied that if Kane was indeed an informant Townsend didn't know it. Some of the SQ officers took a liking to Townsend precisely because he gave the impression that he didn't much appreciate the way the Montreal Mounties did their business.

At the morning meeting of Lauzon's six-man Carcajou unit on Friday, April 18, Lauzon instructed his investigators, among them Pierre Verdon, to pick up Kane as soon as possible. They had Simard's testimony against him and maybe Kane could be turned as well. Through Carcajou's network of informants, Lauzon was confident that they would have Kane within a few hours if he wasn't already working for the Mounties. If he was, Lauzon believed he would be protected by his handlers and Carcajou would

never be allowed to question him. Lauzon wasn't opti-
mistic. When Townsend and Barnett left for the airport to
catch their flight back to Halifax later that morning, they
told Lauzon they intended to arrest Kane as soon as they
could locate him. Lauzon responded that he doubted their
RCMP bosses would allow it.

By ten-thirty that evening Kane still hadn't been
picked up, and any faint hopes Lauzon may have held had
vanished. According to sources, he telephoned Verdon,
and without contravening protocol by demanding the
name of Verdon's informant or naming Kane himself, he
asked why the informant hadn't been able to lead them to
Kane. Verdon reportedly replied that his RCMP superiors
had barred him from contact with his source several days
previously. That was enough for Lauzon. He was sure
then that Kane was the RCMP's "supersource" and that
he was being protected by them.

If Barnett and Townsend, for their separate reasons,
were bent on arresting Kane at that point, they might have
expected help from Verdon and St. Onge: the order that
had come down from above to cut off all contact with and
payments to Kane was at least partially ignored. The two
handlers continued to take calls from him while their
RCMP superiors scrambled to find a solution. Halifax
was intent that Kane be charged in connection with
MacFarlane's death. Senior staff in Montreal were determined to safeguard an enormous investment of time,
money, and hope. Everyone on the RCMP side agreed
that whatever happened, the SQ-dominated Carcajou
squad couldn't be allowed to gets its claws into Kane.

Over the following ten days, however, the force recognized that there was no getting around Kane's arrest for
the MacFarlane murder. They also understood that Kane's

relationship with his handlers—and his need for their
money—was the best bait they had.

On the morning of April 14, Kane heard that Simard
was refusing the services of Pierre Panaccio. He immediately called Patricia at work and said he had to see her.
"Tell them your kid is sick," he suggested when she
protested that she couldn't walk out in the middle of a
workday.

They went for lunch near her office in the north end of
the city, Kane insisting that he had something important
to discuss with her. Still, he wouldn't come out with it
until they'd eaten and left the restaurant. Then he blurted
it out: Simard had been arrested and seemed to be cooperating with the police. He told Patricia not to believe
everything that she might hear about him. Simard, he
said, would be telling the police lies in an effort to get a
better deal.

Patricia didn't probe for details. Ever since she had
happened on the photographs of Kane and his friends in
their colours, she had made it a policy to know as little as
possible about his criminal activities. That was the way
Kane wanted it too, and he had told her nothing about his
trip to Halifax. Patricia knew Simard to be untrustworthy,
though, prepared to say anything that might impress others. She tried to calm Kane, saying that even with the
police on his side, Simard wouldn't be able to prove
something that wasn't true.

Kane and Patricia were getting along well at this time,
and they were about to take their relationship to a higher
level. They had found a house to buy in the town of Deux-
Montagnes, off the northwest tip of the island of
Montreal. It was a healthy distance from the Kane family

in St-Jean and not far up the Mille-Îles River from Scott Steinert's château. The purchase had been made through a real estate agent who did a lot of work for the gang, and the vendor seemed somehow connected as well, although Kane had never met the man. Kane wanted to move in as soon as possible, and the possession date had been set for April 1. But when the day rolled around, the previous owner hadn't yet found a new home. Dany's response was endearing, infuriating, and typical: he proposed that the vendor, his wife, and their two teenage children stay in the house with him and Patricia until they could make other arrangements. "We can't kick them out," Kane told Patricia. "They're nice people and they have nowhere to go."

Patricia wasn't persuaded, but there was nothing she could do. Kane moved in without her, and she returned to her mother's until the house was theirs alone. It wasn't to be.

If Kane was anxious in the days following Simard's arrest, his handlers' debriefing reports do not reveal it. On April 14 Kane told St. Onge and Verdon that "those who might be compromised by Simard" weren't overly worried. They felt that Simard's testimony against them would be no more harmful than Serge Quesnel's against the two Trois-Rivières Hells Angels who had been acquitted the previous week.

Kane was sufficiently sanguine to give his handlers a routine update. The Hells leadership, he reported, had issued a provincewide edict that members were not to wear their colours. "The reason is as much not to be noticed by police as not to be identified by their enemies," Verdon noted. "Also the number of parties will be reduced to avoid attracting attention."

On the business front, a new form of liquid ecstasy was about to hit the streets, Kane said, one that offered a much more intense high. "The drug will revolutionize the market," Verdon wrote, adding that Mom Boucher and his protegé, Guillaume "Mimo" Serra, would have "total control" of Canadian sales.

Lastly, Kane announced the breakthrough that his handlers had been hoping to hear for as long as he'd been reporting to them: Gilles "Trooper" Mathieu, one of the longest-serving Hells Angels in Quebec and the thoughtful éminence grise of the Nomads, had suggested to Wolf Carroll that Kane be officially designated a hangaround and a candidate for membership in the elite chapter.

On April 25, at the next reported contact with his handlers, Kane remained cheery. Only the day before St. Onge had received another strongly worded memo from his superiors ordering him to break off contact with Kane. If he read it he chose not to follow the directive. Kane telephoned him after returning from a spell outside Montreal—where is not indicated—and gave the Mounties an encouraging update. Without revealing where his information came from, Kane reported that Aimé Simard "has said he is changing what shoulder he is shooting from and that he will spare Dany Kane but that the others don't deserve it."

In the days following his arrest Simard had gone through severe emotional turmoil. It wasn't so much the fact that he was committing one of the mortal sins of the criminal world by becoming a rat. Rather, Simard was distraught that he had agreed to testify against his lover and Hells Angels sponsor. His feelings for Kane were conflicted. He knew he had been exploited by the gang and he blamed Kane for drawing him in. At the same time his affections for Kane were genuine, and police who encountered him during this period say that he was greatly pained by the idea of betraying him. Simard's distress came to a head on April 20 when he made an unsuccessful attempt to kill himself in prison by swallowing all the medication he could get his hands on.

Whether Kane or his handlers were aware of Simard's remorse is unknown. One thing is certain: it would have been very difficult for Simard to "spare" Kane at this point. Almost immediately after he had agreed to become a *délateur* police had taken the precaution of videotaping Simard's statement and having him swear to its truthfulness. Under a Supreme Court ruling the content of the tapes could have been introduced as testimony in legal proceedings in the event that Simard might have a change of heart or die before he was able to testify in person.

If Kane gave the impression of indifference in Simard's cooperation with police, the undeserving "others" were similarly unconcerned. Many of the members of the shock squad had, like Kane, left Montreal after Simard's arrest, disengaging their cellphones and pagers to avoid traces. After they'd been away a few days, however, their fear of arrest—or at least successful prosecution—seems to have dissipated. "In the milieu no one is taking Simard very seriously anymore because he is a liar who will be easy to discredit," Kane reiterated.

The report contained an odd paragraph of contradictory metaphors: Kane described the gang's affairs as "floating in oil"—a French expression meaning "doing splendidly"—but said too that "the soup is hot." Nonetheless, he added that if he was arrested as a result of Simard's statements he would do the time necessary to exonerate himself. The fiction that he had nothing to do with MacFarlane's murder was sustained in his meetings with St. Onge and Verdon and in their notes.

The fifteen-minute telephone conversation ended with confirmation of a meeting the next day, a Saturday, for a payment and debriefing session. "The source doesn't want to wait until Monday or Tuesday because he is broke and has lots of information to transmit to us." If the meeting took place, no account of it remains in the RCMP file.

At the regular morning meeting of the full Carcajou squad on April 29, the SQ leadership instructed all sixty or so members of the task force to make the arrest of Kane a priority. It was a provocative move. Many investigators were aware of the rumours that Kane was an RCMP informant, but the SQ members had lost patience with the Mounties, whom they accused of serving their own interests behind the back of the provincial force. If Kane was a source, either he was being badly handled or Carcajou was barely benefiting from the intelligence he provided. It was Carcajou that was under the greatest public pressure to bring the biker war to an end, and they would not be hamstrung by the RCMP's aloof secretiveness. They would go after Kane and make him sweat.

As RCMP members of Carcajou, St. Onge and Verdon normally attended those morning meetings, and while there is no record of their reaction to the order to arrest Kane, it posed a clear threat to their control of the situation. Kane was still free and, it seemed, increasingly confident he would remain so. Now it was only a matter of time before the SQ was grilling him and perhaps scrutinizing very closely the way he had been handled by the RCMP. That is, unless the Mounties moved first.

On April 30, an overcast but warm day, Kane was at the new house in Deux-Montagnes when he was called to a meeting at the Ramada Inn in Longeueil. Wearing jeans, a blue nylon jacket, and expensive running shoes that had never seen a playing field or court, Kane got into the blue Cadillac with the tinted windows and drove the forty-five minutes of autoroutes and bridges between Deux-Montagnes and Longueuil.

He arrived at the customary meeting place just before 4 p.m. St. Onge, Verdon, and three Halifax Mounties had been in place for more than half an hour. The handlers sent Kane a coded page to indicate they were waiting in room 524; the Halifax contingent was in the lobby, monitoring Kane's movements. Less than ten kilometres away at the Canadian Forces airport in St-Hubert, an air taxi waited beside the runway.

The plan was to arrest Kane and take him out of the province before Carcajou could protest or contest the legality of a warrantless RCMP arrest in Quebec. But that afternoon word reached Carcajou that the Halifax Mounties were in town to seize Kane with the complicity of his handlers. While St. Onge and Verdon waited for Kane, their pagers and cellphones buzzed with angry instructions not to proceed. Even St. Onge's superior, hoping to ease tensions with the SQ, told them to wait. Instead they went ahead.

After Kane went up to room 524 and it was established that he wasn't carrying a gun, Constable Townsend and two Halifax officers followed a few minutes behind. They knocked on the door. When it was opened they pulled Kane into the corridor, where they searched him, handcuffed him, and read him his rights. It was four-fifteen. Within the hour Kane was in the air and on his way to Halifax.

In the mid-1970s, when Kane was living with his uncle and aunt, he belonged to the Scouts.
(photo courtesy Kane family)

Due to a congenital eye condition, Kane wore glasses from his youngest days.
(photo courtesy Kane family)

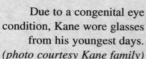

Kane, front row, second from left, with the Demon Keepers, January 30, 1994, at their official founding. Even though they were an Ontario club, the ceremony took place at the Hells Angels clubhouse in Sorel, Quebec. On Kane's right is his good friend Patrick Lambert. Kane would later describe most of the members as "imbeciles who had absolutely no talent."

Roland Lebrasseur, the former armed forces member who became a chauffeur for a Hells Angels–connected stripper agency before being killed by Kane. *(photo courtesy Gisèle Duguay)*

A group shot of Scott Steinert's clique taken while Kane was awaiting trial in Halifax. Steinert is fourth from the right with his arms crossed; Donald "Bam-Bam" Magnussen is on the far right. The two, both good friends of Kane's, were literally hammered to death in an internal purge before Kane would get out of jail.

Deprived of steroids and on a prison diet, Kane lost thirty or forty pounds while incarcerated in Halifax. This photo was taken shortly after his release in November or December 1998. *(photo courtesy Kane family)*

Maurice "Mom" Boucher with his son Francis at a gang ride.
To the left is Gregory Wooley, a former leader of a Haitian street
gang who became the highest-rising black man anywhere within
the explicitly racist Hells Angels organization. Before becoming
active in his father's biker gang, Francis Boucher had been
involved with white power skinhead groups.
(photo courtesy Quebec Justice Department)

The Nomads at their fourth anniversary celebrations, June 1999.
Left to right: Mom Boucher, André Chouinard, Normand
Robitaille, David Carroll, Gilles Mathieu, Michel Rose, Donald
Stockford, Walter Stadnick, Normand "Biff" Hamel, Louis
"Melou" Roy, and Denis Houle. Nine months later Hamel would
become the highest-ranking Hells Angel killed by the Rock
Machine; just over a year later, Roy would be killed in an internal
purge. *(photo courtesy Quebec Justice Department)*

220

Kane, front, sits on a chopper in an undated photo taken during a police stop of the bikers on one of their rides. Police would often use such occasions to harass the bikers, inspecting their modified motorbikes for slight safety violations and the like.
(photo courtesy Quebec Justice Department)

Kane with Normand Robitaille, from whom he would steal secret documents that would eventually lead police to the Nomads' counting house, where hundreds of millions in drug money were delivered and stored.
(photo courtesy Quebec Justice Department)

Mom Boucher and Robitaille relaxing and hamming it up. Robitaille was a favourite of the Hells Angels warlord and considered one of the only people who could talk him down or change his mind when he was angry.
(photo courtesy Quebec Justice Department)

Gregory Wooley with René Charlebois, Pierre Provencher, and Normand "Pluche" Bélanger, all members of the Rockers around the time Wooley was given his Rockers patch, which he received three days after being acquitted on a gang-related murder charge. Bélanger would eventually be excused from standing trial because of a terminal AIDS-related illness. He died in 2004. *(photo courtesy Quebec Justice Department)*

Kane, front row middle, with fellow members of the Rockers. If the date burned onto the photo by the camera is correct, the photo was taken just as he was slipping into a deep depression over the Christmas holidays of 1999. *(photo courtesy Quebec Justice Department)*

Kane, right, "doing watch" as Mom Boucher, convicted cocaine dealer Michel Sylvestre, and Normand Robitaille walk in east-end Montreal, in a police surveillance shot from May 2000. Wary of police bugs, the Hells Angels often did business out of doors. A few weeks after this shot, Robitaille would instruct Kane to start dressing better. *(photo courtesy Quebec Justice Department)*

Kane in the months before his death, in the house in St-Luc where his body was found. He collected African furniture and artifacts, including the Kenyan shield behind him. *(photo courtesy Kane family)*

Denis "Pas Fiable (Untrustworthy)" Houle and his wife, Sandra Gloutney, at René Charlebois's wedding. Less than a year earlier, Gloutney had been ambushed as she left her home in the Laurentians, the only time a spouse or family member was targeted in the biker war. *(photo courtesy Quebec Justice Department)*

The Nomads and their wives at the wedding of René "Baloune" Charlebois on August 5, 2000, Dany Kane's last weekend alive. From left to right: Denis Houle, Normand Robitaille, Walter Stadnick, Michel Rose, Charlebois, Gilles Mathieu, Mom Boucher, Luc Bordeleau, David Carroll (crouching), and Richard Mayrand. *(photo courtesy Quebec Justice Department)*

Kane's coffin. His family had wanted an open-casket ceremony but the funeral director told them the body wasn't in a condition to be displayed.
(photo courtesy Kane family)

David "Wolf" Carroll, Kane's first patron in the Hells Angels, standing beside his Harley-Davidson outside the funeral home. A few weeks before Kane's death, Carroll, who was eager to quit the Nomads, had tried to sell him on the idea of moving to Nova Scotia and going into the drug business there.
(photo courtesy Kane family)

Maurice "Mom" Boucher, the Hells Angels warlord, hugging the Rock Machine leader, Paul "Sasquatch" Porter, at a supper celebrating the declaration of peace between the two gangs in October 2000. The treaty would soon collapse, and Porter would join the Hells Angels.
(photo courtesy Quebec Justice Department)

Another photo of Wolf Carroll, the only member of the Nomads to have escaped arrest and imprisonment in the Opération Printemps sweep and resulting megatrials.
(photo courtesy Quebec Justice Department)

Aimé Simard in a photo taken while he was in prison at the Kent Institution in Agassiz, British Columbia, in 2002. On his arm is a fresh tattoo with the word "Martin"—the name of an inmate Simard knew from the Port Cartier penitentiary whom he hoped to marry.
(photo courtesy Simard family)

16

DAMAGE
CONTROL

The flight to Nova Scotia in the ten-seater King Air took little more than two hours. By 8:30 p.m. local time, Kane had been checked into a holding cell at the Nova Scotia RCMP's Bible Hill detachment near Truro, formally charged with first-degree murder, and readied for a long night of interrogation.

The first Mountie to talk with Kane was Tom Townsend. A well-liked officer with a mildly oafish, good ol' boy approach, Townsend played the role of Kane's best friend, and at first he was concerned that Kane be comfortable, well fed, and in touch with his lawyer. Less familiar with Kane's personal life, he asked if he had spoken to Josée. He expressed interest in the crucifix Kane wore around his neck.

Then, between unhurried disquisitions on subjects such as family, childhood, and loyalty, Townsend subtly tried to nudge Kane toward incriminating himself in small ways. At this stage he wasn't after a confession that he had organized Robert MacFarlane's execution. A simple admission that he had been in Nova Scotia at the time of the murder would be useful for the case they were building against him. But Kane was wise to the game and for several hours did nothing but cough, sigh, stare at the floor, and repeat in heavily accented English, "I don't know fuck-all."

After a frustrating hour Townsend brought in another interrogator, Staff Sgt. Phil Scarff, the designated bad cop. "This is not going away just because you want to sleep!" Scarff shouted when Kane closed his eyes in an attempt to block out the barrage. Scarff suggested that the Hells Angels were already gunning for Kane; that explained the SWAT team that had surrounded his plane when it landed and their presence at that very moment outside the Bible Hill detachment. He added that the gang might very well go after Kane's family if they couldn't get to him. Still, Kane didn't bite, asking why, if the Mounties had such a solid case, they bothered to question him. Why not just take him to trial?

Getting nowhere, Townsend and Scarff decided to reveal that they knew he was an RCMP informant. Before uttering the words they took the precaution of shutting down the video camera recording the interrogation; Kane's defence counsel would have the right to view all such proceedings. But they neglected to disengage the backup system, and this segment of the sixteen-hour session was duly recorded.

Townsend and Scarff told Kane that his work for the RCMP was becoming common knowledge among the various police forces, and once the police knew the bikers would too. At least accept protective custody while you're in jail, they urged him, rather than be vulnerable among the general prison population. Kane wouldn't budge from his position, wouldn't drop the facade of innocence. He claimed not to know what Townsend and Scarff were talking about, but he understood their ploy: force him to become a *délateur* by pretending that he was one already and generate rumours to that effect in the criminal community.

Townsend and Scarff gave up for the night, passing Kane to others in their unit, among them a francophone interrogator. Kane understood English perfectly well, but they hoped he might open up with someone who spoke his native tongue. He did, becoming even more voluble in his contempt for them and their efforts to turn him. Finally, after noon the next day, the RCMP admitted defeat.

Kane's strategy was clear: he would maintain he had absolutely nothing to hide and that all this chatter about him working for the RCMP was just a devious scheme to make it a reality. It was a dangerous gambit, crazy and suicidal in the minds of most of the Mounties involved. In the end, however, it proved to be the smartest move Kane could have made.

Kane's arrest sent the RCMP scrambling in different directions. In Nova Scotia Townsend and his colleagues hustled to assemble their case. After Kane's categorical refusal to cooperate in any way, they had no choice but to proceed as normal with an uncomplicated gangland murder investigation. Simard's testimony would be useful but only up to a point. As Serge Quesnel had demonstrated, *délateurs* in general make poor witnesses. They may have compelling, precise details about the crime in question, but their own criminal pasts, and the fact that their testimony is earning them favourable treatment from the justice system, allows any half-competent defence lawyer to raise serious doubts about their trustworthiness. Simard's long history of petty fraud—including the theft of his own mother's credit

cards—made it easy to portray him as an inveterate liar.
With the deal prosecutors were offering in return for his
testimony, it would be easier still to demonstrate an incen-
tive to lie again.

Townsend had to buttress his case thoroughly, independent of Simard's testimony. To this end his officers had
located the Buick LeSabre at a vehicle auction yard in
Quebec and scoured its interior, looking for gunpowder
residue as well as fibre and hair samples that might link
Kane and Simard to the car. They traced calls made by
Kane from Halifax pay phones to Dominique. They
searched for banking evidence to prove that Kane had used
an automatic teller machine in Halifax, as Simard maintained. They hunted for images, however fleeting, of Kane
and Simard on security camera videotapes from the Halifax
Shopping Centre, the industrial park where MacFarlane
was murdered, and any other monitored locations.

And on May 6 Townsend and a young RCMP constable
named Mark MacPherson did a whirlwind tour of the
Maritime provinces, showing photo lineups that included
Kane and Simard to some of the people who encountered
them on their trip east. Townsend and MacPherson left
Halifax at 6:30 a.m. bound for Charlottetown, P.E.I., and
a rendezvous with MacFarlane's cousin David Roberts.
From there they headed to Shediac, N.B., just outside
Moncton, for a meeting with Claude Blanchard. Then
they travelled to Oromocto to sit down with their colleague, Cst. Gilles Blinn. Finally, just before 9:30 p.m.,
almost fifteen hours into a day of driving and detective
work, they visited Dale Hutley, the volunteer for the
RCMP and Blinn's partner when they stopped Kane and
Simard on the Trans-Canada. MacPherson, a new man
on the force with just a year's experience, had the job of

administering the photo lineups and completing the necessary paperwork. All of the interviews were audio-taped as backup to the notes kept separately by Townsend and MacPherson.

David Roberts had been too busy running for his life on the night of the shooting to be of any help with identification. Blanchard was a very reluctant witness who didn't want trouble with anyone, least of all the Hells Angels. He barely glanced at the photo lineups. But Blinn and Hutley made the long day worthwhile. Both were able to pull Kane out of the photo lineup and provide details about how his appearance had changed since that day they'd first encountered him on a New Brunswick roadside.

Though Blinn had dealt primarily with Simard and was unable to identify him, he was precise in his description of Kane. "When I first stopped him he had round sunglasses, more hair, very clean-cut. There was no beard. He had earrings … lots of jewellery, real expensive jewellery.…" Their identification, placing Kane in the Maritimes in a white car similar to the vehicle caught by security cameras at the industrial park, made a conviction that much more likely.

Meanwhile, in Montreal the RCMP were scrambling not to build a case against Kane but to defend them-selves—institutionally and individually—from the fallout that his murder charge was sure to generate. As an organi-zation the Quebec Mounties had to account for Kane's questionable arrest and his hasty departure one step ahead of agitated local forces. As individuals St. Onge and Verdon had to justify their actions to their superiors and to their colleagues at Carcajou. The enraged SQ investi-gators were calling it a "kidnapping," and at the Carcajou morning meeting the day after Kane's arrest, the squad's

top commander, Capt. Mario Laprise of the SQ, asked
Verdon pointedly whether he had anything to do with it.
In front of some sixty fellow officers, Verdon glanced
around, then looked down at the table and denied any
involvement. It took little time to determine that his statement was utterly false, and Verdon was summarily ejected
from the meeting by Laprise. His time with the elite
Carcajou squad was over.

St. Onge hadn't shown up at the meeting; he had his
hands full elsewhere. Senior to Verdon, he had to explain
their behaviour to his own RCMP bosses. In an internal
memo dated May 6 St. Onge said the arrest hadn't been
planned as the secret operation it appeared. Two Montreal
police were scheduled to take part in Kane's apprehension
as backup to the Halifax Mounties, but at the eleventh
hour "the investigators and I realized that the bosses at the
Montreal police weren't aware of the latest developments.
It was too late and Constable Townsend went ahead with
the arrest."

Regardless, St. Onge maintained, neither Carcajou
nor the SQ had any business getting involved in the bust.
"At the very last minute the SQ claimed they wanted to
interrogate Kane about the murder [of Leclerc] in
Plessisville, which was nothing but a pretext to meet
Kane and try to make him become a *délateur* and only
then send him on to Halifax. Townsend was aware of
these intentions and didn't want to get involved for the
simple reason that a declaration taken after the interrogation by the SQ would never have been admitted in
court." After the fact it's difficult to know if St. Onge's
judicial rationale was foremost in the minds of the RCMP
officers who hustled Kane onto the flight to Halifax, but
he was defiant. "It is clear to me that the SQ, having

tried for years to identify our 'supersource,' as they called him, had a golden opportunity and blew it."

But while Kane's arrest was generating much controversy between the RCMP and the SQ, it was still essentially a side issue; the most difficult questions for St. Onge revolved around the longer-term handling of C-2994. These would come from his own superiors. In what appears to be an attempt to head off this line of inquiry, his memo offered a lengthy explanation of why Kane wasn't really a killer, even if he had taken part in the MacFarlane hit, and how it was that he and Verdon had remained ignorant of his activities. Kane had "voluntarily omitted" to tell them about the Halifax trip; otherwise, they would have forbidden him to go. Yet he had to go if he was to fulfil his responsibilities to the RCMP and help in the fight against criminal biker gangs.

Organizing the MacFarlane hit, St. Onge reminded his bosses, was the fast track to hangaround status, the force's original objective for C-2994. "In this milieu, to climb to the upper ranks, you must help the club in a significant way, that is, by committing one or more serious crimes or in enriching the club and yourself (often the two go together). Those who proudly wear the 'Filthy Few' patch indicate beyond all doubt that they have killed for the club. For them, killing means firing the gun and not driving the shooter or organizing an ambush.... In his head, that of a biker with ten years seniority, he wasn't a murderer in the MacFarlane case, Simard was the murderer, and as [Kane] anticipated, he would be named a 'hangaround.' "

As far as the arrest was concerned St. Onge's boss, Staff Sgt. Pierre Bolduc, backed his man. Referring to Carcajou in his own memo, he commented sharply, "On the date of 97-04-30, the big machine of Carcajou woke up all of a

sudden, a few minutes before the arrest of C-2994, and the
authorities in charge tried to get us to put off the arrest,
which could have had very serious consequences for the
Halifax case. If we had handed over the prisoner to
Carcajou we would have completely destroyed our
chances of obtaining a statement from C-2994 that would
have been admissible in court after he had been interrogated for ten, twelve, fourteen hours by Carcajou."

But Bolduc wouldn't defend St. Onge for long. At the
behest of his own superiors, he spent much of the summer
poring over the hundreds of pages of debriefing reports
filed by Verdon and St. Onge and evaluating the tangible
benefits that had derived from Kane's intelligence. He
then composed a devastating thirteen-page memo that
criticized every aspect of their management of the source.
From the start, he wrote, Verdon and St. Onge were
"bedazzled by the possibility of having under their control the source of the century." As a result they failed to
ask basic questions that should have raised alarms. How
did Kane, "a simple citizen," establish privileged friendships so quickly with such heavyweights as Wolf Carroll
and Walter Stadnick? How did Kane come to be president
of the Demon Keepers? Why was there always a crucial
detail missing from his information that might have led to
an arrest or seizure—the number of the apartment where
drugs and explosives were stored, the licence plate of the
car used by Carroll, the date a shipment was supposed to
arrive or an attack take place?

There was a withering, sarcastic tone to his dissection.
"The source always has information that would be very
interesting if it were provided in time for us to do something," Bolduc commented. He also wondered why Kane
seemed to be so well informed about the activities of

the rival Rock Machine and had no trouble providing their addresses and licence plate numbers. "Was that just a matter of chance?" he asked. "I doubt it!" Another theme of his criticism echoed Carcajou's main concern: how little information was passed on to other police authorities who might have acted on it.

The most scorching charge came in Bolduc's conclusions. Kane was almost certainly a Hells Angels plant, he wrote, passing useless or false information to his handlers while extracting from them the details of what Carcajou knew and what police actions were in the offing. A host of indicators made it hard for him to believe otherwise. There was the fact that the intelligence provided by Kane did not lead to a single drug bust in the two and a half years he worked for the RCMP, despite their knowledge that he had served as a drug courier for the gang "on a good many occasions." There was the tidbit that Mom Boucher was ready to pay a crooked cop twice his annual salary for inside information. "Was this an attempt by the source to corrupt one of his handlers?" Bolduc asked. Considering that Kane had no colours or long-term association with the Hells, why would Boucher "confide in the source his desire to corrupt a policeman?" Finally, there was Kane's refusal to accept protective custody at the Halifax Correctional Centre, even when within a month of his arrival guards were hearing rumours that there was a $14,000 contract on his head. "How is it that C-2994 has such great confidence in the H.A., who need nothing more than a slight suspicion to eliminate any individual who poses a risk to their security?"

Bolduc was especially flabbergasted that in a telephone call to Wolf Carroll from jail, Kane had not hesitated to read him a letter he had received from Townsend, saying

that Kane's status would change after the preliminary
inquiry and that he should still feel free to contact the
RCMP. The message was clear, Bolduc said: Kane's
informant role would be revealed at the preliminary. But
Carroll, who was footing Kane's legal bills, was apparently
unperturbed—proof that Kane was really working for the
Hells Angels while he was on the payroll of the RCMP.

"If we believe the handlers, the source is intelligent
and has good analytical capacities," noted Bolduc. "Either
these qualities have disappeared and he's become a complete idiot," or he was a Hells Angels double agent.
Bolduc stopped short of saying St. Onge and Verdon were
crooked. Rather, he believed that "because of a lack of
experience they had been duped by a source who was sent
to them with a precise goal." But just to be sure, he proposed that the force examine the relationship between
Kane and his handlers more closely. "The various comments from different members of the section suggest that
the source was considered much more as a friend by our
agents than as a source employed by the RCMP."

St. Onge and Verdon wouldn't see Bolduc's report,
dated September 25, 1997, or know of its scathing evaluation for ten months. There would be no official response
to it from Bolduc's superiors—or none that the RCMP
has acknowledged—for twice that length of time. It
seemed the force wanted to forget about the debacle and
focus instead on a more pressing problem: how to hide
Kane's history as a long-time RCMP informant now that
he was in jail awaiting trial for murder.

In mid-June, the Montreal Mounties requested that the
Nova Scotia Crown prosecutor assigned to the case not be
told of Kane's secret role. The request was moot. "In this

province, our dealings with Crown counsel are based on mutual trust," Barnett sniffed. "Therefore the fact that Danny [sic] Kane was a confidential human source for the RCMP at the time of his participation in the murder of Robert MacFarlane has already been made known to Crown counsel."

The Crown's knowing was one thing, Kane's defence lawyer quite another. The Rockers' favourite lawyer, Pierre Panaccio, had been dispatched to Halifax to confer with Kane within a day or two of his arrest. The RCMP were convinced there would be no lawyer-client confidentiality between Panaccio and Kane. If it was disclosed to Panaccio that Kane had been working for the force, Barnett noted, "we believe that ... it will place Kane's life in immediate danger."

Even if a judge gave a dispensation to the Crown to withhold the fact that Kane was an informant, Barnett believed Panaccio would figure it out. First there was the phone call from St. Onge to Blinn after the highway stop near Frederiction. "It may seem odd to defence counsel that Sgt. St. Onge did not contact anyone even after Robert MacFarlane was murdered and investigators had disseminated a message advising that two male suspects operating a white 4-door vehicle were being sought as suspects," Barnett wrote. Then there were the problematic circumstances of Kane's arrest. "There is little doubt that defence counsel will want to know how Danny [sic] Kane came to be in a motel room in Montreal with police officers when Cst. Townsend arrived to arrest him."

Barnett also took his Montreal colleagues to task for their concern about the "significant negative media attention" that would result if it was to come out that one of their informants was moonlighting as a murderer while on the RCMP payroll. "These facts would only be disclosed as a result of actions of the defence counsel and if that should occur the potential negative media attention would be the least of the force's problems."

The RCMP saw two ways out of the mess, both of which called for Kane to plead guilty to the MacFarlane murder. In one scenario he would go through the motions of becoming a *délateur,* agreeing to testify against others in the gang in return for a reduced sentence and a new identity. In the other he would simply enter a guilty plea before any compromising information came out at a preliminary hearing. Neither appealed to Kane. He refused to contemplate even the possibility of pleading guilty or of becoming a *délateur.* His resolve hadn't wavered from his first interrogation with Townsend. He would deny everything and hope to beat the charge.

In mid-August, however, there was a brief moment of panic. Kane called Verdon on August 18 and asked him to come to the Correctional Centre in Halifax. What he wanted to talk about was too delicate to discuss over the phone, however secure the line. Verdon flew down that night with a fellow RCMP officer and met with Kane the next afternoon. It wasn't Verdon's first trip to Halifax for Kane. He and an RCMP corporal who specialized in managing informants had visited on June 10, hoping to persuade Kane to become a *délateur.* He had refused to see them.

This time Kane was less standoffish. Claude Grégoire McCarter, the St-Jean-sur-Richelieu friend whom Kane had brought into the gang (and onto the baseball team) in the months before his arrest, had been murdered a few weeks previous in a style that pointed to the Hells. His girlfriend reported him missing on August 11; a few days later his charred body was found in a burned-out Jeep on a remote gravel road northwest of Montreal. His death sent a chill through Kane. The Hells must have known he'd been an informant; they were killing his friends. Next it would be his family, just as Townsend had predicted.

There were other disturbing signs. Wolf Carroll's attitude had changed, and he seemed less eager to pick up Kane's legal and child support bills. Panaccio likewise was acting strangely, possibly hiding things from him and "not telling him what was really happening." Finally, his former driver, Dominique, had received a telephone call from Aimé Simard in jail in Montreal. Simard said he'd figured out that Kane was a police source. Shortly after he had been arrested and given evidence against Kane, police confronted him with the fact that a .44 Magnum seized from a bus station locker—the gun he'd retrieved from Jimmy Miller in Quebec City—belonged to him. The only person who knew Simard had stashed it there was Kane, and Simard drew the logical conclusion. Dominique didn't necessarily believe Simard—few people did—but if Simard was broadcasting his belief that Kane was an informant, it might prompt some people to entertain the possibility.

"C-2994 is confused and doesn't know anymore what to do," Verdon wrote after the meeting. "He asks what is the possibility of cooperating with us at the same time specifying that he does not want, under any circumstances, to cooperate with the Sûreté du Québec." Yet Kane again refused protective custody, signing a waiver to the effect that he released the RCMP, "its members and agents" from all responsibility for his safety. The meeting ended with Kane saying he would think over his options and phone Verdon a week later. For his part, Verdon would contact Townsend and recommend he prepare a *délateur* deal for Kane's consideration.

Kane's call never came. Scott Steinert stepped in to take care of his various expenses, and this gesture reassured Kane that his situation wasn't so dire. He would continue to hold fast to a fiction: that rumours of his service as an informant were fabricated by the RCMP in a wishful effort to make him one. After all, he might legitimately ask, what was he doing languishing in jail if he was a high-priced police mole?

17

HALIFAX MISTRIAL MYSTERY

Within the Quebec Hells Angels organization, Kane's incarceration raised hardly a ripple. He was widely liked, but fundamentally he was just another minor-league hopeful whose place would soon be filled by someone else. And as long as Kane kept biting his tongue, prepared to take one for the team rather than turn *délateur*, his arrest was a mere inconvenience to the gang.

However, when Simard's revelations led to the arrest of five members of the Rocker shock squad for the Caissy killing, the organization felt more threatened. First Apache Trudeau, then Serge Quesnel, now Aimé Simard. All of them had been offered sweet deals from the justice system to rat out the gang.

These defections, the Hells leadership agreed, had to stop, and Mom Boucher had a plan. It was time to open up another flank in the war, time to go after the justice system itself with a campaign of arbitrary assassination against police, prosecutors, maybe a judge or two, and, of course, prison guards. Boucher's logic had a vicious elegance. Such killings, by their randomness as much as their fact, would sow fear. Fear was the equal of intimidation, and an intimidated justice system would make for police officers who didn't push so hard, prosecutors who thought twice before laying charges, judges who required a little more proof. Inside the walls of Quebec's prisons and jails it would make for guards more acquiescent to the control the Hells Angels already exerted.

But perhaps the real purpose of Boucher's offensive was to ensure internal discipline. Police and prosecutors would never make a deal with a biker who had killed one of their own, he reasoned. If enough soldiers in the Hells organization took out enough members of the justice system, the pool of potential *délateurs* would evaporate. In June 1997, his swelling self-importance overriding his judgment, Mom dispatched two trusted lieutenants to put the strategy into action. Start with prison guards, he told them, the lowest-ranking members on the justice system hit list.

Just before 10 p.m. on Thursday, June 26, with light still in the sky, Diane Lavigne finished her shift classifying prisoners at Bordeaux jail in Montreal's north end, climbed into her white minivan, and headed home to St-Eustache, an off-island bedroom community northwest of Montreal. Lavigne had worked at the prison for eleven years and was one of the first women hired there. For her it was the family business; her father had been a prison guard for almost thirty years.

As she turned onto Autoroute des Laurentides, the highway that would take her north across the island of Laval, a stolen Japanese motorbike with two riders followed her. Driving the motorbike was André "Toots" Tousignant, the Nomads striker; perched behind him was Stéphane "Godasse" Gagné, the shock squad member and Rockers hangaround. A few hundred metres beyond the on-ramp, Tousignant gave the bike some gas and pulled alongside Lavigne's minivan. Gagné looked over and saw the details of a prison guard uniform. Neither he nor Tousignant had noticed that the short-haired, stout figure they had followed from the Bordeaux gates was a woman, and Gagné didn't notice it now. The uniform was enough. He pulled a revolver from his belt and began squeezing the trigger. Two shots hit Lavigne before Tousignant accelerated and the bikers disappeared into traffic.

The minivan slowed onto the highway's shoulder, emergency lights flashing. Another woman guard who had come off shift at the same time as Lavigne and was taking the same route home watched the vehicle pull over. A flat or engine trouble, she thought. She contemplated stopping to help her colleague, but the heavy traffic carried her on. Lavigne's life slowly ebbed away on the side of the Autoroute des Laurentides, while cars and trucks whizzed by, oblivious.

The shock of Lavigne's death had barely subsided when, on September 8, two more guards were ambushed. It was the usual early-morning routine of Pierre Rondeau and Robert Corriveau to take a blue prison bus from the underground parking garage at the downtown Montreal courthouse to the Rivière-des-Prairies jail in the city's northeast to pick up prisoners who were to appear in court that day. They sometimes varied their route, but on this day they took a familiar road across the railway tracks that serviced the industries of Montreal's east end. As they slowed for the level crossing, a short beefy man in a dark outfit stepped out from a bus shelter and in front of the bus.

Paul "Fonfon" Fontaine, another Nomads striker, scrambled up onto the hood of the stationary bus and fired through the windshield at Rondeau. His accomplice and designated driver, Godasse Gagné, shot at Corriveau through the door and side of the bus as Fontaine made for their getaway van parked nearby. Corriveau would escape unscathed; Rondeau was hit three times and died instantly.

No credible claim of responsibility was made in either case, but prison workers had heard the talk inside the walls and suspected bikers in both deaths. More than two thousand staged a twenty-four-hour walkout the day after Rondeau's murder to protest the killings and demand better security.

Other preoccupations that summer helped push Dany Kane from the minds of his biker cronies. Scott Steinert's immigration woes had started off as a low-level irritant, barely worthy of attention in a fast and dangerous life. Yet as slow and plodding as the bureaucratic machinery was, the immigration department proceedings were inexorable, and by mid-1997 deportation back to the United States was an imminent likelihood.

A formal deportation order was handed down in November 1996, but Steinert had appealed it. His chances were slim, and he began investigating other means by which he might stay in the country. If the United States refused to take him, then Canada couldn't send him, so Steinert looked into the idea of renouncing his American citizenship. Through his dealings with Mohawk gun and drug runners, Steinert understood that members of North America's First Nations enjoyed a privileged status with respect to living and working in the two countries. He also knew that in some native communities, money could make miracles. He made efforts to obtain an Indian card, proof of native status and band membership.

Whatever happened, Steinert intended to find his way back to Canada. Even an offer from Mom Boucher to set him up in business in Mexico didn't hold any interest, notwithstanding Boucher's assurance that he would be a millionaire in a matter of months. One reason for Steinert's resolve was his growing power: he had his clique, he had the Château Lavigueur, and he had a solid share of Montreal's drug market. He also had a new romantic attachment.

Steinert had been with a Sorel woman he'd known since his teens for more than a decade. They'd had a child together but never married. Then in 1996 or early 1997 he met a Montreal woman whose parents operated a restaurant patronized by the bikers. He fell head over heels for her. A sumptuous wedding was planned for October, and while police and immigration officials naturally wondered whether Steinert was tying the knot in order to beat the deportation order, there was little doubt of his ardour. Indeed, his overwhelming infatuation with his fiancée distracted him from the gang's business. He began to let things slide, reigniting old resentments.

Steinert never went to see his former protegé in Halifax, nor did any other of Kane's biker friends. His only visitors were Patricia, his parents and children, and Dominique. During the almost twenty months Kane was incarcerated, Patricia visited four or five times. She flew occasionally or drove, either with Kane's parents or with Dominique, listening to his corny comedy tapes the whole way. "Now *that* is love," she says.

Prison officials permitted a scant hour with Kane each visit, hardly worth the effort but enough to allow Patricia to see that Kane was being physically transformed by his time behind bars. His first prison meal had been disgusting—pork chops that were more fat than meat— so Kane claimed to be a vegetarian in the hopes of better fare. It brought him a lot of iceberg lettuce but not much else. On this diet and without steroids, Kane's bulk began melting and his weight plummeted. He had weighed just over 130 pounds in the late 1980s, but thanks to steroids, the gym, and good food, he was a solid 175 pounds or more on a five-foot-seven frame at the time of his arrest. Prison, however, was returning him to his weedy self.

There was a personality transformation under way too, a change that Patricia noticed during their marathon telephone calls. Kane would trade cigarettes for phone privileges and often spent whole evenings calling Quebec, sometimes Wolf Carroll, sometimes Pat Lambert, sometimes Steinert or others from the milieu. Most frequently it was Josée or Patricia on the other end.

The conversations with Josée were reminiscent of those they'd had when he was in prison in Belleville, starting pleasantly but ending with ugly recriminations. Josée claims Kane wanted only "to give me shit and make me cry." The letters he wrote to his children were similarly poisonous. Josée screened them and found the level of hostility he expressed toward her so vile that she allowed very few to reach her kids' hands. Much of his rage had to do with her seeing another man.

The calls to Patricia were mostly largely epic sessions of complaint, sometimes lasting hours. He'd gripe about the food, about other inmates, about not being allowed to watch French television. The police never left him alone, using every scare tactic to get him to turn, though he never mentioned to her the rumoured contract on his life. Patricia could not help noticing Kane's growing sense of persecution. She couldn't know that after the ambush laid by his handlers and his arrest by their Halifax colleagues, Kane understandably felt betrayed. This, combined with loneliness and the fact that he was a francophone in an anglophone institution, fed a self-pitying conviction that he'd been abandoned by his friends and crucified by his enemies. "If he called and I wasn't there, he would tell me that I didn't care about him," Patricia remembers. "He felt that while he was locked up inside, everyone else was out having fun."

She wouldn't stand for the level of control that Kane tried to exert over Josée, but sometimes he couldn't stop himself from making accusations.

"I know you're seeing someone else," he'd charge.

"Tell me who and give me his phone number and maybe I'll give him a call, then," Patricia would respond.

Kane's emotional state was no doubt aggravated by the interminable wait for his case to come to trial. Much of the delay was due to a spate of motions and procedures initiated by both the Crown and the defence. A major concern of the Crown, as well as of the RCMP, was the thorny spectre of the preliminary hearing and the likely disclosure of Kane's history as an informant.

The preliminary had been scheduled to begin July 29, but a week before, Nova Scotia's director of public prosecutions announced that the case would proceed by direct indictment. This meant that the evidence to be used against Kane would not be revealed in open court for testing and examination under oath. Instead the Crown would simply transmit to the defence the evidence it intended to introduce and a trial date would be set. Normally, direct indictments are invoked only in cases where the proper administration of justice might become an issue, complex cases where hearings could drag on for unreasonable periods or where the security of witnesses might be threatened by their appearance at a preliminary. In what appeared to be a relatively straightforward murder case, "the preferring of a direct indictment," as it is formally known, was unusual, but within the Crown's prerogative. And while the Crown was not required to justify its reasons for proceeding in this way, the defence could challenge it.

In the Kane case the Crown was prepared to argue that the price on his head justified the direct indictment. But Panaccio chose not to challenge it, perhaps for strategic purposes. In the event of a conviction, the decision not to hold a prelim might help establish grounds for appeal. He may have allowed it too because Panaccio's role as Kane's lawyer was itself under review.

When Simard was first arrested for the Caissy killing, Panaccio represented him for as long as it took the client to tell the lawyer he had decided to flip and wouldn't be requiring his services after all. That was nonetheless long enough for the Crown to argue that since Simard was due to be its star witness against Kane, Panaccio was caught in an unconscionable conflict. Panaccio duly withdrew as Kane's counsel.

For the next two months, he was represented by Duncan Beveridge of Halifax, the lawyer of choice for many Nova Scotia bikers. But Kane wanted a trial in French and representation by a Quebecker. Just before Christmas Beveridge stepped aside in favour of Danièle Roy, a tough and beautiful woman who was carving a place for herself in the strange and incestuous world of Quebec biker law.

As a young lawyer Roy had fallen under the spell of Jacques Bouchard, a veteran criminal lawyer and a major figure in the murder trials that flowed out of the 1985 Lennoxville massacre. Bouchard and Roy were at one time a couple, then went their separate ways, but thanks to the abundant money and questionable associations that come with it, biker law is a hard field to leave. Roy continued to draw most of her clients from the milieu. When she took on Kane's case, she was also representing Stephen Falls, one of the Rockers fingered by Simard in the Caissy killing. Though she didn't know Kane, she would soon be quite familiar with his former lover and main witness against him.

Roy's first order of business was to request that Kane be tried in French. In Nova Scotia such a request is not easily fulfilled: finding a French-speaking prosecutor, judge, and jury would be a challenge. But Kane had a constitutional right to a French-language trial, and it was granted. Making the arrangements would delay matters still further, as did Roy's representation of Falls in Montreal. Kane's trial was due to begin in the first week of May 1998, exactly a year after he was charged, but the trial of the five Rockers in the Caissy killing happened to be scheduled for that same month. Roy and Simard would be unavailable to appear in Nova Scotia. A new date for Kane's proceedings was set for September 8.

Meanwhile, the RCMP hadn't completely given up on the prospect of persuading Kane to become a *délateur,* despite his repeated rejections of their overtures. In February or March Staff Sgt. J.P. Lévesque, the Mountie with whom Kane had his earliest contacts, according to the RCMP's official history, made an unorthodox approach. On a sheet of plain, lined paper he wrote out a vague note pleading for a meeting. It read,

Hi,
Despite the hard times, I hope your spirits are high.
I spoke to striker (Li'l Red) and he tells me you are

*uncertain about what you are going to do. I think it
is absolutely essential that I meet you in order to
explain certain things so that you might make a
judicious decision.*

> *Good luck,*
> *Your first friend,*
> *Jean-Pierre (Ottawa)*

Striker and Li'l Red were code names for Gaetan St.
Onge. Lévesque tried to send the note through RCMP
channels, but the Halifax Mounties refused to pass it to
Kane—or at least said they did in their complaint about the
letter to Ottawa headquarters. Somehow the note still
ended up in Danièle Roy's hands—the very person
Lévesque had hoped to elude—and she exploded, accus-
ing the force of trying once again to seed rumours that
Kane was an informant and pressure him into cooperating.

According to RCMP documents, Lévesque received a
dressing-down from his superiors. He justified his actions
by saying that Kane might be in a position to help the
RCMP nail a much bigger target—Mom Boucher.

The murders of Diane Lavigne and Pierre Rondeau went
unsolved in the crucial early days and weeks following
their deaths. The police, especially Carcajou, had no leads
and felt obliged to satisfy an impatient public with some
show of action against the bikers.

In the fall of 1997 Project HARM—an acronym for
Hells Angels Rock Machine—began an exercise in old-
fashioned police work, putting on the squeeze at street
level. Beginning at the bottom with retail dealers of quarter-
grams of coke and single grams of hash, they raided bars,
strip clubs, and other businesses that were primarily

fronts for the bikers' drug transactions. One evening in early December, they launched a coordinated series of raids and picked up, among several dozen dealers, an operator named Steve Boies. Boies was already awaiting sentencing on a trafficking charge; police had caught him at it again, and this time with several kilos of coke stashed in his kitchen—serious volume.

While he was being processed, Boies decided he had something to offer the police. One of his close associates was Godasse Gagné, the shooter in the Lavigne murder and Fontaine's accomplice in the Rondeau assassination. Gagné had been promoted to striker status with the Rockers for his efforts. After the Rondeau killing Gagné had called up Boies to ask for help in disposing of any evidence that might connect him and Fontaine to Rondeau's murder. He never told Boies why they were taking a perfectly good car to a junkyard for crushing, or cleaning up a garage, or dumping a nearly full box of bullets; he didn't need to. Coming so soon after the guard's murder, it was obvious. That December evening Boies happily gave up Gagné in exchange for leniency.

One informant quickly made another. Within a day or two police had picked up Gagné and, after an intense overnight interrogation, turned him. Gagné was willing to implicate and testify against Mom Boucher, the kingpin of the Nomads, the biker war's five-star general in the prison guards' shootings. In return Gagné accepted the withdrawal of one murder charge against him, thereby improving his prospects for an early parole, and some meagre financial considerations.

It was the weekend of the Hells Angels' twentieth anniversary in Canada, under any other circumstances an excuse for the most lavish, unbridled of parties. This year,

however, there was a pall over the fun. Godasse Gagné
had been picked and was refusing to speak to the gang's
lawyers. His reasons were not yet known, but they surely
weren't cause for celebration.

It's doubtful that Kane could have provided any testimony of substance in the Crown's case against Boucher.
He was, after all, in prison in Halifax when Lavigne and
Rondeau were killed. More likely, Lévesque's tempting
speculation was an effort to justify his unauthorized and
reckless letter. Either way, Kane was no more receptive to
his latest suitor than he was to Townsend or Verdon.
Everyone awaited the start of the trial in September.

In June the RCMP informed the judge assigned to the
case, Felix Cacchione, that an attempt could be made on
Simard's life during the trial. Halifax's courthouse was
not sufficiently secure, in their view; another location,
one that could be properly cordoned off, would have to be
found. It wasn't until the day after Labour Day that a former school-board building in Lower Sackville—a half-
hour north of Halifax—was secured for the trial.

There was a further delay when the extent of the
Mounties' security provisions became evident. The force
had consulted Cacchione about the number of police,
plainclothes and uniformed, who would be posted to the
building, as well as the use of metal detectors and other
security devices. They had neglected to inform him of the
almost-metre-high, maze-like concrete barrier system that
was to circle the makeshift courthouse.

A visit to the site on September 7 left Cacchione aghast
at what he considered security overkill. His concerns
were shared by both Danièle Roy and Pierre Lapointe, the
veteran Quebec City prosecutor who had been brought in

to handle the case. All were worried that the elaborate security measures would jeopardize the impartiality of the jury as they came and went every day. They might assume that the accused must be guilty for the authorities to take such measures. Cacchione ordered the barriers removed, but that didn't stop Roy from filing a motion for a stay of proceedings on the grounds that media coverage of the security measures had jeopardized Kane's chances of a fair trial. Cacchione dismissed the motion, but it was clear already that the proceedings would be messy.

Cacchione was a former Montrealer who had gone east to study at Dalhousie Law School and then stayed on to make his reputation as a crusading defence lawyer. His most famous client was Donald Marshall, a Mi'kmaq who, thanks to crooked police work, perjured testimony, and illegally withheld evidence, spent eleven years in jail for a murder he didn't commit. Once on the bench Cacchione became a favourite of the local legal fraternity. "I love him. He is prepared *not* to take cops at their word, which can't be said of all judges here," says one. "He looks at police as he looks at other people—capable of lying under oath. With him the word of a policeman is not sacrosanct."

Not surprisingly, while defence lawyers describe Cacchione as fair, gentlemanly, sober, and cautious, prosecutors and police are less flattering. With Cacchione presiding, they expected a conviction against Kane to be that much harder to win. In the early going of the trial, however, Cacchione was even-handed to a fault, impressing both Lapointe and Roy. After the removal of the so-called jersey traffic-control barriers, the judge had two other motions to rule on before the trial could begin in earnest, motions that would determine the outcome of the case and Kane's fate.

The first concerned the RCMP's stopping Simard and Kane on that cold New Brunswick highway two days before MacFarlane was killed. Constables Blinn and Hutley pulled over the Buick LeSabre not because it was speeding, swerving, or missing a tail light but simply because it was a new car carrying two calm young men. Roy argued that this breached Simard's and Kane's constitutional protection from arbitrary detention. She maintained that everything to do with the highway stop should be ruled inadmissible. Cacchione agreed in part. He ruled that the detention was arbitrary and thus the CPIC identification, plus Kane's voluntary offering of his name and date of birth, could not be entered as evidence. However, Blinn and Hutley's visual identification of Simard and Kane at the time of the stop and in the later photo lineups could be presented, as could their testimony about what they saw in the trunk of the Buick, since Simard had freely allowed them a look inside.

The second motion came from the Crown and was necessarily obscure. Lapointe requested that certain documents he would normally be obliged to turn over to the defence be considered privileged, exempted on the grounds that they would identify an informant, reveal police investigative techniques, or possibly compromise an ongoing investigation. The documents in question, of course, identified Kane as an RCMP source. Cacchione acceded to the motion. This set the stage for an extraordinary piece of legal theatre where the accused's double life as an informant was known to the judge and the Crown but not to his own lawyer.

Jury selection, at least, went smoothly. By the end of the first full week of October, twelve bilingual jurors had been chosen. On October 13 they began to hear evidence. The testimony of the first dozen witnesses was given in about four days, almost all of it devoted to the scene of the crime and the technical details of MacFarlane's death. Nine of the witnesses were RCMP employees; the other three were a pathologist, a security company supervisor, and a man who duplicated a videotape for the investigators.

Then, at 9:35 a.m. on October 20, the Crown's star witness was sworn in. For a full day and part of the following morning, Lapointe had Aimé Simard tell the court about his past, how he had met Kane, been introduced to the nasty world of Quebec's warring bikers, and come to kill MacFarlane. Lapointe's questioning was interrupted twice by lengthy objections from Roy and subsequent discussions on points of law, but overall Simard's testimony was concise and effective. The prosecution felt that he had done as well as might have been hoped.

It was Roy's job to trip him up and demonstrate his unreliability to the jury. She had witnessed Simard's performance at the Caissy murder trial a few months earlier and had reason to feel confident: the Rockers' trial had been a disaster for the prosecution. It began in early April and should have lasted perhaps two months; instead, it stumbled on until mid-July. A month into it the Crown prosecutor, Lucie Dufresne, who was widely regarded as seasoned and no-nonsense, quit the case after reportedly suffering a nervous breakdown. Her collapse was attributed to overwork and the stress of facing five well-paid biker lawyers alone and with few resources.

Perhaps fortunately she was gone from the courtroom before Simard took the stand. He contradicted himself on countless points. He said he had done surveillance on Caissy at the recreation centre on a snowy day two weeks before the killing. When a defence lawyer pointed out that two weeks before the killing Simard had been in Jamaica and that the last snowfall had been six weeks prior to the murder, Simard suddenly recalled events differently. On other occasions he was confronted with major discrepancies between his testimony and earlier statements given to police. Asked why something had been true earlier but wasn't any more, Simard responded lamely, "It was true that day."

Even his body language undermined his credibility. After every question put to him, Simard mutely refilled his glass from a pitcher of water, took a slow sip and then, as often as not, asked the lawyer to repeat the question. At one point, when Simard requested yet another bathroom break, the judge suggested he drink less water. On his return from the toilet, Simard sat down, locked eyes with the judge, and took a long gulp from his glass.

On July 18 the jury rendered not-guilty verdicts for all five men charged, including Simard's former boss Daniel St-Pierre, Gregory Wooley, Roy's client Stephen Falls, and the Rockers leader, Pierre Provencher. Simard promptly phoned a *Journal de Montréal* crime reporter and declared that the jury had either been bought off or intimidated. He called for an inquiry into the decision. It was more likely that Simard had simply not been believed by the seven-man, five-woman jury.

Roy was sure she could raise similar doubts in the minds of the Nova Scotia jury when she began her cross-examination of Simard on October 21. She grilled him for four days, leaping forward and backward in time and from one episode in his life to another. Remarkably little of her questioning pertained to MacFarlane's murder; instead, she focused on Simard's petty crimes and his propensity to lie and deceive in order to obtain what he wanted. "Simard lies as easily as he breathes," Roy remarked afterwards.

The cross-examination was suspended for two days after an article in the Halifax *Daily News* broke the publication ban on coverage of the security measures surrounding the trial. Cacchione scolded the paper for the transgression, but that didn't satisfy Roy. She made another application for a stay of proceedings, insisting that Kane's constitutional rights were being incrementally sliced away like so many pieces of salami. Lapointe countered with the argument that publication ban or no, the elaborate security provisions were hardly news to the jury. Cacchione sided with Lapointe and dismissed the stay application but not before threatening the *Daily News* and its reporter with contempt of court charges.

It appeared Simard had learned from his experience at the Caissy trial, and he'd been better prepared by Lapointe. Roy found him a steadier witness this time out. Toward the end of her cross-examination she seemed to be grasping at straws when she asked about the medication he used—he'd briefly been prescribed Prozac and took a sleep aid—and questioned him about a book that had been found in his cell on how to testify effectively. Finally, on October 29, Roy finished with Simard and he stood down. Lapointe breathed a sigh of relief.

The next witnesses Lapointe called were the last people to see MacFarlane alive, his cousin David Roberts, Roberts's buddy Claude Blanchard, and two employees of the Spy Shop, including Paul Macphail. Blanchard was an especially reluctant witness; the prosecutor's office had had to chase him for months to get him to testify. When he was compelled to do so, he had no interest in reviewing earlier statements he had given to police. He was

afraid of the Hells Angels and wasn't willing to say anything that might draw their ire. Even on the morning of
November 2, the day he was due to appear, Blanchard
refused to meet with Lapointe in advance. So after
Roberts and the two Spy Shop employees gave what the
prosecutor considered strong testimony, he decided to
scratch Blanchard as a witness. Roy objected to this last-
minute change, and Blanchard was forced to take the
stand.

Kane's lawyer did her best to raise doubts about
Blanchard's credibility even though he'd been of minimal
value to the prosecution. She went through his extensive
criminal record of armed robbery, forcible confinement,
assault, using a firearm in the commission of a crime, and
drug trafficking. She suggested that the real reason he and
Roberts had gone to Halifax was to score cocaine from
MacFarlane, a charge Blanchard denied. She had him
admit that he had been working as a male stripper for two
years at the time of the shooting. But the testimony that
most helped Kane was evidence that he volunteered freely
and had reiterated consistently since his first statement to
police: he was sure that the car driven by MacFarlane's
killers was a white, four-door Lumina—a Euro-sport
model with a fin on the back—rather than a Buick
LeSabre. He also said that he thought that the primary
shooter was dark enough to be "Lebanese."

The next witness was Const. Tom Townsend, the lead
investigator on the case. His testimony was taken in a voir
dire hearing, what lawyers describe as a trial within a trial.
A voir dire allows the judge to hear arguments in order to
determine whether certain evidence is admissible. For that
reason all voir dires take place in the absence of the jury
and are subject to publication bans.

Townsend's voir dire was in response to a request from Roy that the photo lineup identification of Kane by the highway officers who stopped him in New Brunswick be excluded. Cacchione had earlier ruled the CPIC hit inadmissible, as well as Kane's and Simard's willing self-identification. Roy wanted more. She maintained that the only reason the highway cops remembered Kane and Simard was that the CPIC check alerted them that Kane was involved with criminal bikers. If the CPIC check violated the Charter of Rights and Freedoms, so too should the memory that resulted from it.

Cacchione didn't buy her argument. He ruled that the police had laid eyes on Kane and Simard before their arbitrary detention breached the Charter and thus their photo lineup identification could be entered. Crucially, however, Townsend testified in the voir dire that without consulting his notes he could remember only Auxiliary Const. Dale Hutley identifying Kane in the photo lineups; Const. Gilles Blinn, he said, did not.

The voir dire testimony, subsequent submissions, and the ruling consumed two days. When the trial proper resumed, it heard from two minor witnesses, the woman who managed the Montreal car rental franchise where Simard had done business and the woman whose licence plate Kate had stolen in the Halifax Shopping Centre. Then it was time for the much-debated testimony of the New Brunswick RCMP highway patrol.

Const. Gilles Blinn took the stand first, and after being told very firmly by Cacchione that he couldn't mention the CPIC check or Kane's self-identification, he briefly described the circumstances of the highway stop. He recognized the passenger in the car to be the man "sitting behind the counsel for the defence," Dany Kane. "His hair has grown," Blinn said. "He seems also to have lost some weight. And he has no earrings. But it is 100 percent the same person. There is no doubt about that."

Under questioning by Lapointe, Blinn began to testify about the photo lineups that Townsend and Mark MacPherson showed him and Hutley at the end of that marathon day eighteen months earlier. Before Blinn could say whether he had picked out Kane or Simard or both, Lapointe abruptly asked for a recess.

That morning Lapointe had hoped to meet with MacPherson to discuss his testimony. For weeks he'd been trying to get together with him, but since the crash of Swissair Flight 111 into the waters off Peggy's Cove on September 2, MacPherson and almost every other Nova Scotia RCMP officer had been recovering debris and body parts from the Atlantic. MacPherson had missed the morning meeting, and Lapointe proceeded with Blinn's testimony. He requested the recess when he was informed that MacPherson had finally arrived.

Lapointe wasted no time in asking the young Mountie about the photo lineups. MacPherson said that Blinn hadn't identified Kane; indeed, he maintained he hadn't even shown Blinn the lineup that included Kane because Blinn had told him something to the effect of, "Don't bother showing me a photo of the passenger. I only dealt with the driver."

That information was a bombshell to Lapointe. It was contrary to what MacPherson had stated months earlier to his superiors and to Blinn's previous statements as well as testimony he had given in at least one pre-trial motion. And it was contrary to what Blinn, sworn in and on the stand that very morning, was about to repeat in front of a jury.

Lapointe decided his only course was to share this twist with Cacchione and Roy and be completely transparent while he tried to sort out the discrepancies. Both the judge and defence lawyer heard MacPherson's revised version of events. Lapointe then pleaded for the weekend to straighten out matters, but Roy objected that she didn't want to give anyone time to exert pressure on MacPherson to change his story. She insisted MacPherson testify in a voir dire then and there.

By this time Cacchione was becoming very concerned and, it seems, experiencing an uncomfortable flashback to the Donald Marshall case. "During my years as a defence counsel I was a bit paranoid," Cacchione told Lapointe and Roy. "I had truly thought that I had put this behind me. What has just happened is so upsetting that it makes all this paranoia reappear."

Cacchione said his confidence in all the testimony given at the trial up to that point had been weakened by this development—an alarming signal to Lapointe—and he agreed with Roy that MacPherson ought to testify immediately in a voir dire.

The clean-cut MacPherson spoke in full sentences and gave the impression of absolute certainty in his testimony. He said that after the Simard photo lineup for Blinn had been administered, he had shown Blinn a photo of Kane "just for his information." But he had not shown him a photo lineup of Kane, since Blinn had told him not to bother. He added that according to the photo lineup sheets he filled out, Blinn hadn't even been able to make a positive identification of Simard. "There was nothing worthwhile to us as investigators" in Blinn's results, MacPherson testified.

As MacPherson stepped down, Cacchione thanked him for his candour, an indication that he regarded MacPherson as the upstanding cop telling the truth where others were happy to bend or even fabricate it. Before he recessed the court for the weekend Cacchione again expressed his unease. "This is completely uncharted territory," he said. "All I know is we are facing this terrible situation and we don't know what is behind it. Maybe I am paranoid. I hope that's all it is."

Though Cacchione didn't mention the word, both Roy and Lapointe were experienced enough to know that there now existed the distinct possibility of a mistrial.

Lapointe went back to the audiotape of the photo identification session more than a year and a half earlier in Oromocto. It was immediately clear that Blinn had indeed picked Kane out of a photo lineup.

"You identified him over here on this picture here," Townsend says.

"Uh-huh," confirms Blinn.

"Photo number…?" asks Townsend.

"Number five," answers Blinn, before going on to give a precise description of the change in Kane's appearance between the roadside stop and the more recent photograph.

Lapointe now understood that it was MacPherson, and to a lesser extent Townsend, who were mistaken. MacPherson had been barred from talking with anyone about his testimony over the weekend, including, of course, Lapointe. That left Townsend who, in consulting his notes, realized that yes, Blinn had picked Kane out of the photo lineup. Lapointe prepared himself to go into court Monday morning to argue against a mistrial. Armed with the taped proof he was sure he could clarify the issue.

Cacchione likely spent much of the weekend wondering what the RCMP was up to. He was well aware that Kane was a prized informant for the force and that he had accompanied Simard on the trip east that ended with

MacFarlane's murder. Was this an intentional attempt by the Mounties—or some Mounties—to torpedo the trial? This wasn't another Donald Marshall case, an RCMP attempt to railroad an innocent man. Rather, it looked like just the opposite, an attempt to spring a guilty one.

On Monday, November 9, Danièle Roy's luggage and legal files went missing during her flight from Montreal, necessitating the cancellation of that day's session. When the court resumed sitting on Tuesday, Cacchione had no time for Lapointe's arguments that since the jury hadn't been "contaminated" by evidence it hadn't heard, there was no reason for a mistrial. (Even Blinn didn't know why his testimony had been so suddenly interrupted.)

Cacchione seemed to side with Roy's argument that Lapointe was approaching the trial as if it were a movie shoot. "Scene one, take two. It didn't work the first time. Let's try it again" was Roy's characterization of Lapointe's suggestion that MacPherson and Townsend be allowed to testify again in an effort to resolve the photo lineup confusion.

"The inescapable conclusion I am left to draw is that the officers are prepared to change their sworn testimony as the need arises," Cacchione declared. "To allow this trial to continue when serious doubt has been cast upon the veracity of a key Crown witness would be, in my opinion, to invite a miscarriage of justice."

And with that, Cacchione declared a mistrial. Whether by a fabulous fluke or an artful perversion of justice, the RCMP's informant was about to go back on the street with his biker bona fides miraculously intact.

18

A NEW
MAN

Judge Cacchione's mistrial call on November 10 did not exonerate Dany Kane of the murder charge against him. The Crown could schedule another court date and Kane would go through the process a second time. But the declaration of a mistrial opened the way for Roy to file for a stay of proceedings that, if granted, would make another trial highly unlikely. Police would have to come up with substantial new evidence to convince the court that a new trial was merited. Roy didn't waste any time; she followed Cacchione's clearly expressed suggestion and filed for a stay within a few days of his ruling.

In the meantime Kane was released on bail. Gemma and Jean-Paul Kane, who had driven down to Halifax when a mistrial seemed imminent, agreed at once to the bail conditions imposed by the judge: Kane would live with them in St-Jean-sur-Richelieu and they would post a bond of $20,000. In addition there was a cash deposit of $10,000 required and a long list of undertakings to be observed. Kane had to report to the RCMP's offices in Montreal every Monday; he was to have no contact with Wolf Carroll, Paul Wilson, or any Hells Angel or biker associate; he couldn't own or use a pager or visit a bar; he wasn't to possess any weapons, nor was he to visit Nova Scotia for any reason except further legal proceedings.

Kane drove straight to St-Jean with his parents. One of his first acts back home was to go to Josée's apartment and, in her words, "confiscate" the children. He told her that after his twenty months in jail, they hardly knew him any more. He didn't deny that he was troubled by the presence of Josée's live-in boyfriend and the possibility that the kids would soon look to this new man as their surrogate father.

Kane also told Josée that he was through with crime in general and the gang in particular. She was skeptical but thought he might be expressing at least a wish if not the truth. While he'd been in jail, Josée had consulted a seer who had said of Kane, "Maybe his friends aren't really his friends." Josée reported this to him, believing the seer referred to the gang. She hoped he might have taken the observation to heart.

In some ways Kane's biker cronies certainly acted like friends. They had passed the hat and collected several thousand dollars, money for a vacation, they said, after his long prison ordeal. Kane accepted the cash gratefully but didn't take a holiday. Instead, says Patricia, he spent the money on his children, buying his way back into their affections.

Kane's welcome-home reception from the gang didn't extend much beyond the monetary gift. Twenty months was an eternity in the bikers' world; he had been out of sight, out of mind, and hardly missed. Besides which, in mid-November 1998, all of the gang's attention, and much of the country's, was focused on a courtroom in Montreal's austere and imposing Palais de Justice. There, Mom Boucher was on trial for the first-degree murders of the two prison guards, the main witness—indeed, the only real witness—against him being Stéphane Gagné.

Kane felt snubbed for other reasons. A matter of days after Gregory Wooley's acquittal for the Caissy killing, he was awarded his patch as a full member of the Rockers. No such honour awaited Kane after winning the first round on the MacFarlane murder charge. On the contrary, when he returned from Halifax there was no more talk of making him an official hangaround of the Nomads. He was back in the limbo of the Hells' outer orbit, not a real member, not a business associate, not anything he could name. It rankled and he shared his frustrations with Patricia, to whom he didn't pretend to be giving up the criminal life. "He often felt cheated by the gang," she says. "He said he was always going back to square one … having to prove himself over and over again."

Kane didn't discuss with Patricia the reasons for his demotion within the gang's hierarchy, but she might have guessed. Simard's testimony that he and Kane had been lovers would have fuelled abundant speculation. Few might admit to believing a stool pigeon like Simard, but it still led to whispers, ridicule, and doubts about Kane. When teased about it, Kane played along in his good-natured, jokey way. Still, he can't have been amused when senior gang members ribbed him that he'd never be a full patch because, as they said, fags weren't allowed to be Hells Angels. Blacks weren't supposed to be Hells Angels, either, Kane brooded, but there was Wooley, a full-patch Rocker, the next best thing. Kane wasn't granted even that distinction despite almost seven years of service.

His disenchantment with the gang was fostered by more than personal insult. An ugly if inevitable finale had befallen his good friends and partners-in-crime, Scott

Steinert and Donald Magnussen. In late 1997, less than a month after his lavish wedding, Steinert had phoned Magnussen to say that they were being summoned to a hastily called meeting with members of the Nomads and Montreal Hells Angels. Both seemed to have known what was coming; each cried as they said goodbye to the women in their lives. Neither was heard from again.

Various legal actions against Steinert continued in his absence. Most of his assets—including the Lavigueur property—were confiscated in proceeds-of-crime seizures. When he didn't show up for his immigration hearing he was again ordered deported to the United States. "Maybe it's the weather," pleaded his lawyer, trying to forestall the deportation order. "Maybe he was confused about the date." A few Hells knew better, and most others suspected that Steinert was well beyond the reach of immigration authorities. Magnussen's body floated to the surface of the St. Lawrence River in May 1998; he had been literally hammered to death. Scott Steinert, whose body bobbed up almost a year later, had suffered the same fate.

On November 18 the court in Halifax reconvened before Judge Cacchione to hear Roy's arguments for a stay of proceedings. Arguing against the stay Crown prosecutor Pierre Lapointe called five witnesses—Townsend, MacPherson, and Blinn, as well as two other RCMP officers who played administrative roles in the case.

Of the principal players Townsend was the first to testify. He immediately acknowledged that his notes on the photo lineup sessions were sketchy and incomplete. They didn't indicate which of the various photo lineup boards had been shown to Blinn. They did, however, suggest that Blinn had "recognized" Kane. Townsend explained his earlier testimony that Blinn had not "positively identified" either Kane or Simard by saying that he made a distinction between positive identification and simple recognition. "It wasn't a definite 'This is him,'" stated Townsend. "To me there's a difference when someone says 'This is him without a doubt' and [when] someone says, 'Well, I recognize this person here.'"

The explanation was credible, considering that in none of the photos of Kane shown to Blinn or Hutley was he wearing the same haircut as when he'd been stopped. Combined with the tape-recorded statement in which Blinn clearly recognizes Kane in a photo lineup and speaks of his changed appearance, it helped clarify Townsend's earlier fogginess.

MacPherson's testimony was much more confused. Like Townsend's, his notes were inconclusive. What's more, the photo lineup forms that were his job to fill out were of no help whatsoever. A photo lineup showing Simard had been labelled A-1; another showing Kane was A-2. MacPherson had Blinn viewing photo lineup A, which didn't exist.

From memory, MacPherson stood by his earlier testimony in which he said Blinn had vaguely recognized Simard but not made a positive identification and hadn't been formally shown a photo lineup of Kane at all. His notes, however, contradicted him. They read that Blinn "felt he recognized both Simard and Kane." His notes also suggested he was confused about which of the two men in the photo lineups was Kane and which was Simard. He wrote that Blinn selected Simard from another photo lineup labelled K, when it was Kane and not Simard who was featured in that lineup.

Finally the tape of Blinn's statement was played to him. It was the first time MacPherson had heard it since the May 1997 evening it had been made, and he had to admit that all of his earlier testimony was discredited and essentially worthless. "That tape proves that I'm wrong," MacPherson acknowledged.

Despite that admission, Cacchione persisted in believing that Blinn and Townsend were the unreliable witnesses, and in his ruling, rendered on December 18, he again lauded MacPherson. There was "a deliberate attempt by certain officers to influence the outcome of this trial by misleading the Court as to the reliability of the identification evidence," he wrote of Blinn and Townsend. "These officers displayed a propensity to change their evidence as the need arose. Had it not been for the candour of Constable MacPherson it is very likely that no one would ever have discovered that Constable Blinn had not made a positive identification of anyone."

With that, he granted Kane a stay of proceedings, effectively an assurance that unless the Crown successfully appealed his ruling, Kane would never again be tried for Robert MacFarlane's murder. The bail conditions Cacchione had imposed were lifted. Kane was free to consort with the Hells once again.

Of all the evidence to come out at the stay proceedings, the most intriguing detail had nothing to do with the photo lineups and went unmentioned in Judge Cacchione's ruling.

It came in the testimony of Cpl. Vernon Fraser, the first Halifax Mountie to contact Blinn after Simard had confessed to the MacFarlane murder. Fraser made the telephone call on April 17 on behalf of Tom Townsend, who had flown to Montreal with Gordon Barnett the day before to look into Simard's claims. Fraser tracked down Blinn in St. Louis, Missouri, where he was vacationing. Astonishingly Fraser testified that Blinn had been expecting a call about Kane and Simard. "He had followed the MacFarlane murder in the newspapers," Fraser said. "He put two and two together."

If Blinn had known or suspected that the two men he stopped in New Brunswick had gone on to Halifax and killed MacFarlane, why hadn't he reported it earlier? The explanation Blinn gave Fraser "was that [Simard's] was a different type of vehicle than what we were looking for." Indeed, Claude Blanchard had always insisted that the killers' car was a Lumina with a fin on the trunk. But then why had Blinn been expecting a phone call about Simard and Kane? His explanation made little sense.

Many suspect that Blinn didn't inform his colleagues of the two dubious young men he'd pulled over on the Trans-Canada Highway that cold February day because of the phone call he received shortly thereafter from Sgt. St. Onge. What St. Onge said to Blinn is unknown. Blinn suffered a serious head injury in the line of duty in 1999 and can't remember even talking to St. Onge; St. Onge himself has never spoken publicly about the call. It is conceivable, however, that his words to Blinn amounted to "Kane is involved in something that you can't know about but don't want to mess up. Forget the stop ever happened."

Such a conversation could have had the effect of keeping Blinn—a patrolman with a reputation for straightforward honesty—as quiet as he was.

Gaetan St. Onge did record the details of a telephone conversation he had on his first full day back at work after the New Year's holiday in 1999. That call came at just after 11 a.m. and was from Dany Kane. He was phoning, St. Onge wrote in his report of their exchange, to "find out what was going on."

St. Onge hadn't spoken to Kane for well over a year. His former source had been recently on his mind, however. Less than a month earlier, on December 11, he, Pierre Verdon, and Jean-Pierre Lévesque had submitted their rebuttal to Staff Sgt. Pierre Bolduc's excoriating evaluation of their handling of Kane. In it St. Onge described how he had learned of the existence of Bolduc's evaluation only after meeting a prosecutor who, he said, had been sent it by mistake. "So by pure chance I discovered the report of this study."

In an attempt to defend their reputations, St. Onge, Verdon, and Lévesque spent five months preparing a twenty-three-page response. Paragraph by paragraph they answered his interpretations, speculations, and allegations with denials and justifications, concluding somewhat sulkily, "This whole affair has greatly diminished our interest in again developing sources of this calibre."

Much of their memo was tit-for-tat sniping. One section, though, would be especially pertinent when Kane's stay of proceedings was announced. Addressing the question why Kane refused to flip after his arrest, or accept protective custody, St. Onge wrote, "The source is not an idiot. Very analytical and intelligent, he risks everything for everything. If he confessed and changed sides, he would go to prison. If he was found guilty, he would go to prison. If he is acquitted, he would be free and a biker hero."

In early January 1999 Kane was not exactly a biker hero, but he was a gang associate with solid credentials.

And he was on the phone. In his report of the conversation St. Onge says he made it clear to Kane that their relationship was over:

> *I took advantage of the occasion to inform him that we could not do business together for the following reasons:*
>
> • *That he would be easily identified since when he was arrested we stopped transmitting information and in resuming once he was freed that would as good as confirm his identity. Also some police with an understanding of the milieu think he is already a source....*
> • *That we have no more money and even with a new budget the RCMP would never authorize such substantial amounts*
> • *That my superiors have no more confidence in him following what had happened.*

St. Onge was following an edict issued on December 21, three days after Judge Cacchione granted Kane his stay. The order came in a stern memo from the RCMP's source coordinator in Montreal, Capt. Jacques Houle. "We can't at the RCMP have confidence in this source," he wrote. "C-2994 lied to us, hid things from us, and it would not be prudent to continue to do business with this person, whatever happens in the future; this individual must be classified as undesirable by our organization."

Houle omitted another major reason the RCMP couldn't have anything to do with Kane, namely the circumstances of his deliverance from the MacFarlane murder charge. In one sense the mistrial and stay were the perfect outcomes for the RCMP. What had seemed impossible eighteen months earlier had been accomplished: Kane was out of prison and his cover was secure. In another, it was too perfect. Senior brass knew that Kane was a walking scandal. The fact that he had taken part in a murder while serving as an RCMP informant was bad enough. His mistrial, thanks to confused and contradictory testimony by RCMP officers, made their involvement with him look particularly suspect. The headlines that might have been written were horrifying to imagine.

In the last paragraphs of his source report St. Onge suggested that the RCMP might be passing up an opportunity by blacklisting Kane. "He repeated to me that he had done hard time but said that it now played in his favour vis-à-vis his biker colleagues," St. Onge wrote. He may have been thinking that the police would soon be needing all the help they could find in their campaign against the bikers.

On November 27 Mom Boucher had been found not guilty of the prison guards' murders. The verdict hadn't been unexpected by those who followed the trial closely. Boucher's razor-sharp and ice-cold lawyer, Jacques Larochelle, had demolished Gagné in his cross-examination, chronicling his life of crime and contempt for the truth, forcing the nervous, mumbling witness to acknowledge that based on his word, the jury should have more than a reasonable doubt.

Kane referred to Boucher's trial and the money it had cost. "He said we can't imagine how much Boucher profited from that trial and the power that he has acquired," St. Onge reported. "He is considered like a god. The source said that the prison guards affair is nothing compared to what is coming."

Toward the end of their call St. Onge told Kane that he would likely be approached by other police forces to become their informant. He urged Kane to be careful. "He responded that he would deal with no one but us."

If the conversation was really as friendly as St. Onge represented it, Kane's attitude had undergone a sea change. He had felt utterly betrayed by the RCMP after his arrest in April 1997. The force for which he'd risked so much had turned around and thrown him in prison. So why did he gamely report back for work barely two weeks after his stay of proceedings was made official? Did he believe that, far from abandoning him, his Mountie friends had engineered the mistrial in order to get him back into harness again?

At the time Kane's expenses were low. He was still living at his parents', despite the lifting of his bail conditions, and Wolf Carroll and Pat Lambert were spotting him money while he regained his footing. But Kane wanted back in the game. After the Boucher acquittal the Hells felt they were on the ascendant as never before, and Kane relished the fun as well as the expected financial bonanza. Bitter he may have been about starting again at the bottom with the gang, but he was prepared to do it.

One revenue stream that Kane began pursuing more actively was debt collection. The largely cash economy of the criminal underworld presents problems as far as banking and money laundering are concerned. In those problems, however, lie opportunities. If interest can't be earned legitimately through deposits in above-board financial institutions, then it has to be earned illegitimately. That's done through loan-sharking operations, an enterprise that appealed to many of the more affluent, more established Hells Angels. Without the power to foreclose on a house or garnishee wages, these banker-bikers looked to enforcers to collect on overdue accounts. And at weekly interest rates that were often in the double digits, accounts tended to become overdue rather quickly.

Kane took on a lot of this work in the early months of 1999. Usually he found borrowers to be willing, even eager, to pay up promptly but not always capable of doing so. His job was to convince them that it was very much in their interests to sell their cars, cottages, or houses, and sooner rather than later. It was rarely necessary to threaten debtors and even rarer to resort to physical punishment. Much more compelling were their own morbid imaginings.

Occasionally, if only to keep up appearances, muscles had to be flexed and heads cracked. Shortly after returning from Halifax Kane set out to regain the body he'd had before prison. His scrawniness might have played well in the courtroom, rendering him a far cry from the pumped-up menace Blinn recalled. But it wouldn't do on the streets and in the bars where he made his collections. Kane went back on a steroid regimen himself and sold the product to others. His client base was close to hand: almost all were fellow Hells associates.

Patricia had no illusions about Kane's embarking on the straight and narrow after Halifax and didn't protest his return to gang activities. As before she didn't want to know the details. But there was change of another kind in Kane that did surprise her, one that sprang from his months in the Halifax jail where he had marked his thirtieth birthday and had time to reflect on his life.

Kane wanted to become a new man not in terms of career path but in terms of his personal relationships.

Patricia discovered the post-prison Kane, transformed physically by jail, to be transformed emotionally as well. "He wanted to be like everyone else. Do family stuff," she remembers. "It was strange at first. He was doing what I used to do, things that were my territory. All of a sudden I was with a family man."

It was all the more strange because Kane and Patricia had mutually agreed to a separation after Halifax. They had decided to take advantage of Kane's residence in St-Jean with his parents to re-examine their lingering doubts. Patricia had found Kane's jail time difficult to bear. She had learned, the hard way, about the domestic hazards of life with a criminal. Valentine's Day dinner wasn't the same with two of her boyfriend's buddies who were lucky enough not to be incarcerated. For Kane's part he sometimes thought Patricia intransigent and high maintenance and wondered whether he shouldn't find a more compliant woman, the kind most bikers chose as partners.

Even so, Patricia hardly expected the new Dany Kane to be so touchy-feely. "After Halifax our life became like *Oprah*. It was all about *communication*," Patricia says. Quite quickly she grew weary of Kane's self-help enthusiasms, bringing up issues that she regarded as long resolved or completely forgotten. "He had this recipe about how to make a relationship work and really wanted to try it out. I said, 'Maybe that kind of thing works for white folks but not for me.'"

Separation would give most men an excuse to sleep around, especially a man in the hyper-macho biker world and one who had just come out of a stretch in prison. But Kane wasn't interested revelling in the pleasures that had been denied him so long. He seemed genuinely interested in remaking himself. Patricia was convinced of it when he confessed to a slip-up some months after his Halifax detention. "I slept with the babysitter," Kane blurted out one day.

"And?"

"I *slept* with the *babysitter*."

"Was she good?" asked Patricia, feigning indifference. She knew that the best way to keep Kane—and other men—in line was to act as if she didn't care. She had erected some necessary self-protective defences with Kane, but she could not help being moved by his contrition.

Kane's self-improvement kick extended to etiquette and clothes. Patricia found herself instructing him in the fundamentals of civilized conduct, how to greet every person individually when entering a room, what to bring for the hostess of a dinner party or barbecue, what to wear and when to wear it. His heightened appreciation of clothes led to shopping trips in the Gay Village where Patricia's favourite menswear stores were located. On these excursions her unspoken questions about Kane's sexual orientation were quelled. If Kane wasn't exactly homophobic, she found him at least homo-fearful. When trying on a garment Kane would resist any attempts by the store clerk to groom him; when strolling along Ste-Catherine Street he would squeeze her hand extra-tight when they passed a male couple.

If Simard had lied about his relationship with Kane, he must also have lied about Kane's involvement in the MacFarlane murder, Patricia reasoned. But Kane's new emotional transparency and eagerness to communicate stopped short of confessing his more serious criminal acts. He said that the RCMP and Simard had teamed up to frame him and that they had been undone by their own crooked scheme. "I asked him, when he and I were alone," Patricia remembers, "'Just whisper in my ear. It's just between you and me.' But he said 'Trust me, I'm not a killer,' and I went with it."

Kane was back in the milieu with her acquiescence, but she wasn't happy about his renewed appetite for steroids. The drugs made him edgier, more aggressive, and more prone to irrational behaviour. And for a couple who rated sex a high priority, steroids had an ironic effect: they might make a man look more virile, but they reduced libido and impeded performance.

There was another, more fundamental, reason for Patricia's wariness. In the early months of 1999 they were resolving their differences and once more speaking of a future together. For Kane that future included having a millennial child with Patricia, a fantasy he had shared with her while he was in prison. Kane's steroid consumption gave her qualms, but in the spring of 1999 she agreed to the idea, in part because of all that persuasive communication Kane revelled in.

He implicitly acknowledged his failings as a father to the children he'd had with Josée when he told Patricia, as he frequently did, that things would be different with their child. He would do it right this time: be the father that he hadn't been to Benjamin, Nathalie, and Guillaume; be the parent that he himself, split between his mother and father and his aunt and uncle, had never experienced. He'd be involved and active, a real presence playing a significant role.

They had a few cursory conversations about setting up house together and then, in late spring, Kane had taken her to see the home in St-Luc on the banks of the river L'Acadie. At $250,000, it was overpriced in the sluggish real estate market, but with the help of a crooked real estate broker and the broker's connections to a local bank

Kane got a mortgage for all but $3,692.50 of the asking price. The house wasn't in Kane's name, of course; in the age of proceeds of crime laws, that's not the biker way. Rather, Kane registered it in the names of Dominique and Serge Tremblay, an acquaintance who sometimes served as a *prêt-nom*.

Eager to get out from under his parents' roof Kane was in the new house by July. Patricia followed in September but spent the summer weekends and occasional week-nights with him there. It was during one of these visits that she tried a home-testing kit to see if she was pregnant. When the plastic wand showed the undeniable blue of a positive result Kane could not contain himself. He reached for the phone to call his friends and family. There would be no waiting for the first trimester to pass safely.

Around this time Kane was given even more welcome news: he would at last receive his patch as a full-fledged Rocker. The honour lost some lustre with the knowledge that the gang was on a major recruiting drive to expand its numbers, with plans to subdivide into various chapters in the Montreal area. It seemed there was a new member patched at every second gang meeting.

Still, once he was finally *patché* Kane felt a surge of pride and immense relief. It proved he was moving up, that he did really have the right stuff. The fact that he had brought a traitor into the gang, one who had exposed him to endless ridicule as well, wasn't going to curse his biker career forever. Patricia remembers having to pretend to be as happy as Kane. It wasn't that she didn't want him to become a full member of the Rockers; it was just that she didn't understand its significance.

"Does it actually pay to be a Rocker?" she asked.

"No, it costs money," said Kane, referring to the 10 percent tithe of their criminal earnings and the monthly minimum, now set at $500.

"Then why be a member?"

For the status and power, Kane explained. "It opens doors and people respect you for it."

With a baby on the way, a spacious new home, and a defined position in an expanding, highly profitable business, Kane had all the trappings of a suburban family man. The missing element was a dependable, steady source of income. The patch, no matter how coveted, couldn't deliver that. Kane knew full well that while there were multimillionaire bikers in Quebec, there were others who didn't know where next month's rent, let alone their monthly gang membership fees, were coming from.

Strong-arming deeply indebted schmoes for a percentage and dealing minor-league quantities of coke and steroids brought in respectable money but not enough for Kane. Enlarging those operations was not an option either, even with the new patch. The entire city, indeed the whole province, seemed to be spoken for by men more senior to him in the Hells organization. Other spheres were equally competitive or demanded a skill set that he didn't possess. Kane knew nothing about truck hijacking, fraudulent telemarketing, or hydroponic marijuana growing, all popular among other members and associates of the gang.

So with summer winding down and the corn high in the fields around St-Luc, a reminder that after the season of plenty leaner times lay ahead, Kane decided to return to a familiar enterprise. One that didn't require an investment of cash that he, a terrible financial manager, couldn't muster. One that brought in steady money and allowed him to live the life he desired. One that afforded much greater thrills than simply being a small cog in the criminal machinery with questionable prospects for advancement. Kane decided to go back into the informant business.

19

IN THE
OLD JOB

The exact circumstances surrounding Kane's reprise of his informer role are murky. Again, there's an official story that is highly questionable and widely doubted.

According to it, Montreal police detective Benoît Roberge was sitting in his office in mid-August 1999, lamenting the spotty and unreliable intelligence his sources were providing him. He needed an informant for his unit as good as Dany Kane had been for his RCMP pals, Pierre Verdon and Gaetan St. Onge. Roberge apparently pondered for a while and then, like the simple Zen resolution that solves a complex problem, realized that only one person could be the new Kane: the old Kane.

The Montreal police, including Roberge, had pulled out of Carcajou while Kane was in prison in Halifax pointing to a six-month lull in biker hostilities as evidence that peace had been restored to the streets of the city. In reality few people doubted that the real reason for their withdrawal was the poisonous mistrust between the SQ, the SPCUM, and the RCMP representatives within Carcajou.

But after the not-guilty verdict in the prison guards murder case and Mom Boucher apparently invincible, the Hells had once more gone on the offensive against not only what remained of the Rock Machine and the Alliance but the justice system as well. In April bombs had been discovered outside five police stations around Montreal. Par for the biker course, their munitions man had installed dud detonators, and the bombs would never have exploded. Still, the message was chilling and seemed to support Kane's New Year's warning to St. Onge that worse was to come.

Now, however, the police had a new arrow in their quiver in the form of Bill C-95, the anti-gang legislation that was set in motion by the bombing death of young Daniel Desrochers in August 1995. The law made its way through Parliament in 1997, and prosecutors were keen to test it, despite their reservations that the burden of proof to establish membership in a criminal organization was too onerous.

In mid-1999, after the police station bombs, the various police forces in Quebec made another attempt to work together when they set up a series of Escouades Régionales Mixtes (ERMs), regional task forces. Roberge, the top biker cop on the Montreal force, was assigned to Montreal's ERM just as he had been assigned to Carcajou.

Not long after he joined the squad Roberge says he telephoned Kane's parents' home *"sous l'anonymat"*—without saying who he was—and left a message that he was looking for their son. His mother apparently called right back and gave Roberge her son's number without hesitation.

There are many—other police officers, bikers, and biker lawyers—who doubt this version of events, and not simply because Gemma Kane has no recollection of Roberge's message. (In any event she says she would have given Roberge's number to Dany and left it to him to return the call or not.) They feel that Kane's ties with his police investigator friends were never entirely severed, and they view the eight months after Halifax as a cooling-off period during which Kane re-established himself with the gang and police authorities got over their aversion to relations with a killer. They suggest that even if there was no official contact between Verdon and St. Onge and Kane during that time, there were almost certainly occasional chats.

They also see it as no accident that Roberge came to be Kane's handler. Of all the investigators in Carcajou he was closest to Verdon and St. Onge. He had very likely met Kane long before he was arrested and imprisoned in Halifax and was fully aware that the boyish-looking biker was the RCMP's C-2994. The police in this group contend that more often than not when Verdon or St. Onge scribbled *"Carcajou avisé"* beside important pieces of information in their source reports, it meant nothing more than that Verdon had whispered the details across his desk to Roberge. One senior SQ Carcajou employee thinks that just as Kane was a coded source for Verdon, Verdon was a coded source for Roberge, transmitting intelligence that largely originated with Kane. These skeptics compare the official August commencement of the Roberge-Kane relationship to the day that a secretly trysting couple decides it's acceptable to go public. The difference, of course, is that this relationship was still secret; only Roberge's superiors would judge its acceptability.

If this was indeed the way things transpired, Kane was soon doing his best to woo the ERM brass. During his first documented phone call with Roberge on Wednesday, August 18, he was apparently receptive, and they agreed to meet the following Monday. Before that rendezvous took place, Kane phoned Roberge at eight-thirty on

Saturday morning to tell him that the Rockers had just tried to whack one of their own, Stephen Falls, the man Danièle Roy had defended in the Caissy murder trial.

Kane didn't give Roberge the back story to the attempted hit. He didn't reveal that just days before he had been with Falls and Wolf Carroll in Nova Scotia, conducting surveillance on Randy Mersereau, a former Hells Angel turned independent dealer, whom Carroll had decided to eliminate. He didn't explain how Falls had come to lose favour with the gang. But this nugget of information, this simple phone call, signalled that Kane was eager to return to work and not necessarily intent on squeezing money out of the police at every turn. The gesture went some distance in rehabilitating Kane's reputation with Roberge's superiors.

On August 23, once again in a hotel room in Montreal's peaceful, largely anglophone West Island— *terra incognita* to most of Montreal's bikers—Kane spent four hours with Roberge and Sgt. Robert Pigeon, an SQ investigator with long experience in organized crime. Kane ran through the membership of the Nomads and the Rockers, outlining not only their criminal activities but whom they did business with and how long they had been involved in the milieu.

He described in detail the Rockers' tithing system and the monthly meetings—*les messes* or masses—at which the 10 percent was collected. A Nomad was always present to oversee the meetings, the location and time of which were never known until the night before when strikers for the gang were dispatched to deliver the details to all the members. Where the proceeds from the tithing went beyond the club's minimal operating expenses, lawyers' bills and the cost of the occasional party, Kane didn't know.

He had, however, learned why Stephen Falls, nick-named Sandman, had been targeted: he owed the gang too much money. Kane also knew why Claude Grégoire McCarter, his friend from St-Jean, had been killed in the summer of 1997. The Rockers had become suspicious when McCarter consistently escaped arrest despite a police crackdown on the baseball team, of which he was a member. They concluded he had to be an informant. "He was also known as a thief," Kane added.

These tantalizing goods displayed, Kane had a pro-posal for Roberge and Pigeon. Just as he had moved up the biker ranks he was prepared to climb a rung in the informant business, he told them. Now he would become an *agent source,* another term for which no adequate English equivalent exists. Rather than simply gathering intelligence and relaying it to police, he would wear a lis-tening device, a wire, to collect physical evidence, and after arrests were made and charges brought he would tes-tify in court against his former brothers. Of course, Kane stipulated, this service wouldn't come cheap. First he wanted police to pay all the expenses attached to his lifestyle as a full-patch Rocker. In addition he wanted a weekly salary. Kane claimed to be bringing in about $4000 a week from criminal activities, and he suggested he expected that and more from them. He insisted too on a major payout at the end of the investigation in which he was involved. He didn't name a figure but implied he was thinking in the millions. Beyond financial recompense, he expected a new identity and relocation to western Canada or the United States, plus help in learning a trade and finding a regular job. Finally, he wanted them to ensure that he would have the right to carry a handgun for his own protection when it was all over.

Roberge and Pigeon were duly impressed, at least with Kane's overview of the Hells Angels organization in Quebec. "A very nice look at their activities and associations," Roberge wrote. Fifteen pages of notes on the subject—half in Roberge's tight little scribble, half in Pigeon's looping hand—immediately went upstairs to senior ERM officers in an effort to convince them that Kane, however tainted, was essential. Of Kane's demands for compensation, Roberge and Pigeon said nothing; it seems they kept those five pages of financial and other details to themselves.

Kane phoned Roberge with more biker tidbits the next day and the day after met with Roberge and Pigeon for another two hours. This session was more business oriented; they discussed what the police wanted from Kane and what he wanted from them. Whether Kane cited precise numbers is unclear. Regardless, Roberge and Pigeon said it wasn't up to them to determine his remuneration. His contract would have to be negotiated with ERM's money men. Kane wouldn't have pushed it; he knew that his first task was to make himself indispensable, and he agreed to work for what he considered a pittance—$750 a week plus certain expenses.

If Roberge's notes are accurate, no monies would be paid to Kane for at least two weeks, yet he continued to be generously forthcoming. He told his new handlers about the Rockers' plans for expansion through associations with the east end's Pelletier family, the southwest's Dubois clan, and "les Italiens." One of Kane's chores in this drive was to find the gang a clubhouse on the South Shore, as well as order customized gang sweatshirts and jewellery.

The first task he shared with Francis Boucher, Mom Boucher's twenty-four-year-old son and heir apparent. To

prove himself worthy of promotion from his current status as a Rocker to full-patch Hells Angel, Francis had to
diversify and enlarge the organization's business. His
chosen field was "chemicals," man-made drugs like PCP,
LSD, and various types of amphetamines. It was an industry the Hells had long neglected and so was still controlled by the otherwise much-reduced Rock Machine.
Francis suggested to Kane that he become a partner in the
enterprise with him and his father, a proposition that
might have been a show of faith in the new Rocker or an
attempt to exploit him.

Another business opportunity was offered by Kane's
old patrons Wolf Carroll and Walter Stadnick. Along with
Donald "Pup" Stockford, they were preparing for another
assault on the bastion of Ontario and wanted Kane's help
in advancing down the 401. First they'd work to control
Kingston and Belleville; ultimately, Toronto would be
theirs.

Kane also confirmed to his handlers what he'd long
ago suggested to his RCMP contacts: that Walter Stadnick
was responsible for the demise of Steinert and
Magnussen. The accumulation of grievances had become
intolerable: the pair wanted too much, too soon; their
"appetites" were too big; they stepped on too many of the
senior gang members' toes; they lacked respect.

Kane's information was much like the intelligence he'd
provided to the RCMP. Most of it could be classified as
nothing more than "nice to know" by a hard-ass superior.
But Roberge and Pigeon had learned from the mistakes of
St. Onge and Verdon. They would not allow Kane to pull
them into the same quagmires that had almost sunk their
RCMP colleagues. This was made clear in the last week
of September when Kane was given a familiar assignment

by the gang: kill a Nova Scotia drug dealer who was causing grief to the Hells Angels and their friends.

After the Hells' botched attempt on his life, Stephen Falls had apparently allied himself with their remaining enemies. In Montreal it was the Rock Machine and elements of the West End Gang; in Nova Scotia it was Randy Mersereau and his associates. At home the Quebec Nomads and Rockers took Falls's defection very seriously. He knew their addresses, their haunts, and their routines. Consequently, underlings were assigned to guard the Nomads around the clock, even while they slept, and were told not to skimp on the firepower they packed.

The extra protection measures didn't prevent a near fatal attack on the wife of Denis Houle, who despite his nickname, "Pas Fiable"—Untrustworthy—was considered the number-two man in the Nomads behind Mom Boucher. His thirty-two-year-old wife, Sandra Gloutney, was leaving their luxury home in the lower Laurentians early in the morning of Monday, September 20, 1999, when an assailant hidden in the woods fired several times at her car with a semi-automatic rifle. One bullet struck her shoulder, another missed her head by centimetres. Gloutney had the right reaction: she hit the gas, but then lost control of Houle's brand-new metallic blue Corvette and flipped it when she hit the ditch. Houle himself wasn't at home. The word was he was off on a hunting trip. Wolf Carroll, who lived nearby and had appeared on the scene within minutes of the incident, wearing a baseball cap reading "Hells Angels—Nomads," told Kane that Houle was really in Europe with a mistress.

Falls, predictably, was blamed for the attack, and Kane reported that the *"H.A. veut réagir"*—the Hells wanted revenge. Two days later Kane reported that Carroll had asked him to go to Halifax to kill Randy Mersereau. Not only was Mersereau's growing drug business costing the Hells, and especially Carroll, dearly in Halifax, but the gang was convinced he was working with the Rock Machine. "The H.A. think that Randy is financing the R.M.," Kane reported. "The H.A. know that Falls is on vacation paid for by Randy."

There was talk that Mersereau had taken out contracts on Carroll and Mom Boucher as well as the president of the Hells' Halifax chapter, Mike McCrea, justification enough for his death. That he, like Falls, had once been a fellow Hells Angel and even served time for the gang after the Lennoxville massacre just made things worse. Carroll decided it was time to take out his former friend from the 13th Tribe. He told Kane to be prepared to stay as long as three weeks; they wouldn't be back until the job was done.

"The source doesn't know what he will do exactly, but Randy and his main associates must be eliminated," Roberge noted. "Afterwards the Rockers and the Scorpions"—a small gang of street dealers based in Montreal's Gay Village—"would have the job of trashing the bars and hangouts of Randy's gang."

Kane knew he couldn't simply tell Carroll he'd rather not participate and pass on the job without some repercussions. However, when he informed his handlers of the plot, there was no indication that he appealed to them for a way out of it. Perhaps this was an example of Kane's often surprising and unexpected candour. But if he had been so transparent with his RCMP handlers—informing them of his assignment to kill MacFarlane, for example—the details never appeared in their source reports, and they hadn't tried to stop him. Roberge wrote everything down. Then he put together a plan to prevent Mersereau's killing. The target would not be warned; that could very well blow Kane's cover if Carroll got wind of a tipoff. Rather, it had to look like a case of pure serendipity.

At 5 a.m. on Friday, September 24, Kane picked up Wolf Carroll at his downtown pied-à-terre. Soon the two bikers were driving east toward the dawn in a green GM Alero Kane had rented the day previous. Before calling for Carroll, he'd given Roberge the make, colour, and licence plate of the car.

On the road Carroll was his usual chatty self. He confided to Kane that neither he, Stadnick, nor Stockford had much time for Guillaume "Mimo" Serra, an up-and-comer in the gang. Serra was just into money and power, Carroll complained. It was the gripe of a veteran Hells Angel, one that was heard about many of the younger members. Some of these upstarts weren't even into motorcycles, Carroll lamented. But Boucher and Serra were close, so what were the traditionalists to do?

On the subject of Boucher, Carroll confided that Mom wasn't much of a businessman. A strong leader, sure, but he was lucky to have Normand "Biff" Hamel as a partner. The two had been friends from their days in the SS and had received their full Hells Angels colours on the same day in May 1987—a reward, police believed, for a hit carried out a few days earlier. Hamel, however, had always shied away from the limelight that so attracted Boucher, concentrating instead on business. Carroll also told Kane that the 10 percent tithe that the Rockers passed up to the Nomads was beginning to form a substantial pile of cash; something in the neighbourhood of $2 million sat in the club's coffers.

Having started out early, the bikers were making good time. Kane left Quebec City in his rear-view mirror before most of the city's bureaucrats had arrived at the office.

Two hours later they were close to the highway divide where Maritimes-bound traffic turns south, away from the St. Lawrence, and on toward Edmundston, New Brunswick. Their time was helped by highway officers of the SQ, who, applying pressure in contract negotiations, were said to be ignoring speeders on the province's roads. Or so the radio reported.

Not far from Rivière-du-Loup, Kane and Carroll saw the flashing lights of an SQ patrol car behind them. They pulled over. The patrolman chatted with them for a while, then checked the trunk. There the officer found the silencer-equipped machine pistol that Carroll had been carrying ever since Houle's wife had been shot, plus a fully loaded .38. Just as Kane had told Roberge he would.

Carroll and Kane spent the weekend in jail in Rivière-du-Loup. There they were surprised to learn that the day before they set out to kill Mersereau, someone else had almost beat them to it. A large bomb had devastated the used car dealership that Mersereau had opened in Bible Hill, Nova Scotia, just six weeks earlier. Seven people, including Mersereau, were injured, two seriously. One man was blown out of his shoes and out of the building. So far, no one was willing to cooperate with the police investigation.

In jail Carroll kept chatting, revealing to Kane and thus the ERM more about the Nomads' inner workings. He spoke of Michel Rose, an established drug importer before he became a Hells Angel, who gave each member of the Nomads ten kilograms of hash when he was given his patch the previous June. "Mike is well regarded," Carroll told Kane. "He makes a lot of money for the H.A."

Carroll described a consortium within the Nomads of six bikers—Boucher, Houle, Hamel, Rose, Gilles "Trooper" Mathieu, and André Chouinard. He didn't give it a name, though it would later be widely known as "la table." This was where the real money resided, Carroll said. These were the men who, as the Hells Angels moved more heavily into drug importation and solidified a vertically integrated empire, sat at the top of the food chain. They were the ones who would establish relationships with Colombian organized crime groups, among others, to bring in literally tonnes of cocaine. Their position would be all the more lucrative when the Nomads fulfilled their intention of establishing a cross-country monopoly and obliged all other chapters to source their supplies from them.

Carroll also gave Kane something of a pep talk. If he really wanted to rise above the Rockers and become a full Hells Angel—with its elite chapter, no less—he should approach the Nomads individually, tell them about his dream, and make it clear he wanted to become a hangaround. All the Nomads liked him a lot, Wolf told his underling.

Kane appreciated Wolf's confidence, but he knew this not to be true; Denis Houle had always been wary of him for reasons he couldn't explain. Houle, described by an acquaintance as "the most animal" of Quebec's Hells Angels, would fall silent whenever Kane was within hearing distance and had told others of his visceral distrust of him. With Kane himself, he made no pretence of civility. He regularly instructed him to have his Hells Angels tattoos removed. Kane wasn't a full member, let alone a striker, and so wasn't entitled to wear them, according to the gang's rules.

On Monday morning Kane and Carroll were released on just $1000 bail, an amount that surprised the two Rocker colleagues who had been dispatched to Rivière-du-Loup with $10,000 cash to buy their buddies' freedom.

Carroll's wife and mother-in-law drove up to take him home; Kane took care of the Alero.

Back in Montreal Kane continued to deliver a steady stream of information. The Rockers were "off balance" because of police pressure and the Falls affair. Normand Robitaille, a newly initiated Nomad who had the job of overseeing the Rockers, told the gang members not to wear their colours or carry guns. They were to leave the weaponry in the hands of the strikers and hangarounds. The Halifax president, Mike McCrea, had claimed responsibility for the Bible Hill bombing and reported that since it hadn't accomplished its purpose, a team of hit men was now on the trail of Randy Mersereau.

Much of the time Kane spent with his ERM handlers was consumed by negotiations over the fine points of his *agent source* deal. He encountered a much more rigorous process than had been the case with the RCMP. At one of his first meetings in early September, Kane gave eight pages of personal details, including the names and addresses of all of his family members, to Pigeon. By the end of the month, these had been scrutinized by the senior officers who were to decide whether or not to make Kane a formal offer. Various sessions—essentially a series of job interviews—were also scheduled, in preparation for which Kane received extensive coaching from Roberge and Pigeon.

At the first of these on September 30, Kane met with Capt. Bruno Beaulieu and Sgt. Robert Dubé of the SQ's Service de protection des témoins, the Witness Protection Service, the division responsible for vetting and taking care of informants and *agents source*. It was an informal, get-acquainted meeting, with Beaulieu and Dubé explaining the role of the SPT and how it functioned. They described how they evaluated potential *agents source* and—with an eye to containing Kane's expectations—how they determined what they were paid. For his part Kane gave a broad outline of what he was after. He knew it wasn't the moment for hard bargaining, but it wouldn't hurt to prepare the ground. All he wanted, he said, was enough money to buy a house, a bit of wooded property and a lot of peace in a place like Jamaica for him and his family—his extended family, including not just Patricia and the children but his parents, his sisters and their families, and Josée as well.

Kane was asked for a summary of his financial circumstances, which he portrayed as substantially rosier than they were. He was earning about $5000 a week, he now claimed, and had fixed expenses of about $3500 a month. He said he had a portfolio of high-tech stocks worth over $2.5 million. As the session drew to a close, he raised a final item, which he requested be "off the record": might it be possible for a side agreement to be negotiated, one that would never be revealed in court, that would guarantee him an extra $1 million? Beaulieu told him to forget it.

The next meeting was with Roberge and Pigeon's boss in the ERM, Capt. Pierre Lebeau. According to notes taken, he made it clear that the SQ was still wary of a repeat of what had happened under St. Onge and Verdon. Lebeau explained that as an *agent source,* Kane could commit only crimes that had been pre-authorized by his handlers. In an eloquent explanation of the biker credo, Kane said that would be very difficult.

"The Rockers have to be respected and demonstrate that they have power," Roberge quoted him as saying. "A member can't allow himself to be given lip or insulted. If that happens, he has to respond immediately, exact revenge, never lose face. If someone insults a Rocker, a Hells, or what they represent, that person must be punished and brutally so, to ensure that the whole world is scared of bikers. It's all based on intimidation."

At a second meeting with Beaulieu, Kane was introduced to SPT officer Sgt. Yvon Drouin. This session was expected to lead to a deal, and for the first hour they discussed a new identity for Kane and how he might otherwise be protected. Then they turned to money. The SQ offered $500 a week and a $1 million payoff at the end. Kane replied that he would not budge below $2 million. Beaulieu and Drouin explained that they were authorized to offer a sum that would "allow [the informant] to resume living a normal life, not a life of luxury comparable to his criminal life." Kane wasn't impressed, and the three-hour session ended uncomfortably with his lengthy and derisive rant on the quality of the SQ in general and the force's diminished credibility since an evidence-tampering scandal several years earlier.

Another negotiating session was scheduled for the next evening, October 14, and Kane went into it hoping to convince the SQ that it couldn't afford not to come to terms. "The Hells Angels are on top everywhere. Canada belongs to them, as does the whole world," Drouin quoted him. "They don't ask permission from anyone. It's the others who ask their permission. It's like opium. The Hells aren't interested in opium. The Chinese are. But if the Hells became interested in opium the Chinese would have to give it to them."

The strategy didn't succeed. The meeting lasted little more than an hour since Kane had to rush off to a gang supper where he was to deliver the patches for two new members, and the SQ bosses decided that they could live without Kane as an *agent source*. It was partly a question of budget—at the end of the year money was tight—and partly a question of confidence in Kane. For the time being the SQ said thanks but no thanks.

The failure to reach a larger deal didn't end Kane's informant relationship with Roberge and Gaétan Legault, a young SQ investigator who had taken over from Pigeon as his force's handler on the Kane file. For $750 a week, the ERM continued to buy some very useful intelligence.

Shortly after Stéphane Gagné had flipped and agreed to testify against Mom Boucher, his two accomplices in the prison guard murders, André "Toots" Tousignant and Paul "Fonfon'" Fontaine, had disappeared. Toots, a one-time spokesman for the Hells organization who maintained with a straight face that he made thousands a week with a network of peanut-dispensing machines, was later found charred and without the tips of his fingers in a forest a hundred kilometres from Montreal. It was believed that Boucher had ordered his execution to prevent him from corroborating Gagné's version of events; Fonfon had probably met a similar end. Kane reported otherwise. Fontaine was alive and well and had been made a Nomad for his services. The Hells, Kane added, were hoping to negotiate a deal with police whereby Fonfon would plead guilty to the guard's murder and be eligible for parole after ten years.

Kane also had information from out east. Mike McCrea, perhaps prompted by the example of the Rockers in Montreal, wanted to set up his own puppet gang for the Halifax Hells. They'd be based in Cape Breton "in a city with a bizarre name like Ingonish," Roberge noted. "The new club would have about twenty or twenty-two members, including some of Scottish origins." Whether

McCrea had a sense of history or had been inspired by Mel Gibson's *Braveheart,* his choice of name for the gang was oddly dignified. They were to be known as the Highlanders.

On November 3 Kane reported that Randy Mersereau had finally been whacked, on Halloween, in fact. The assassins had done an impeccable job, killing Mersereau with a 9 mm silencer-equipped machine pistol, like Carroll's, and burying the gun with him. "They didn't leave a trail or a clue," said Kane. "Randy just disappeared." For their efforts, the killers were immediately made prospects for the Halifax Hells Angels. It would be a month before Mersereau's family reported him officially missing.

Locally the Rockers had been given a stern lecture at a recent "mass" on how they should conduct their financial affairs. To keep the authorities at bay they were told to "make themselves legit" by filing their tax returns, "even going back a few years, to justify their standards of living. To be legal, show that they have jobs or own companies." Carroll was being investigated by tax officials, and the Rockers were told to prepare for their own audits. The instructions were to "do business with accountants, financial managers, or any professional to make yourselves legal," Kane said. The Rockers were also cautioned about maintaining their reputations within the criminal community. They were told to fulfil their obligations or face serious consequences. "If a member doesn't pay his debt to the Italians, the West End Gang or whoever, he'll be kicked out of the Rockers," Kane reported.

Recent initiates to the Rockers were required to submit lists of their immediate family members—children, parents, spouses, brothers and sisters—along with dates of birth, drivers' licence details, and social insurance numbers.

These weren't for the Rockers' benefits plan. "All of this is to discourage members from becoming rats." In other news, old friend Pat Lambert, who had cut much of his contact with the gang while Kane was in prison, made a brief reappearance. Apparently he had moved into the hydroponic marijuana business. Stephen Falls had been located in Costa Rica; "a team would be put on his case."

Overall, however, Kane's information grew sparser as winter closed in. There were fewer phone calls to his handlers and less frequent meetings. Kane did the minimum for his $750 weekly pay, rather than exceed expectations as before. After little more than three months, it seemed the source was drying up.

In reality, Kane was falling into a bleak depression.

20

DARK DAYS
AND A DONE DEAL

In late fall and into December of 1999, Kane became increasingly glum and uncommunicative. After a meeting with Benoît Roberge and Gaétan Legault on December 14—a meeting that moved them no closer to agreement on his terms for becoming an *agent source*—Kane dropped out of touch completely for more than three weeks. He was equally unsociable with the gang and with his family, holed up in the house, refusing to see or talk to anyone. He slept, watched television distractedly, or just sat around. Even Patricia heard little more than grunts and monosyllables from him. When calls came in she would answer and convey the message that Dany was fine, he just didn't feel like chatting.

As the days passed, members of the Rockers became suspicious of Kane's silence, as well as his absence from the gym and the gang's usual haunts. He wasn't attending the gang's meetings or paying the 10 percent tithe. A junior member was dispatched to the house in St-Luc. Patricia answered the door and repeated what she'd told everyone else: Kane was alive and well, but he didn't want visitors.

"Sorry," said the biker, "I'm not allowed to leave until I see him with my own eyes."

Patricia conferred with Kane for a minute or two. He consented to show his face but volunteered no more than that. It was enough for the gang, and Kane was left alone to get over his depression.

The condition was endemic to the family, according to Patricia. "You couldn't be a Kane and not be depressed sometime or other." But she could only guess at the reasons for the bout that afflicted him throughout that holiday season.

The family itself could have been a source of distress. Proximity to his parents and sisters had been one of the attractions of the St-Luc house, but Kane began questioning the wisdom of the decision not long after he and Patricia settled in. His parents often dropped by uninvited—"snooping," to use Patricia's word—and they became an even greater drain on Kane's finances. For years he had helped them out financially in various ways; once he was in St-Luc, he and his wallet were closer to hand. There was the lease on a new Volkswagen Beetle for his mother, plus the $100 a week he gave her to ferry Benjamin, now living with his parents full time, to and from school. Gemma charged her son for babysitting services, not something that was expected when her other grandchildren needed minding, and Jean-Paul had been hired to help with renovation work on the house. Kane understood that being paid for such favours allowed his parents to accept his handouts while maintaining their self-respect; nonetheless, the situation gnawed at him.

His relationship with his parents, in particular his mother, was inevitably complicated by his childhood exile to the home of his aunt and uncle. Years later he still felt himself cast out and haunted by what he had done to deserve it. "Why me?" Patricia remembers Kane's asking over and over. There were no answers that satisfied him, and he nursed a simmering resentment against Gemma, fed by a suspicion that she was primarily interested in his money. This was accompanied by a feeling of pity toward the easygoing, though sometimes spineless, Jean-Paul, for whom Kane felt real affection but who didn't fit his vision of a manly role model.

There were other factors that could have contributed to Kane's sense of despair. After the first rush of gratitude for his Rocker colours, he may have wondered if the patch wasn't small compensation for his years of service to the gang. More recent arrivals had enjoyed more stellar careers—Guillaume Serra, to name one—and the Rockers seemed willing to recruit anyone for the sake of expanding their numbers and increasing their tithe revenues. Kane's disenchantment with the gang was evident as early as October, when he told his handlers that he was contemplating an application for hangaround status not only with the Nomads but with the Halifax Hells Angels as well. If he made overtures to the Hells Angels chapters, there had been no response by mid-December, the last contact with Roberge and Legault before the holidays.

Their debriefing sessions resumed in early January and followed the desultory course of those in December. In his notes for the January 14 session, the third of the new year, Roberge observed that "the source is going through a phase where he has no motivation and is questioning things on the personal front." In truth the dark cloud over Kane had already begun to lift. The forced jollity of the Christmas season was behind him, and every day was a little longer and brighter than the one before. Then, too, the simple fact that he was still alive in mid-January likely lifted his spirits.

In early December the Hells Angels and associated bikers from across the country had congregated in a Sherbrooke hotel to celebrate the gang's twenty-second anniversary in Canada. Two police biker specialists—one from the Sûreté du Québec, the other from the Ontario Provincial Police—took rooms in the same hotel as a show of defiance, a calculated gesture intended to send the message that the Hells Angels' every move was being watched. It proved to be a foolish and costly bit of bravado.

While the cops were having breakfast one morning two members of the Scorpions broke into one officer's room and grabbed his laptop. The bikers were sure the computer belonged to the SQ man, Guy Ouellette, Canada's leading police expert on criminal bikers. That's what Kane had reported to his handlers on December 7. (Authorities have always maintained it was the OPP investigator's computer.) Kane must have wondered what information might be found in the computer about him. He knew that the police were sometimes sloppy. Although his name was never mentioned in reports—he was always referred to as "the source" or as IN-3683, the informant number ERM had assigned him—some of the bikers would have been able to identify him by the information he was providing.

By mid-January, however, there had been no attempt made on his life and no indication that he was under suspicion. If his work for the police was to be discovered by the bikers, it didn't look as if it would be thanks to the stolen laptop. Kane slowly emerged from his depression and the house in St-Luc.

Not all was well between Kane and the gang, however. He had missed paying his tithe for two months running and had reneged on other obligations while in seclusion. It was a bad time to run afoul of the Rockers leadership. They realized that the gang's hasty expansion had led to a loss of discipline among the membership, and they intended to restore order. In early January one member was kicked out for owing too much money. A few days later two more, including Mom Boucher's top flunky, were suspended for neglecting to pick up two B.C. Hells Angels at the airport as instructed. A fourth member lost his patch when his cocaine habit got out of hand. Kane knew that he was on the bubble and could be the next to go.

Roberge and Legault may have been aware of his tenuous position; it is almost certain that the SQ's Witness Protection Service was not. It wouldn't have been in Kane's negotiating interest—or that of Roberge and Legault who very much wanted Kane promoted to *agent source*—to admit as much. If Kane lost his patch, he would lose access to the *messes* and the intelligence he gathered there. At best he would be back to doing watch, standing in hotel corridors or on the sidewalk outside restaurants, holding the more senior members' handguns so that if there was a bust, Kane would take the fall.

Unaware that he was on the verge of demotion, the brass had returned to the idea of engaging Kane as an *agent source*. It was a new year with a new budget, and Kane had provided insight into the activities of the Hells organization that the ERM wasn't getting anywhere else. As of early January almost every meeting Kane had with his handlers included some conversation about his *agent source* potential. By the twentieth, he was ready for another encounter with Captain Beaulieu and Sergeant Drouin of the Witness Protection Service. Again Kane said he wouldn't budge below $2 million, on top of which he wanted a car and a house and $5000 a week for the duration of any legal procedures in which he was expected to testify. The SQ offered a total payout of not more than $1.4 million, plus $2000 a week. Kane rejected the SQ's offer and, as a negotiating gambit, said he was thinking of quitting the biker business altogether and handing in his patch to Pierre Provencher in the next day or two. Applying some pressure of his own on his superiors, Roberge counselled Kane to do just that.

The threat wasn't fulfilled; a week later Kane met again with Legault for more *agent source* discussions, and he was given $1000 to cover his missed tithes. "His criminal earnings are at present insufficient," it was noted. "The source missed the last two *messes* because of financial difficulties."

Two weeks after that, Kane had another session with Beaulieu and Drouin, at which he upped his demands substantially. Now he was asking for a tax-free payout of $10 million and a weekly salary of $10,000, as well as unspecified tax-free amounts for his parents and sisters. He wanted the firearm permit, an official pardon for past crimes, and sensitive security for the denouement of his work for the police, the busts, and the ensuing trials—no *"gros show."* When the raids came down, Kane said he didn't want uniformed police spiriting his family into protective custody, possibly traumatizing his children. "At the same time I want there to be a procedure in place so that their studies don't suffer. Everything in a climate of calm and not of war."

It was now the SQ's turn to reject a proposal, though they stood by their earlier offer of a $1.4 million payout and $2000 a week. They remained open to further talks at more realistic levels.

Kane came down to earth the next day when, at the Rockers *messe,* he was told that he had been suspended from the gang. "Not enough watches or availability," went

the explanation. "Lack of work and not enough 10 percent." He was told to surrender his patch and club jewellery
immediately. Patricia remembers Kane being discouraged
by the suspension but not devastated. The dark depression
that had so recently plagued him didn't return.

The SQ's offer was still on the table and looking
increasingly attractive after the dramatic drop in his own
bargaining power. Over the next two weeks Kane met
with his handlers five times in a push to iron out the
details. He itemized all his debts, the largest and most
pressing being $70,000 he owed Wolf Carroll for two
kilos of cocaine. (The transaction had been pleasantly col-
legial: Wolf secured the coke for $35,000 a kilo and sold
it to Kane for $37,500. Wolf then referred Kane to a
dealer in Ontario who bought both kilos for $40,000 each.
Everyone made his profit, but Kane failed to pay Wolf
anything more than a deposit for the merchandise.)
Another debt was owed to the club itself. Kane had been
given $3500 to have gang sweatshirts made but spent the
funds on his own needs. Legault handed over $4000 to
cover the sweatshirts and to pay his current tithe.

Roberge and Legault also performed what might be
considered due diligence. On the last day of February
they visited the RCMP's Montreal headquarters to review
the bulging RCMP file on C-2994. They dealt with Capt.
Jacques Houle, the force's source coordinator, who
allowed them to make notes but not photocopies. Houle
didn't hesitate to give them the official RCMP line on
Kane, whether they wanted to hear it or not. "We question
the integrity of this source who gave us a lot of interesting information but always, or rather usually, after the
fact. We felt that C-2994 sometimes tried to acquire information rather than deliver it."

Houle was skeptical of Kane's ability to reintegrate so seamlessly into the biker fold when there had been suspicions raised about his being a police informant. "We know biker groups don't need certainty before eliminating [someone suspected of being] a source." He added that no member of the RCMP, including those who were then with the ERM, could have any contact with Kane. Roberge and Legault listened to his concerns, Houle wrote in his notes of the meeting, but did not seem to agree with his assessment.

Roberge and Legault weren't interested in having Kane's career as an ERM *agent source* derailed by the RCMP's caution. They had high expectations for him, and they knew that there was another, unofficial RCMP position on Kane that was more in tune with their own. Between July 1999 and early 2000 the RCMP looked seriously into rehiring Kane—seriously enough that a member of the force completed an eight-page RCMP *agent source* evaluation form about him and attached another eight pages of background documentation. Nothing seems to have come of it, however, and by late February, Kane was apparently talking only to the ERM and its SQ masters. Finally, after a twelve-hour bargaining marathon on March 3, four years to the day since he had killed Roland Lebrasseur, Kane and the SQ reached an agreement-in-principle.

At one point in the talks Kane asked for legal counsel to review the deal. The only lawyers he'd hired previously were biker lawyers, people like Danièle Roy and Pierre Panaccio. Of course, he couldn't consult them on such a matter without soon having a very different contract on his head. Kane had been much impressed by Pierre Lapointe, the Crown prosecutor at his Halifax murder trial. Perhaps he thought that Lapointe had something to do with his being a free man. He told Beaulieu and Drouin that he wanted Lapointe, a Quebec justice department prosecutor, to study the contract being offered by the SQ, an arm of the Quebec government, on his behalf. That notion was quickly shot down with a lesson in basic legal responsibilities and conflicts of interest. Kane accepted the fact that he would have to trust his own best judgment.

That judgment proved to be solid. Eleven days later, on March 14, Kane signed probably the most generous informant deal in Canadian law enforcement history. It ran to thirty pages, each initialled by Kane and Beaulieu, and bore no resemblance to the boilerplate waivers the RCMP had Kane sign every few months. Each of the ninety-seven paragraphs of the SQ contract seemed specifically written for Kane, laying out the targets he was to pursue and how he was to pursue them, and detailing precisely how much he would be paid and when. It was a purposeful, results-oriented document, written by lawyers for a squad that by all appearances was intent on breaking the back of the Hells Angels in Quebec. With six months of intelligence delivery and eager cooperation in the bank, the ERM had concluded that Dany Kane was going to do it for them.

The contract named the three groups Kane would report on—the Hells Angels Nomads, the Rockers, and the Scorpions—along with sixty men—eighteen Nomads, thirty-three Rockers, and nine Scorpions—whom the police were especially eager to convict. Their suspected crimes were also itemized.

The contract specified that Kane wasn't permitted to incite others to commit crimes. Any revenue or goods he derived from criminal activities had to be turned over to the SQ "in the interests of conserving evidence." He couldn't pick and choose what information he shared with police; if he learned anything about the named groups or persons, his handlers must learn it too. This intelligence was to be communicated to them verbally but Kane was also required to keep handwritten "true and complete notes about all the activities, criminal and not, of the people targeted by this investigation." These notes were to be recorded as often as possible, ideally daily. Kane could be subjected to a polygraph test at any time.

The second half of the contract, the part that most interested Kane, explained what the SQ would do for him. By any measure, except perhaps that of the professional athletes whom the bikers so often cultivated, emulated, and in many ways resembled, it was immensely lucrative. On signature of the contract Kane would be paid $2000 every week for general living expenses; every month he would receive an additional $1649 to cover the mortgage on the St-Luc property and almost $600 for his Harley payments.

But the serious money came when the big busts were made and the targets brought to court. As soon as the police, advancing in a single sweep, moved on the Nomads, Rockers, and Scorpions, making arrests and seizing evidence, Kane would be paid $590,000. When he finished testifying at the preliminary hearings (or when the Crown decided to proceed by direct indictment) he would receive a second payment of $580,000. And once he left the stand for the last time at the subsequent trials he'd be given the final instalment, another $580,000. For at least eight weeks after the end of the trials Kane would continue to pocket the $2000 weekly stipend. If he was required to testify at an appeal, he'd receive another $200,000 plus $2000 a week for the duration of his involvement.

The success or otherwise of the Crown's prosecutions were not Kane's concern. Nor was there a provision in the agreement that all or even a majority of the listed bikers had to be apprehended. If his work as an *agent source* resulted in any arrests, Kane stood to make in excess of $2 million.

Yet this was just a fraction of the amount that the SQ had allotted for Kane's role. According to an almost entirely blacked out budget document, the total cost—which presumably included the expense of relocating Kane and his family with new identities and the salaries, overtime, and operating costs of his handlers—was estimated at more than $8.6 million.

Kane began recording his "true and complete notes" on the gang's activities a week before the contract was formally signed. He was in a hurry to consummate the deal, and with good reason: there was a "signing bonus" of $63,000, money that was earmarked to help pay his debt to an increasingly impatient Wolf Carroll.

Even though he was a senior member of the Nomads, Carroll hadn't been invited to join *la table,* the chapter's money-spinning importing circle. While he still operated a large and rich wholesaling operation in areas of Ontario, Quebec, and much of the Maritimes, he always seemed to spend more money than he made. The result was that he himself was heavily indebted—much more than Kane—and needed to collect his receivables to meet his payables.

On March 7, the first day of his formal note-taking, Kane received an early-morning summons from Carroll and in turn called Dominique to drive him to Carroll's home in the Laurentians. In St-Sauveur, Kane accompanied Carroll to his weekly check-in at the police station, a bail provision from the Rivière-du-Loup gun charge. Then, over a meal, Carroll told Kane he had to come up with at least $55,000 of the money he owed him by the next day. Kane kept his panic to himself, returning to Carroll's house and playing a bit of ball hockey with Wolf and his son. But he knew there was no way he could meet Carroll's deadline.

Once he was back in Montreal providence seemed to step in. A Mafia connection of Kane's beckoned him to a café in the city's north end. The man had 1500 kilos of hash to unload and could let the lot go for $6300 a kilo. It was a deal worth almost $10 million, much larger than any Kane had done before. He could not pull it off himself, but if he could act simply as a middleman, making a couple of hundred dollars on each kilo, his money problems would be resolved. Sure, there was that proceeds-of-crime clause in his *agent source* contract, but that agreement wasn't due to be formally signed for another week, was it? And Wolf might not wait that long.

Kane spent the next day or two trying to find a buyer for the Mafia contact's hash. Normand "Pluche" Bélanger, a money man for the Rockers, said the hash deal was too big for him and recommended Kane take it to Mom Boucher. But Boucher was out of town and Kane had to wait most of the week for an audience, all the while dodging urgent messages from Wolf and Pat Lambert, still a close associate of Carroll's.

Finally Mom returned to hold court at the Pro-Gym. Kane arrived in time to deliver some steroids to a client, then dutifully waited his turn. "I asked him if he had two minutes for me," Kane noted later in his new journal, adding with a hint of pride, "He said he had four." Mom was interested, but not if the product was "repress"—low-quality hash made of leftovers—of which there was an abundance on the streets of Montreal. In fact, Mom had just bought substantially more than 1500 kilos of repress for only $5000 a kilo. Kane said he'd check out the quality.

Some of Kane's financial pressures were relieved later that day when he was given the signing bonus attached to his SQ contract. He hurried over to Carroll's pied-à-terre on Boulevard René-Lévesque, catching Carroll just before he left for Halifax with Paul Wilson. Carroll's mother was ailing and her son was worried. Wolf took the money, folded $2000 into his pocket, and put the rest in a drawer, while scolding Kane for not returning his calls and pages. Then he had Kane drive him and Wilson to the airport.

The next day Kane received another cash payout from his handlers to take care of neglected, though less threatening, creditors: $6600 for four months of mortgage payments, almost $1900 for hydro bills, more than $900 for three different phone accounts, and $1800 in accumulated payments on his Harley-Davidson. The total came to $11,192.06, all transferred to Pierre Tremblay, a pseudonym that Kane adopted as a precaution against biker moles in the police accounting department. He was also given a bank card for the account into which his weekly pay was automatically deposited.

Kane's first experience wearing a body pack to record conversations had come the day before, when he met with his Mafia hash connection. The occasion must have given him some pause. Just two weeks earlier another SQ *agent source* in the biker world had been murdered in the Laurentians. Claude De Serres was a pot dealer associated with the gang whose secret sideline had been revealed by the police laptop stolen in Sherbrooke. Normand Robitaille, who had done business with De Serres, invited him to a chalet north of Montreal, purportedly to discuss a marijuana grow operation. Police installed a wire on De Serres for the meeting. When they found De Serres's corpse, the body pack was still in place, his last grim moments recorded for posterity. De Serres's demise may have convinced the SQ that they needed Kane as an *agent source* all the more.

It didn't discourage Kane from taking the job or wearing a wire, and the tryout went smoothly enough, although much of the conversation was unintelligible and the rest produced nothing incriminating. Those with any experience in the milieu knew better than to talk about drugs or business transactions except in the most oblique way. The clearest parts of this particular conversation caught Kane rhapsodizing about his fully equipped Harley and complaining about the endless meetings he was obliged to attend.

He had bought the bike the previous June, and it was loaded—cruise control, an intercom system, a stereo, saddlebags, and a windshield. It was so heavy with options, Kane said, that he was planning to buy another one, *"plus sport."* Still, he loved the big machine. He'd already put 14,000 kilometres on it, tootling around New Brunswick, Ontario, and up to the Saguenay–Lac-St-Jean region. He dreamed of taking it out to the Rockies, maybe that summer, if he could put his work aside for a few weeks, get out of the meetings that filled his days. "I went to a meeting at one o'clock today. It went on until five. I had another one this morning. It just doesn't end," Kane said. "My life is one long meeting."

Kane and his criminal cohorts tried to avoid set routines; in their world, a predictable schedule is an invitation to a predictable end. Still, as an *agent source,* Kane saw his days develop definite patterns. He would wake early, usually between 5 and 6 a.m. and be out of the house soon after. Almost every day the first item on his agenda was a call to Roberge or Legault to check in and confer on the day's events. If an interesting meeting was scheduled Kane would rendezvous with his handlers and a police technician at a secure location—usually a hotel room in the suburbs—to have a body pack installed. Most days that early-morning call would be the first of at least a half-dozen, sometimes ten or twelve. Kane would then head to Montreal, to the Hochelaga-Maisonneuve district and the Pro-Gym. Occasionally he would pick up Normand Robitaille at his house in Laprairie, also on the South Shore, on the way into town.

If he wasn't wearing a body pack, Kane would work out at the gym, chat with his fellow bikers and, if the opportunity presented itself, shmooze Mom Boucher. One day in early April he found Mom in a particularly expansive mood, boasting that he had financed a major public inquiry—known as the Poitras Commission—that had just spent more than a year looking into questionable policing methods at the SQ. He'd paid the lawyers to dig up all sorts of dirt on the force, Boucher said, adding that the next commission of inquiry he bankrolled would examine the shameful abuse of prisoners' rights in the province's jails. "He said he had already succeeded in getting a lot of things changed," Kane noted.

Mom claimed to spend his money in other public-spirited ways. He said he'd bought a plot of land in downtown Montreal on which he would erect a monument to those who had been killed by police. It was one of the few extravagances Boucher allowed himself. Any obvious self-indulgence—a lavish house, a flashy yacht, an expensive car in his name—would have drawn the close scrutiny of Revenue Canada and Revenue Quebec. He related the story of his son Francis once pulling up to the family home in a new Cadillac. The father told the son to get lost. That kind of car attracts police attention, the last thing Mom needed. Francis would have to learn these lessons and in due course make it on his own, he pronounced. It would be good for him.

Mom commiserated with Kane about the loss of his Rockers patch. He was glad to see it hadn't prompted Kane to drop out of the gang altogether. He'd proved he wasn't a *lâcheux,* a quitter; Kane would get his patch back soon, Mom said. Pierre Provencher had already told Kane as much two weeks earlier, at the end of March, and Normand Robitaille had taken him aside to say, "There are some guys who have the stuff to advance and some guys who don't. You have it." But reassurance from the big boss was like no other.

After a morning at the Pro-Gym Kane and the other biker regulars often went for a meal. Sushi was a favourite, but they spread their patronage around. If there was a group of Nomads present, as there usually was, the underlings, including Kane, sat at a nearby table, doing watch well away from conversations they weren't supposed to hear.

Afterwards Kane was free to pursue whatever criminal enterprise he was working on. The huge hash deal eventually came to naught: it was indeed the low-quality repress Mom had feared. Then for a day or two Kane was seized by a project that would have sent his Hells Angels stock soaring. A friend of a friend had bumped into Apache Trudeau in a bar—he knew it was him from photos and the telltale scars of surgically removed tattoos. If Kane had scored the scalp of the biggest rat in the gang's history, entree into the Nomads would have been his. But the hunt soon hit a dead end and Kane turned to another drug deal. This was for a shipment of ecstasy brought into the country by a contact who worked at Toronto's Pearson Airport. Kane's interest lasted only as long as it took Francis Boucher to explain to him that the ecstasy business in Quebec belonged to *la table*. If Kane wanted to move a large volume of the drug, he'd have to do it outside the province.

His days were filled with those endless meetings and his nights with biker social events, all opportunities for networking and business development. One such occasion was held in Sorel when the Death Riders from Laval were patched over to become the north Montreal chapter of the Rockers. The turnout was impressive, drawing Nomads and other Hells Angels and members of all the affiliated gangs from the Montreal region.

There Kane and Pierre Provencher spoke again of the riches that lay just down the 401. Provencher told Kane that he wanted to find himself a steadier business "because that"—Provencher made his hand into a gun—"is all very well, but it doesn't last long." Kane agreed and tried to interest Provencher, whose wealth was a source of speculation and envy to other Rockers, into taking another run at Belleville and Kingston. With a little effort, he said, they could move two or three kilos of coke into those towns every week.

Other outings were business-free, such as visits to Provencher's sugar bush, sometimes with their families where the kids ran loose, sometimes alone with their fellow bikers, tackling the work that needs to be done at a sugar shack in spring. A few social occasions were more obligatory than fun. In early April Normand Robitaille, a serious body builder, entered a competition to which all Rockers were pointedly invited. Robitaille was their main Nomad overseer, after all, and their supportive presence was expected. They might also influence the judging. Most of the Rockers found something better to do that evening, only to hear from Provencher two days later that Robitaille had been insulted by the weak turnout. Kane's absence may have cost him his early return to full membership. After the bodybuilding episode Robitaille tempered his previous warm words by telling him that his patch wouldn't be returned as soon as expected. He claimed it was because of an unpaid debt Kane had guaranteed.

Kane's relationship with Wolf Carroll had been strained by the delayed payment of his debt; it was also being tested by Robitaille's increasing demands. Kane had become Robitaille's regular driver and bodyguard, which meant that he was on call to chauffeur or run errands five days a week. The situation was reminiscent of the earlier clash between Wolf and Scott Steinert. But Robitaille was more sensitive to internal politics than Steinert had been, and he acknowedged that Carroll had established claims to Kane's allegiance.

While in Halifax at the end of March Carroll had met with Randy Mersereau's brother, Kirk, in an effort to normalize relations between the Hells Angels and the family. From Nova Scotia Carroll had phoned Kane to say things had gone well and that he and Kirk "were now friends." After Carroll's return, however, Kane made the trip to St Sauveur to see his old mentor and heard a very different story about the Mersereau meeting.

Wolf said that Kirk hadn't got the message and was vowing revenge for Randy's murder. Carroll tried to explain why Randy had to die, telling Kirk that his brother "had done some bad things." He asked Kirk directly whether he had been involved in putting out the contract on Boucher, McCrea, and himself. Mersereau denied any part in the plot, but Carroll didn't believe him. He decided Kirk would have to die too.

Kane, quite correctly, took this as advance notice that Wolf would soon ask him to take part in another hit down east. No dates were discussed, but Kane knew the call could come at any time. Before then, however, Wolf came up with another job for his protegé.

21

LIFE, DEATH,
AND DEBTS

In mid-April 2000, Patricia's due date was fast approaching. She had been off work since February, and Kane was particularly solicitous of her well-being in the late months of her pregnancy. He urged her to rest frequently and eat more; he telephoned every few hours and often came home in the middle of the day to check on her.

The winter months had brought them closer than ever. Kane came to appreciate and respect the rules Patricia set down for the home in St-Luc. No guns or drugs in the house. No gang members dropping in unannounced. No talking business in the house when they did visit. Most important, Kane learned to leave his work-related stress on the doorstep when he stepped inside. No downloading his frustrations or disappointments on innocent parties.

Kane's evident devotion both to Patricia and to becoming a model dad was such that despite the babysitter episode, she didn't question his fidelity. In fact, his monogamy became something of a running joke among his fellow bikers, almost all of whom kept at least one mistress. They would tease Kane about Patricia's hold on him, and occasionally when Kane was out partying with them and the usual complement of strippers and escorts, a friend would phone Patricia to ask if Kane could have sex with another woman. "He's a grown man," Patricia would answer permissively. "He can make up his own mind."

Having been in jail for the births of his second and third children, Kane was determined to be present for the arrival of this latest and much-wanted child. Those intentions were almost derailed on April 17, when Wolf asked him to go to Toronto to meet with members of the Para-Dice Riders. At last, it seemed, the Hells Angels were about to make real headway in Ontario. The first step, Wolf told Kane, involved some ugly but necessary business against rivals of the Para-Dice Riders in the Toronto and southern Ontario market. The Loners all have to die, Kane reported, and their president, Jimmy, first and foremost.

Kane was relaying this information to his handlers later that day when he was interrupted by another call. Normand "Biff" Hamel, Mom Boucher's longstanding confidant and the Nomads' de facto chief financial officer, had been gunned down in the parking lot of a Laval shopping centre in front of his wife and son. It was the highest-ranking hit that the Rock Machine had pulled off, and it sent a shock through the Hells organization. Kane delayed his departure to Toronto for a day, picking up and passing on to Roberge the buzz about plans for a counterstrike.

At 6 a.m. on April 19, after securing $4900 from the ERM for miscellaneous expenses, he headed south on the 401, Roberge and Legault close behind. He went straight to a restaurant in Woodbridge, a largely Italian suburb on the northern outskirts of Toronto, where he met a Para-Dice biker named Gino. They took a walk while Gino told Kane what he knew about members of the Loners, especially Jimmy, the club's president, and Peter, its principal hit man. He provided the address of the gang's recently purchased clubhouse, but other details, including photographs of the leaders, would take another day to assemble. Even then it might be delicate; no one could know that Gino was Kane's source. The Para-Dice Riders were still divided on the question of joining forces with the Hells Angels. Gino said he was already regarded by some as an "undercover" Hells.

They arranged to meet again the next day, and Kane drove into downtown Toronto to check in at the Colony hotel. Roberge and Legault followed suit. At nine-ten that evening Kane received an urgent page from Gisèle. Patricia was at the hospital and in labour. She'd gone in for a checkup that afternoon and been told she was already dilating. Kane conferred with his handlers, then grabbed a taxi for the airport—but not before phoning Gino to see if they could meet at Pearson so that Kane could collect those photos of the Loners. Gino suggested they connect in Montreal instead; he was planning to go up himself the next day to fly the Para-Dice colours at Normand Hamel's funeral.

Kane arrived back in Montreal at about 1 a.m., in time for the birth of a baby boy some nine hours later. It wasn't an easy delivery, and Patricia's blood pressure plunged precipitously afterwards, causing her to lose consciousness. She awoke to find Kane calling everyone he knew to announce the joyful news. "It was like it was his first. To say he was happy isn't enough," Patricia recalls. "He actually took a few days off."

Not immediately, however. The gang comes before all, and there is no more important biker event than the funeral of a slain brother. A few hours after the baby was born and with Patricia out of danger, Kane slipped away. First stop was Dorval airport to pick up Gino and several other Para-Dice Riders. He accompanied them to their hotel in Longueuil and took them out to supper. Then he went home to collect his Harley for the ride to the Hells Angels South clubhouse and a memorial party for Hamel.

The next day was the funeral service, and Kane was back on duty, calling for the Para-Dice Riders at 9 a.m., taking them to breakfast, then again to the South clubhouse. Finally the group made their way into Montreal and to the Magnus Poirier funeral home on Sherbrooke Street East where the diminutive Hamel was laid out in his Hells colours. There Kane ran into Wolf, who, in a show of old-time biker respect, had ridden his motorcycle to the funeral home through pouring rain. He was soaked and asked Kane to drive him back to his apartment for a change of dry clothes.

On the way Wolf spoke about the Loners job. It was a better idea to whack Peter the hit man first because, well, he was the gang's assassin. Then he mused about killing the whole gang at once with some well-placed dynamite at their new clubhouse: a great coup if they could pull it off, but the risks of collateral damage were high. The last thing anyone wanted was another Daniel Desrochers, Wolf said. However they decided to do it, he would first send a few anglophones to do the surveillance. A francophone like Kane would only attract attention in Ontario. Still, he said, it would be up to Kane to "finish the job."

Having received his orders from Wolf, Kane drove the Para-Dice Riders back to the airport and then went home to get acquainted with his new son. For three days Kane did little but spend time with Patricia and the baby. His handlers hoped he'd see Wolf on Monday, April 24, for another discussion of the Loners plot, but Wolf had himself decided to take a day off with his son.

On Tuesday it was back to work in earnest, with Kane donning a body pack for a meeting with Pierre Provencher and another Rocker. If the police hoped to capture incriminating talk of drug deals and murder schemes, they were disappointed. The conversation was largely mundane chit-chat. How much water a person should drink over the course of a day and whether it was possible to drink too much; whether it was necessary to diet to achieve the ideal body ("I want *un shape* skinny but muscular," said Kane, "it really gets women wet"); what kind of exercise they'd take up that summer (Kane planned lots of in-line skating). The three men lamented that the Rock Machine, once well structured and worthy opponents, were now "a bunch of bums." They grumbled about the difficulties of getting by on anything less than $5000 a week. And they discussed the advantages of blending in with the crowd. Kane credited his survival to the fact that he didn't have a memorable face.

An obviously proud new father, Kane did most of the talking and at several points brought the conversation back to the birth of baby Jesse. He described Patricia's ordeal and told his friends that for the sake of their girl-friends they should always wear condoms. He joked that Jesse didn't look like him. "I laughed like hell when the baby was born," Kane said. "He had a huge sac and a tiny little dick. I took him when the cord wasn't even cut and I looked at him and I said, 'It's not me, the father, because I've got little balls and a big dick.'"

Kane returned to Toronto that week for more meetings with Gino, including a tour past the Loners' clubhouse and the homes and hangouts of Jimmy and Peter. At a lunch organized by Gino one afternoon Kane encountered two bikers he knew from the Hells Angels Sherbrooke chapter. As they chatted it became clear the men were in town for a hit of their own. The Rock Machine had recently succeeded in opening a chapter in Toronto, and they were after one of its prominent members.

In the presence of the Sherbrooke Hells Gino was forthcoming to a fault, revealing his long association and subsequent falling-out with Peter. Gino had taken care of his wife and kids financially while Peter served a long prison sentence. After Peter's release, Gino fell into difficulties, but Peter had flitted off to Italy, abandoning him. Gino recommended that Kane first kill Peter, then Jimmy, and he handed over their photographs to ensure easy recognition.

Back in Montreal Wolf was enraged by Gino's lack of discretion and declared him an idiot for being so public about the job he wanted done. Wolf said that next time he saw Gino he'd stick a gun in his hand and tell him to do the job himself.

It was an uncharacteristic outburst for Wolf, the biker who seemed to have excellent relations with almost everyone, but there was good reason for his testiness. Not only did he have serious health concerns but his financial problems were reaching a critical point. Wolf admitted that he was $500,000 in the hole to *la table*. If he didn't come up with the money soon, his fellow Nomads would cut off his drug supply. And if his drug supply was cut off Carroll would only find himself in worse financial shape. Kane still owed him $2000, he said, and he wanted the cash now.

Wolf's humour improved a few days later when he, Kane, their lawyer Danièle Roy, and two Rockers— serving as bodyguards in case the Rock Machine made another surprise attack—chartered a small airplane to fly to Rivière-du-Loup for their court date on the firearms charges. Wolf had proposed driving, but Roy rejected the idea, forcing Wolf to shell out $2800 he didn't have for the charter. He soon decided it was money well spent. After negotiations with the Crown, Roy struck a deal that would see Kane plead guilty to possession of the two guns (despite one being discovered in Carroll's bag) and receive a sentence of four or five months. Charges against Carroll would be dropped. Kane wouldn't have to enter his plea— and thus not begin his sentence—until late October. "Wolf was very happy," Kane reported, as were the two Rockers. They were pleased "that I took the fall for Wolf because he is very sick." Kane didn't welcome more jail time, but if he had to, he would serve it for Wolf's sake and for the credit it would earn him with the Nomads.

Twelve days later Carroll underwent surgery to remove what Kane called a *caillou*—a pebble, but likely some sort of tumour—from his thyroid gland and was out of action for a few weeks. By then Wolf had pulled the plug on Kane's assignment with the Loners, saying he would give the job to two hangarounds from Halifax. Thanks to Gino, Kane had already been associated with the hit in the minds of some. Wolf proposed an alternative: the murder of an independent dealer who was running drugs out to Nova Scotia and cutting into Carroll's monopoly. But Kane resisted this time. "I told him I wanted to concentrate on getting a business going," he reported to his handlers. He'd lost time while in prison in Halifax, and it appeared he'd lose more later that fall. "It was now my turn to make some money." Others in the gang were sympathetic to Kane's money worries, among them Pierre Provencher and Normand Robitaille, two bikers who were doing very well dealing cocaine and who found it difficult to understand why Kane wasn't more flush. They had to acknowledge that his duties for Robitaille didn't leave much time for his own affairs. He often picked up the Rocker overseer early in the morning and found his day taken up with ferrying him around: to the health club so Robitaille could play racquetball, to a series of restaurants so Robitaille could conduct his business, then to the daycare so Robitaille could collect his daughter. Robitaille recognized the problem and thereafter expected Kane's services only three days a week, leaving him time to develop his own income sources.

In mid-May Kane told Provencher he wanted to establish an enterprise that had first attracted his interest in 1994—his own little gang of dealers "who would mostly work with pot and a little coke in Ontario, about ten guys who would make me about $500 a week each." It would take time to build his network, however, and in the interim Kane needed everyday operating funds, more than he was being paid by the ERM.

In late April the SQ's Witness Protection Service had asked Roberge and Legault whether Kane was handing over the proceeds of his criminal activities, as his contract stipulated. The response was no, because there weren't any. "Before he was doing 'collections' and had to resort to violence on occasion," went the explanation. "The SQ having forbidden him to use violence, IN-3683 is not doing 'collections' anymore, so he hasn't made any money." There was no mention of his steroid and drug-dealing activities, and the SPT didn't push it.

A month later, though he'd still made no remittances from these pursuits, Kane was pressuring his handlers for more cash. His technique was similar to that used with the RCMP: whine about being underpaid for a few days and, if the money wasn't forthcoming, play hard to get. For a

short period in May Kane reduced his contact with his
handlers to a minimum; on one day he failed to return any
of Roberge's or Legault's pages, thereby violating another
provision of his contract. Roberge relented and arranged
for an SQ superior to hear his complaints. "His professional double life is very demanding with the constraints
of his family," Roberge noted.

At the meeting Kane again reminded his employers
that the financial demands of being a biker were difficult
for someone in the straight world to comprehend. All his
peers routinely carried between $5000 and $10,000 cash
in their pockets. The fact that he didn't could be disastrous. "He explained that image is very important and that
he needs a minimum [amount of money] in order not to
raise any doubts." There was no immediate response, but
over the next few weeks the SQ's purse strings loosened,
and Kane was reimbursed thousands for what he claimed
to be job-related expenses.

Kane had argued that he wasn't making any money from
crime. His handlers knew that wasn't true, given his drug
dealing, but Kane was refusing substantial sums by not
accepting murder contracts. Kane's notes from this period
make it clear that within the Hells organization he was seen
primarily as a hit man, and not just by Wolf. On May 22
Kane was told by Provencher that he and another Rocker
associate would be given the contract to kill two leaders of
the Ruff Riders, a street gang that had unwisely declined an
alliance with the Hells. The same day he was told that if he
should come across a man named Fritz, he should kill him
on the spot; Fritz was a suspected police *agent source*. Two
days later Provencher asked Kane to make a remote-control
detonator for a bombing he had in mind. A week after that
he was offered $20,000 to kill a woman who was selling

drugs for the Rock Machine. Another Rocker had been given the assignment, but two or three weeks had passed with no results. Kane was known to be more reliable.

In the meantime Wolf had asked Kane to eliminate yet another of his aggravations. Dédé, or D.D., as Carroll called him, was a member of the West End Gang who specialized in armoured car robberies. Apparently he was quite successful and thus very wealthy. He was also a friend of Kirk Mersereau's and was rumoured to have been party to the contract put out on Mom Boucher and Wolf to avenge the death of Randy Mersereau. Wolf's request came the day after he had called Kane late at night to say the Rock Machine seemed to be circling Denis Houle and extra surveillance was needed. "He wanted to catch [the Rock Machine] in the act and kill them like the dogs they are," Kane wrote in his journal. "And he wanted to chop off their heads to set an example."

Kane refused the hit on the female dealer, explaining he didn't want to risk finding himself back in prison, at least not before he had made himself a whole lot richer. Saying no to Wolf wasn't as easy. Wolf was his superior in the gang and increasingly his friend and confidant. In conversations from this period that were recorded on Kane's body pack, the younger biker went on at length to Carroll about his pleasure in parenthood and in the solidity of his relationship with Patricia. The baby permitted Kane to see new qualities in her, ones he didn't know existed and had never known in his own mother.

For his part Wolf opened up about his financial and health difficulties and used Kane as a sounding board for his increasingly desperate schemes to pay off his debts. He would go into the hydroponic marijuana business, which, at the time, was hotter than the high-tech stock market and looked far more promising. He would go down to Sarnia to whack a Rock Machine member, a killing for which *la table* would reward him. He'd even go back to street-dealing.

The shared confidences, however, didn't mean that debts were forgotten; Carroll repeated his demands that Kane level up with him. It was money the younger man didn't have, and by mid-June he was again avoiding his mentor and telling his handlers that "Wolf is sick and fighting with everyone."

Kane had another, more complex, money issue that looked to be escalating from the nagging to the nasty. In the fall of 1999 a friend named François Houle (no relation to the Nomad Denis), received death threats from members of the Italian mob to whom he owed something in the order of $120,000. Kane came to his rescue, negotiating with the Mafiosi and eventually guaranteeing a loan to Houle from a member of the Sherbrooke Hells Angels. Houle repaid the mob and his life was spared. But he proved less grateful than Kane had anticipated and soon started to miss his loan payments to the Sherbrooke biker, Guy Rodrigue—always referred to as "Malin," shrewd or sneaky.

On June 12 Malin had had enough and phoned Kane to say he wanted no further dealings with Houle, that thereafter Kane was responsible for the loan and would have to pay him a minimum of $1000 a week and that was just the loan's interest. Kane was concerned, but not yet prepared to obey Malin's every instruction: he called François Houle to tell him to sort it out with Malin.

Kane may have drawn hope from the expectation that his work for the police was nearing its end and that the first payout of $590,000 would soon be in the bank. Since

November, shortly after he began giving police advance
warning of the times and locations of the Rockers' masses,
ERM investigators had been planting microphones and
hidden cameras in the hotel rooms and banquet halls where
they were to take place. Like most organized criminals,
members of the Hells Angels units were infuriatingly
guarded and obscure when discussing their illegal activities,
even among themselves. Over time, however, investigators learned the code they used to discuss drugs and
killings. Supplemented by the occasional indiscretion,
the *messes* were a rich mine of evidence for the police.
With Kane's debriefings and the evidence gleaned by
other ERM investigators from wiretaps, surveillance,
crime scene investigations, as well as the testimony of
other informants, the authorities were assembling a solid
case against the entire organization in the Montreal area
by early summer 2000.

A sign that the investigation was in its home stretch
came in mid-May, when Kane spent two days recording
videotaped statements known as "KGBs." Before the
camera Kane swore to tell the truth and then essentially
read the contents of his notebook, adding the occasional
detail. The recordings were a form of insurance for the
police, one endorsed by the 1993 Supreme Court of
Canada ruling (*R. v. K.G.B.*) that statements voluntarily
given by a witness prior to a trial can be entered as testimony as long as certain standards of truthfulness are
upheld. The decision was directed at cases of domestic
violence or trials involving child witnesses where a witness's version of events recounted before a judge might
be substantially different from what it was hours after the
crime had been committed.

Some prosecutors realized that KGB videos could also prove useful in instances where a witness disappears or dies before a case comes to trial. Even so, it was not common practice in 2000 for organized crime investigators to take the precaution of recording an informant's testimony. The ERM's decision to make the tapes may have been motivated by the killing of Claude De Serres two and half months earlier, but the timing of the sessions suggests the squad was in the process of tying up loose ends.

Another indication that the police felt the end of the operation was in sight came the day of Malin's demanding telephone call, when Kane met with his handlers for a long talk about the status of the investigation. "Discussion about the file, its functioning, its future, and its timetable" is how Roberge succinctly described the meeting. "About the pieces of evidence we are looking for." No other information is given, but one thing is known: the police were at that stage planning a massive and concerted series of raids, arrests, and seizures most likely for September, possibly for October.

If Kane wasn't sweating over Malin's loan, it might have been because he believed he could stall until the big bust, when all his criminal debts would be effectively erased, as would the jail sentence he was due to serve for the firearms charges. One way or another, deliverance seemed imminent enough that Kane was able to persuade Roberge and Legault to give him an advance of $86,000 against future earnings to cover a host of accumulated household debts and family obligations. These included $9000 for new carpeting and tiles in the St-Luc house, $6000 for a new garage door, $5000 for landscaping, and $6000 for furniture and appliances. There was $15,000 to pay his parents and Dominique for work done on the basement and $25,000 to repay Josée's mother for expenses Josée had incurred during Kane's imprisonment in Halifax, plus $3500 in back child support, $3000 for clothes for the kids and $2500 to cover an unexplained debt to a man at a downtown Montreal sunglasses boutique where Kane sometimes had his kilos of coke delivered. Kane's handlers gave him the funds in mid-June, slipping in an extra $2500 with no strings attached. It went to repair his Harley, a job-related expense the SQ agreed to wearily.

His family remembers that it was during these weeks that Kane increasingly mentioned his desire to start a new life and his expectation of an imminent financial bonanza.

It was to Patricia that most of these cryptic messages were directed, out of the blue, in the car, in bed, over a meal. She recalls one occasion particularly well. Jesse had been a pukey baby from the beginning, eating abundantly but throwing much of it back up. Though he was otherwise healthy, Patricia began to think something was wrong. Kane told her she was overreacting, but she insisted on taking the infant to the hospital. There he was kept overnight for tests, despite Kane's insistent assertions that she and the doctors had no cause for alarm. The next day Patricia was told that a valve in Jesse's stomach wasn't closing as it should and that he would need surgery to correct it. When she phoned Kane, he began to cry and apologized for so adamantly opposing her decision to have Jesse examined. The operation went well, and the baby was released from hospital on a Saturday. They returned to the hospital for a checkup the Monday following and afterwards went out for breakfast.

There, at the restaurant, Kane brought up the idea of moving away, beginning afresh, all ties severed with their former lives.

"You're going to rob a Brinks?" Patricia asked.

"Something better than that," Kane answered.

He asked if it would bother her if he quit the biker milieu. Patricia thought it a silly question; she knew no one in that world other than Kane and hardly found it appealing. But she could not imagine severing ties to her family, as Kane seemed to be proposing. The conversation ended with Patricia frustrated by Kane's coy refusal to give any more details about why he was asking these questions and Kane stymied by Patricia's insistence that she couldn't conceive of losing contact with her mother and sisters.

22

HAZY, LAZY LAST DAYS

Quebec's patron saint is John the Baptist, and June 24, his feast day, is traditionally one of the principal holidays in the province. In modern secular Quebec its religious significance has been dispelled and the day officially designated as the *fête nationale*. But it remains what it has always been: a holiday to kick off the summer. The school year has ended, offices close for the day, and a huge parade snakes through downtown Montreal. People pull chairs and tables out into the streets, pile them high with food and drink, and celebrate with their neighbours.

For the Hells Angels the *fête nationale* was trumped by the Nomads' anniversary on the same day, an even better excuse for a party. In 2000 the honour of hosting the celebration went to Michel Rose, the long-time drug importer and member of *la table* who had made his fortune well before becoming a Nomad. Rose's home was in the suburb of Repentigny, off the eastern tip of the island of Montreal. Neither the house nor the property was excessively large, but Rose's was a waterfront lot on the St. Lawrence, and his toys were on prominent display in the driveway and at the dock.

Kane's notes and wiretapped conversations always betrayed a preoccupation with fancy machines (as well as the monthly payments it took to own them), and his handlers no doubt wished he would apply the same eye for detail to a cohort's physical appearance or an incriminating conversation. That day at Rose's Kane noted a 1996 Mercedes convertible as well as a more recent, top-of-the line Mercedes four-door sedan parked in front of the house. In the garage sat two high-end Harleys, and in the yard, his prized bike—a "full chrome" Harley softail, its gas tank customized with an engraved Nomads logo. The covetous Kane estimated its value at a minimum of $80,000.

At the dock floated the true extravagance: two Sea-Doos and three speedboats. Kane was mesmerized by a twelve-metre *Miami Vice*–style cigarette boat, worth $400,000, and a fourteen-metre dual-cockpit racing craft that carried a $500,000 price tag, according to its pilot. It was called *El Rapido* and rightly so: it could clock over 220 kilometres an hour. Rose's guests were offered rides, and Kane eagerly jumped in, abandoning Patricia and Jesse to mingle with the other wives and girlfriends.

Usually uncomfortable at biker gatherings, Patricia found that her three-month-old baby was an irresistible conversational subject, and she was able to connect with some of the women more easily than before. In particular Mom Boucher's wife, who gently rocked Jesse to sleep, impressed Patricia with her warm, down-to-earth manner.

For Kane the party was more than a good time. The event was the occasion for the restoration of his Rockers' patch, proof that he was fully accepted by the gang once again, whatever his missteps in the past, whatever his current financial problems.

Wolf Carroll was notably absent from the celebrations. The previous Sunday, June 18, Carroll had beckoned Kane, as he often did, to St-Sauveur, not to pressure him about money owed or propose yet another hit but simply to unload his discontent. He'd managed to bring his debt to *la table* down to $400,000, and he was optimistic that he'd pay off the balance before too long. Still, Carroll was thoroughly disenchanted with the Hells Angels in Quebec, the Nomads and *la table* especially. It wasn't just that bikes and brotherhood were no longer central to the gang, though Carroll complained about that. The real problem was that everything was *"business et seulement business."* Money had become the only criterion by which people were measured. "You have no money, you're no good" was the Nomads' philosophy, Carroll said.

Since Carroll had no money, he was judged solely by the size of his indebtedness. The gang had forgotten all he had done for them, and he admitted to feeling threatened, sidelined in obvious ways. He hadn't been consulted on the promotion of René Charlebois to full-patch Nomad, for example, a violation of the code that gave every full member of a chapter a veto over the membership of any aspirant. Instead, Carroll had been informed of the decision two hours before the patching ceremony. He believed, too, that his territory was under siege. In fact, he objected to the whole business approach that the Nomads were promoting, seeking to impose an across-the-board price for drugs and establish clearly delineated territories in which everyone plied his exclusive trade. In Wolf's view this cartel system ran counter to the libertarian, free-market ethos of real bikers.

In Halifax, he said, things were different. There were no territories, no set prices. It was still like the frontier, and he was thinking of returning East for good. "I'm at a turning point," Carroll told Kane, as they strolled through the woods of the lower Laurentians. "I can't live here. It's pretty and all, but I can't make any money."

Kane was sympathetic, venting his own gripes about the Hells, especially how long it was taking to advance up the ladder. *"Fuck, ça fait longtemps,"* he complained. "Things change and it counts for nothing now. Everything you do, it doesn't count, Wolf."

Carroll asked how he found working for Normand Robitaille. "He's pissed off all the time," Kane said. "If it isn't one thing it's another. He's always riding me." A few days earlier Robitaille had started ragging on Kane's appearance, ordering him to get "some classy clothes for my days with him."

So Carroll popped the question, or rather announced his intentions. "If I call you, I'd like you to come down," he said. "You know what the biker trip is all about, Dany. You've got it in your heart more than the rest, you know."

Carroll's excuse for missing the Nomads' anniversary party was, in fact, that he had to be in Nova Scotia. He called Kane from there on June 22 with an invitation to visit for his summer holidays. Over the next three days, however, be became increasingly insistent, saying at one point that he had important documents for Kane to see. Kane thought it was a code for something he didn't understand, but he was nonetheless obliged to respond. On the afternoon of June 26, he headed east, driving a rented minivan, Roberge and Legault following at a discreet distance.

The three men spent the night in Fredericton, and the next day Kane arranged to meet Carroll at a McDonald's in Truro. Wolf's son was with him, but that didn't deter him from talking business. Things had turned ugly with Paul Wilson, Wolf reported. An underling of Wilson's had given a statement to police implicating Kane and Carroll in the murder of "McFerland," and Wolf suspected that Wilson, who was apparently "chattering" about them, might become a police informant.

"Wolf told me that Paul had to die," Kane told his handlers. Wilson was aware that Carroll had it in for him; he'd already taken flight and was apparently hiding out in British Columbia.

Kirk Mersereau's time was up as well, Wolf said. Not only had he put out a contract on Wolf, but he and a couple of cronies, including D.D., the armoured car robber from the West End Gang, had been doing surveillance on Wolf's home and family in St-Sauveur. "He had to die for that," Kane informed his handlers.

Carroll again pitched Kane on the idea of relocating to Nova Scotia and, perhaps to whet his appetite, took him to Halifax for a few days of fun at the Hells Angels clubhouse. Kane went to the beach, did some shopping, borrowed Mike McCrea's Harley for a ride around the city, and enjoyed a few good meals as well. He seemed to like Halifax. He reported to his handlers that he was *"très respecté"* by the Hells Angels community there, as evidenced by the provision of a hangaround or "friend" to accompany him throughout his visit.

Kane had been given $600 to cover his Halifax expenses even while his handlers paid his gas and hotel in Frederiction. Still, within a couple of days he was wheedling more in surreptitious phone calls from the Hells' clubhouse or while he was out and about. Roberge and Legault arranged a drop of $400, which they taped under a sink in the bathroom of a Tim Hortons.

There was some business discussed among the bikers, specifically the hit on Kirk Mersereau. McCrea informed Carroll and Kane that Mersereau was en route to Montreal, presumably on the hunt for Carroll. It was then decided that Kane would return to Montreal with Jeff Lynds, a Halifax hangaround who would be the trigger man. Lynds, however, didn't know Montreal, so Kane's job was that of a guide or a gillie: show Lynds around, flush out Mersereau, and let the one shoot the other. But before they could leave, Carroll came back with word that Mersereau had had a serendipitous highway accident in New Brunswick. His car was scrapped and so too was the planned hit. On Canada Day Kane climbed into the mini-van and drove back to Montreal alone.

Things were quiet in the biker world in July. People were off on vacation, and the war between the Hells Angels and the Rock Machine showed signs of being over, the Hells' dominance no longer questioned. Indeed, Normand Robitaille had told Kane some weeks earlier that even the Italian mob, which had always disliked the Hells Angels, had recently accepted the inevitable and resigned themselves to doing business with the gang and with *la table* in particular.

Shortly before Mike Rose's June 24 bash, there had been an unprecedented summit between Vito Rizzuto, kingpin of the Mafia in Montreal and across Canada, three of his lieutenants, and members of *la table*. Mom Boucher was expected to attend but never showed up, a calculated snub of Rizzutto. But Rizzutto hadn't walked; rather, he agreed to a division of territory—the Italians would get the north end of the city and Little Italy but not much else—and to a fixed price for cocaine. It would wholesale for no less than $50,000 a kilo.

Members of the Rockers would be granted a 10 percent discount when buying from the Nomads, Robitaille informed them later, but under no condition were they to pass on the savings. Even if they cut the coke to a fraction of its purity, they were not to charge less than $50,000. Within two weeks the effects of so steep a price began to show in sluggish sales. It didn't greatly affect Kane; he wasn't moving more than a kilo every month or so. Some Rockers, however, were getting an earful from their smaller dealers.

Kane was more concerned with his newly minted Road Warriors, the gang he was assembling to deal pot and cocaine into Belleville and Kingston. The Nomads had approved the scheme in mid-June, along with the gang's name, logo, and motto: Only a Matter of Time. Kane's main drug courier at the time, Ghislain "Coyote" Guay, was earmarked to be president. Kane would be the gang's godfather, their contact with the Nomads, and sole source of the Road Warriors' supply. Until the police launched their major offensive and Kane's role in the operation was exposed, the Road Warriors would be his ride into the biker bourgeoisie. Just as Wolf had the Halifax Hells and Mom had the Rockers, he would have the Road Warriors. There was the small cloud of Wolf having had a falling-out with Coyote and telling Kane that "he had to die," but Kane didn't take it seriously. These days Wolf seemed to be making such declarations all the time.

Kane was surprised when Normand Robitaille cut him in on another enterprise, a fraudulent telemarketing scheme of the kind that was then booming in Montreal. Smooth-talking callers would phone Americans, often elderly citizens with a penchant for entering contests, and inform them they had won a car. Before receiving the prize, though, they were required to pay the applicable taxes and duties. The sooner they sent the money, the sooner they'd be enjoying their new vehicle. In reality, of course, there was no prize, no car, and no contest.

Such scams had a long history in Montreal—some say because of its large, underemployed English population—and in the 1990s when long-distance telephone rates plummeted the business thrived. The Hells Angels and the Mafia were quick to enter the market. The particular operation that Kane became attached to was a Hells-Mafia co-production that had been negotiated at the summit with Rizzutto. Kane had done watch on that occasion, well away from the meeting table, yet Robitaille set his share at an eighth of a third, or slightly over 4 percent. His involvement in the operations of the phone room didn't seem any more onerous. Once up and running, the enterprise was expected to bring in $1 million every week.

With what appeared to be the promise of good money with little effort—the way he liked it—Kane took off a week off in early July. He and Patricia had talked of a trip, but instead spent the time doing a bit of work around the house and generally taking it easy with the new baby.

Only once that week did Kane contact his handlers and that was to tell them that Louis "Melou" Roy, a wealthy Nomad from the Trois-Rivières chapter, had been the victim of an internal purge. Roy had kept his distance from the biker war; like a lot of Hells Angels, he thought it a dangerous strategy, one that would only arouse the police and hurt business. Under pressure from Mom Boucher, he had come around somewhat, and with a respected track record that dated from the Missiles, he was eventually invited to join the Nomads. But he hadn't accepted an invitation to join *la table* when it was offered in early June. Melou was a traditionalist like Wolf and preferred to have his own business. *La table* was too corporate, membership too much like a straight wage job with its $5000-a-week salary. Even a share of its substantial profits above and beyond the paycheque didn't appeal to him, nor did the concept of price fixing. Melou had his own contacts in Colombia and used them to great profit, which he wasn't prepared to give up or share.

Carroll had told Kane about Melou's refusal to sit at *la table* during their heart-to-heart on June 18, and both hoped the decision wouldn't prove to be hazardous. Three weeks later word circulated that it had been fatal. Eventually it emerged that Melou's real crime was to sell coke to the Mafia for less than he did to his Hells Angels brothers. That was likely why they tried to recruit him to *la table* and killed him when he refused to join.

When Kane returned to work the following week Roberge and Legault were themselves on vacation, and the gang continued to observe the Hells Angels' equivalent of summer hours. Kane picked up Robitaille later in the day and often knocked off in the early afternoon to ride his Harley with other gang members.

Robitaille kept Kane informed of a few significant developments. André Chouinard, a Nomad and *la table* member, was abruptly forced out of the gang; he didn't have the stuff to be a Hells Angel, according to Robitaille. Then came the news that Wolf Carroll's debt had been forgiven by *la table*. Kane never heard Wolf's version of events, but some said it was Wolf who took care of Melou. It would have been logistically difficult, however: Wolf was in Nova Scotia in the days before and after Melou's disappearance. (He was last seen going to a Nomads meeting held directly across the street from Mom Boucher's father's home in Hochelaga-Maisonneuve.)

Others in the milieu maintained that Mom himself killed Melou, strangling him with his bare hands.

Kane also relayed the details of a scheme by Pierre Provencher to wipe out the Ruff Riders, the street gang that had resisted closer affiliation with the Rockers. The plan was to send as many Ruff Riders members as possible to Nova Scotia on the pretext of doing a job for the Hells Angels there. Somewhere along an isolated stretch of highway in New Brunswick, they would drive into a *"trap shot"*—an ambush—laid for them by the Rockers. The reason: "they were liars, traitors, and troublemakers," Kane told his handlers.

Most of the information Kane transmitted in late July was of the "nice to know" variety. On the eighteenth, he had a chat with Boucher at the gym, and the warlord shared his sense that a major police action against the Hells Angels was imminent. It had been too long since they'd been hit, he said. Later that day Normand Robitaille confessed to a similar intuition, though his concerns were more personal. "I'm starting to do business with all sorts of people and I'm afraid of getting nailed," Robitaille told Kane. "At a certain moment everything will be going well and then a *délateur,* an informant, will give me up."

At the same time Robitaille couldn't resist some self-satisfied gloating about how well he was doing. He occupied a privileged senior rank in a criminal organization that was indisputably *"le tops."* What more could he ask for?

A week later Kane was chauffeuring Robitaille from one meeting to the next, from a high-end Italian restaurant in Laval to a decrepit diner in Verdun to a chain coffee house downtown. After six hours of criss-crossing the city. Robitaille made an odd request. He asked Kane to drop him at the South Shore terminus of the *métro*, Montreal's subway system. Bikers never availed themselves of public transit, and Robitaille didn't explain why he was doing so then. It may simply have been that it was rush hour and the bridges were clogged.

Perhaps wary of being mugged or spotted by Rock Machine thugs, Robitaille removed his rings and gave them to Kane for safekeeping. He handed Kane all three pagers he was carrying as well as two of his three cellphones. Finally he asked Kane to look after the small satchel or, as Kane called it, men's handbag, which contained the few papers he carried with him during the working day. Then he instructed Kane to pick him up at a *métro* stop in the east end just under four hours later.

Kane promptly rendezvoused with Roberge and Legault and passed over the satchel. While Kane took a break his handlers sped directly to a South Shore police station, where they spent half an hour at a photocopier with Robitaille's documents. The papers appeared to be accounting records, pages filled with handwritten numbers, initials, and code names. The ERM investigators had no idea what intelligence the paperwork might provide, only that they had never before seen such material from the Hells Angels.

Kane picked up Robitaille at the appointed hour and returned his pagers, phones, jewellery, and satchel. Robitaille was with two members of the Trois-Rivières Hells Angels and all three were tipsy and good-humoured. They climbed into Kane's minivan and made for the South Shore. Robitaille's buddies had left their cars at the *métro* in Longueuil. Kane then drove Robitaille home, stopping at the IGA, where Robitaille dashed in for a few items.

The last week of Kane's career as an *agent source* differed little from any previous week. His reports to Roberge and Legault contained the same sort of details he had been relaying to them for months.

The Ruff Riders ambush idea had been scrapped; instead, a competing street gang called the Bo-Gars would take care of them in return for certain indulgences from the Rockers. Normand Robitaille was especially pleased at the prospect of one street gang going after another; it would divert police attention from the Hells Angels.

Kane's Road Warriors were roaring ahead. The gang-in-chrysalis was given territory north and west of Montreal, which meant its drug-dealing business would not be limited to Ontario alone. Kane supplied the ERM with a list of all the founding members, including their social insurance numbers and driver's licence information.

He reported on an evening visit to Mom Boucher's compound in the South Shore municipality of Contrecoeur. Mom had offered the grounds for the wedding of Nomad René Charlebois the following week, and the event was raising security concerns. As Francis Boucher told Kane, "Because three hundred people were invited to the wedding, three hundred people knew where the wedding was." Mom had assigned his son watch duty on the property every night that week. Giving Kane a tour of his own quarters Francis showed him the machine gun and night-vision sight that he had ready in case anyone should be foolish enough to abuse Mom's hospitality.

The most gratifying development that week for Kane was the resolution of the unpleasantness surrounding Malin's loan to François Houle. On July 28 Robitaille himself had told Kane to pay off the debt and settle the matter; it was his second reminder. Kane's continuing obligation was making the Rockers and the Nomads look bad in the eyes of the Sherbrooke Hells Angels. In case he didn't get the point Malin repeated his demand that Kane cover the loan on July 31.

On the evening of August 1 Kane made his way to Laval to sit down with François Houle and sort out the details of how much had been borrowed and how much repaid. Some progress had been made: the debt had risen as high as $130,000 in late 1999 but now stood at about $80,000. For the time being Houle's arrangement was to pay $2000 a week, $1000 against the principal and $1000 in interest.

Two days later Kane spoke again with Malin, who demanded that the loan be paid at once; even for a loan shark, chasing errant creditors was no fun. That night the same message seems to have been delivered to Houle, though in a different manner. He called Kane in a panic after two heavyset men came to his door. Wisely, he didn't answer their knock.

The next day, Friday, August 4, Kane met with Roberge and Legault a few minutes after 10 a.m. They gave him $1000 to present to Charlebois as a wedding gift—the figure the Rockers had been told was appropriate for them—and $650 for a lawyer to take care of his driver's licence, which had been suspended once again. Just before the session wrapped up at ten forty-five, Kane raised the subject of the Malin loan, how it was causing him headaches, threatening to undermine his credibility in the biker milieu and thus his usefulness as a productive *agent source*. There was no resolution, but Roberge and Legault argued Kane's case to their superiors later that day.

By four-thirty that afternoon they were able to telephone Kane with the happy news that the ERM would pay the debt. Better yet, they assured him, it would not be taken "out of his account," in other words not deducted from the $1.75 million promised by his *agent source* contract after the police arrests and subsequent trials. The funds would be available the following Monday or by Tuesday at the latest. The only hitch—and it was a small one—was that the ERM proposed to give Kane the money to pay off Malin in two instalments. Kane wanted it all at once, but Roberge and Legault observed in their notes that either way he was happy and relieved that this burden would soon be lifted from his shoulders. They hung up, agreeing to speak on Sunday.

At seven-thirty on Sunday evening, as Kane lay on the couch listening to the Doors, Roberge's notes indicate that he paged him twice with no response. He tried his cellphone numbers but found both phones had been turned off. Despite Kane's silence, by seven Monday morning Roberge and Det. Sgt. René Beauchemin, an ERM investigator who was filling in for Legault, were "in position to meet" Kane. At seven-fifteen Roberge paged him and again ten minutes later, affixing a numeric "semi-urgent" code.

When there was no response they took a drive by Kane's house in St-Luc. "Blue minivan in the yard and garage door closed," Roberge noted later. "Observe no activity." They then went by Robitaille's house in nearby Candiac but saw nothing out of the ordinary. All they could do was drive around Kane's haunts on the South Shore, hoping to spot him or Robitaille and to have various wiretaps monitored for Kane's voice or mention of his whereabouts.

They had no news until word came in to ERM headquarters from the St-Luc police. As Roberge noted dispassionately in what would be his last entry in the handlers' notebook for IN-3683, "10H30 … we learn of the death of the *agent source* by suicide in his garage."

23

COMING TOGETHER, FALLING APART

His double life a well-kept secret and his apparent suicide a sidebar to the main story of the biker war, Dany Kane's demise received scant attention beyond the circle of his fellow gang members and those few policemen who could not publicly acknowledge their close relationship with him. Whatever his private dramas, the greater world regarded Kane as nothing more than a loyal, if somewhat star-crossed, foot soldier for the Hells Angels in the hostilities with the Rock Machine. In the final months of 2000, those hostilities escalated, erasing Kane's memory all the more quickly.

Barely a month after his death, Michel Auger, *Le Journal de Montréal*'s senior crime reporter, wrote a series of articles about the seething power struggles in Montreal's underworld. Portraying the Hells Angels as duplicitous among themselves and in their relations with other criminal organizations, the articles provoked Mom Boucher to make the most ill-advised of many reckless decisions in his conduct of the biker war: he ordered Auger assassinated.

Auger's reputation as an investigative journalist was largely based on his extensive contacts in the Montreal police department; most of his scoops came from leaks from friendly cops. As far as Montreal's criminal community was concerned, this led to a pro-police bias in his reporting, even if such a tilt was little noticed by the reading public. As Cmdr. André Bouchard, a senior SPCUM officer who regularly dealt with Auger put it, "Everything he wrote we gave to him. Journalists, they use us and we use them too. He used to come down and have a coffee with us at nine o'clock every morning. [He'd ask,] 'What have you got?' ... We'd say something like, 'Yesterday two arrests and, hey, publish this....' We'd give him stories, and it helped us at the same time."

Whether Auger was aware he was used in this way isn't known, but it persuaded Montreal's hoods that the *Journal de Montréal* reporter was less objective observer and more police propagandist and agent provocateur. His pieces in that second week of September were based on solid information, but still they were the final straw for Boucher, who, thanks to a corrupt contact in the province's vehicle licensing bureau, already had Auger's home address and licence plate number.

Whoever carried out the job—police have never charged anyone with the shooting but claim to know who he is—didn't dilly-dally. Shortly before 11 a.m. on September 13, the day after the articles appeared, Auger returned to *Le Journal*'s offices in Montreal's east end following his regular morning briefing with officers of an SPCUM major crimes unit. He stepped out of his Subaru station wagon and went around to retrieve his laptop from the rear compartment. As he bent over he was hit in the back by the first of six bullets that the shooter pumped into him. Remarkably none hit Auger's spine, lungs, or other vital organs, and he survived without any permanent injury. He was back at work four months later.

The consequences of the attack for the criminal world were more lasting. Public and media anger at the attempted assassination of one of the province's best-known crime reporters equalled and even surpassed that which had followed the bombing death of young Daniel Desrochers five years earlier and the shootings of the prison guards in 1997. This wasn't an accident, like Desrochers's death, or the sort of occupational hazard borne by those whose daily work brought them into contact with nasties like Godasse Gagné, Toots Tousignant, and Fonfon Fontaine.

The shooting of Auger was a calculated attempt to intimidate the media and impose a reign of fear on society at large. For Quebeckers—many of whom shared the police sentiment that thugs killing thugs was no great tragedy and few of whom were touched personally by the bikers' violence—the Auger incident crossed a line. When police revealed they had come across a long list of targets for assassination by the Hells Angels months earlier—a list that included Auger's name—the clamour increased. Was Auger just the first of many? people wondered. Needless to say, the province's journalists, who felt themselves suddenly under assault, eagerly encouraged this sense of outrage. Protest marches were held, indignant editorials written.

As with the creation of the Carcajou squad five years earlier, the Quebec government took swift and decisive action—after the fact. Carcajou had addressed deficiencies in front-line policing; now the government intended to tackle its failures in the legal prosecution of the bikers. Several trials, including that of five Rockers for the Caissy murder in which Aimé Simard was the disastrous star witness, had demonstrated that the existing machinery was no match for the formidable legal teams hired by the bikers and other mobsters. So within a week of the Auger shooting the ministry of justice created the Organized Crime Prosecution Bureau.

No longer would regional prosecutors, often already burdened by dozens of cases that they handled alone, be required to carry organized crime cases without assistance. Now a special team, comprising many of the best and brightest prosecutors in the province, would be given the responsibility and the resources to mount thoroughly prepared cases against the Hells Angels, the Rock Machine, and other organized crime gangs.

That wasn't all. Although Bill C-95, the anti-gang law passed in 1998, had yet to be seriously tested by police and prosecutors, the cry went up that Canada's laws still weren't tough enough. Federal legislation allowing for harsher penalties with a lower burden of proof of involvement in gang activities was needed and widely demanded.

If the scale of public reaction didn't immediately impress on Mom Boucher the gravity of his blunder, the unhappiness of other crime lords with whom he did business soon did. They had been content to have police attention diverted by the antics of the Hells and the Rock Machine, but the bikers' excesses—and the shooting of Auger was inanely excessive—threatened to make life more difficult for all organized crime. The displeasure of the Italian mob, the West End gang, and other criminal groups were conveyed unequivocally to Boucher. Even Hells Angels heavyweights

from the U.S., who had little to fear from tougher anti-gang
laws in Canada, bluntly warned their Quebec cousins to act
more like businessmen and less like outlaws straight out of
a blood-soaked Western.

The head-office scolding was all the more remarkable
given the laissez-faire ethos that traditionally governed
relations between different Hells Angels chapters, especially those divided by borders. The international brand
might be sullied by one particular franchise, but rarely
were the offending chapter's actions judged or criticized
by the others. Only the most egregious infractions of the
Hells Angels' code—too much friendliness with police,
say, or discourteous treatment of fellow Angels—was
cause for bringing a chapter to heel. The Auger incident
was deemed so grievous that the American Hells wanted
an end to the war with the Rock Machine.

The shooting had made international news; a headline-
grabbing truce between the Hells and their Rock Machine
enemies wouldn't undo the damage, but it might help stall
the building momentum for more stringent anti-gang
laws. To this end a summit was organized between Mom
Boucher and Fred Faucher, the young hood on whose
shoulders the leadership of the Rock Machine had fallen
after the assassination and imprisonment of most of the
gang's senior members. The ninety-minute meeting took
place on Tuesday, September 26, in Quebec City's main
courthouse. This surprising choice of venue was heavy
with symbolism, but there was also a practical aspect to
salle 409 of Quebec's Palais de Justice. It was a room
reserved for meetings between lawyers and their clients
and the last place police would receive permission to
plant a bug. More important, the meeting could not go
unnoticed by the Quebec media.

Both sides had the same response when asked about the subject under discussion—*"pas de commentaires pour le moment"*—but the logical conclusion was easy to draw: peace. Less than two weeks later it was confirmed when an agreement to end hostilities was formalized at a well-lubricated dinner at Bleu Marin, a downtown Montreal seafood restaurant that had recently lost its most illustrious regular, the former prime minister Pierre Elliott Trudeau.

The *Allô Police* star reporter Claude Poirier was given the scoop. A journalist who was the antithesis of Michel Auger insofar as he met regularly with Mom Boucher and was considered a patsy of the bikers by police, Poirier was paged on the evening of Sunday, October 8, and told to make his way to Bishop Street with a photographer. There he was met by two men and escorted to the nearby restaurant where, in a private upstairs room, a dozen or more senior members of the rival gangs, including Boucher, Robitaille, and Richard Mayrand of the Hells Angels, were partying as if no bad blood had ever flowed between them. The photographer was instructed to get snapping, and he did, catching, among other shots, the de rigueur handshake and hug between Boucher and Faucher.

In the absence of a larger threat it was an unlikely moment for peace to break out between the two gangs.

The Rock Machine had borne the brunt of the Hells Angels' expansionary ambitions and of police efforts to end the war by knocking at least one of the antagonists out of the game. But in mid-1999 the gang received a fillip when the Bandidos, the Hells Angels' main rivals on the international scene, agreed to "affiliate" with them. Some biker experts had predicted that such a deal would never be formalized and that the Rock Machine would eventually fade away, but talk of affiliation, however vague, was the first step toward full association with, and absorption by, the Bandidos. At the very least it was a sign of solid international support.

There were other signs of renewed Rock Machine vigour in Ontario. In 1999 a chapter was established in Kingston (comprising mainly Montreal émigrés), and some independent Toronto bikers began wearing the gang's patch. In the summer of 2000 there was more progress when the Rock Machine entered a formal alliance with the remnants of Ontario's Outlaws and with the Loners. The Loners may have been attracted by the strong Italian connections they shared with the Rock Machine, or by the knowledge that Kane and Carroll had been gunning for their leaders, or simply by their mutual and absolute antipathy for the Hells Angels. Whatever the reason, the Rock Machine had won the wooing contest for the Loners and appeared to be on the verge of winning Ontario as well.

Walter Stadnick and other senior Hells weren't in a position to do anything quickly in Ontario, but much progress had been made with Los Brovos in Manitoba since the killing of David Boyko four years before. With a little effort—and an offer to elevate all Los Brovos members to prospect status immediately and to full-patch Hells Angels in a year's time—Stadnick persuaded the gang to sign up. In mid-July the Hells could claim a presence in all four Western provinces. With Quebec largely under their control and the Halifax chapter, however dysfunctional, holding down the Atlantic provinces, Ontario alone eluded their grasp. In the fall of 2000 the Hells Angels and the Rock Machine were poised for a showdown, not for peace. Only the menace of a stricter anti-gang law that would adversely affect them both brought them to a much trumpeted but uneasy truce.

Yet if the bikers expected their declarations of armistice to lower the official heat, they were sorely mistaken. Two days after the evening at Bleu Marin, Mom Boucher's acquittal on the prison guard murders was overturned by three appeal court judges. They agreed that the instructions given to the jury by Superior Court Justice Jean-Guy Boilard had inaccurately represented the Crown's case against the biker. The Court of Appeal ordered a new trial, and Boucher was re-arrested and returned to his tailor-made cell, isolated in an empty wing of the Tanguay prison for women in Montreal's north end. Two days after that it was the Rock Machine's turn, when police raided a storage locker the gang had rented for the warehousing of explosives and firearms and seized a sizeable stockpile of dynamite and machine guns.

The busts continued on an almost weekly basis through the fall in Montreal, Quebec City, and in the *régions:* the North Shore, the Eastern Townships, the Abitibi, Saguenay–Lac-St-Jean. In response the bikers endeavoured to keep their heads down, but they were incapable of containing their more psychopathic elements. An appalling episode occurred on October 17 when members of a Hells Angels puppet gang beat to death Francis Laforest, a twenty-eight-year-old bar owner who had refused to let the gang's dealers sell drugs in his suburban Montreal club. Coming just five weeks after the botched hit on Auger, the fatal assault erased any public relations points that might have been scored at the Bleu Marin celebration. Again people marched in the street, this time led by a frail Michel Auger.

In late November the Rock Machine was formally designated as a Bandidos probationary club. Boucher et al. had hoped that the Hells Angels–Rock Machine pact, even if motivated by pure survival instincts, would put an end to the Rock Machine's romance with the Bandidos and ultimately lead to the nominally independent gang being absorbed by the Hells. The possibility had been raised at the Quebec City Palais de Justice summit, but the Rock Machine wasn't enthralled by the idea of merging with the gang that had been its constant mortal enemy. Indeed, it could be argued that the raison d'être of the Rock Machine was to battle the Hells Angels. So when the Bandidos offered to take them aboard, the gang leaped at the chance. Or rather ninety-odd members did; three senior bikers, who had likely held private negotiations of their own with various Hells Angels, refused. They were immediately accepted into the Nomads.

Granting full-patch rank to Salvatore Brunetti, Paul "Sasquatch" Porter, and Nelson Fernandez—all of whom came with strong networks in Ontario—was just the start for the Hells. Next came the confirmation of their Manitoba prospects, the former Los Brovos, more than six months ahead of schedule. On December 16, ignoring the rule that specified a year's service between Hells Angel prospect and full patch, the Winnipeg chapter was welcomed into the fold as equals. Less than two weeks later the rationale behind fast patching was made clear. Hurried negotiations with four Ontario clubs had borne fruit: to win coveted control of Ontario at last, the Hells Angels offered an unprecedented patch-for-patch deal. There would be no slow climb from friend to hangaround to striker to prospect to full member. Instead 168 members of Satan's Choice, the Para-Dice Riders, the Lobos, and the Last Chance were told that in exchange for burying or burning their old patches, they would receive immediate full membership in the Hells Angels. The fact that it was a with-us-or-against-us proposal was understood. The Hells didn't have to spell out the alternative: that if they refused to sign up, a brutal war for Ontario, long expected by some police, would almost certainly follow.

Around suppertime on December 29, a convoy of buses, SUVs, and luxury cars rolled into Sorel and up to the Hells Angels clubhouse at 153 Rue Prince. Out of the vehicles poured a stream of men of all shapes and sizes and a single colour—white. Many wore or carried unadorned leather jackets and vests. Inside, after minimal ceremony and no pomp whatsoever, the men were handed their new Hells Angels patches, insignia flown in from Austria, home of the exclusive manufacturer. These they carried with their vests and jackets to a table where the only woman present that evening sat behind an industrial sewing machine.

The Hells Angels thus added ten new chapters to their Canadian operations, three in Toronto, one each in nearby Oshawa and Woodbridge, and four others stretching from Thunder Bay to Windsor. The tenth chapter was to be Ontario's own Nomads.

Again, *Allô Police*'s Claude Poirier and a trusted photographer were briefly invited in to document the event. Poirier's account was couched in the breathless, overblown prose that characterized the tabloid. But the coverage couldn't hide the fact that the evening was remarkable for its lack of joy and celebration. There was little boisterous laughter and only half-hearted partying. Any pledges of eternal friendship and loyalty rang hollow. Many bikers left early, heading back to their homes and hotels rooms. Twenty-three years after first arriving in the country, the Hells Angels had secured the prize of

cross-Canada conquest—not through a love match with
the Ontario gangs but thanks to a shotgun wedding.

The Rock Machine, now formally the Bandidos, could
not hope to outdo the Hells Angels in territorial expansion. They could, however, try to raise their profile to
prove they were still players, and the next week they
hosted an Allô Police reporter at their Kingston clubhouse.
A hundred-odd Bandidos from Canada, the U.S., and
Europe were present. Billed as a party to mark the recent
affiliation, it had as its true purpose a show of force.
Nonetheless, when asked about relations with the Hells
Angels, Bandidos spokesmen were as diplomatic as their
Hells counterparts. "All we want is peace" was the stock
reply from both sides. "We're not looking for trouble. We
won't back down if it presents itself, but we won't be the
ones who start it."

There was no mistaking a heightened tension below
the surface of these public utterances, and the postings to
various biker websites, usually written anonymously by
bikers themselves, made it plain. The shaky truce was
broken on January 18, 2001, when Réal "Tintin" Dupont,
a lesser-known Bandido, was shot to death in the parking
lot of a bar near Montreal's Dorval airport. Dupont had
always disliked the Hells Angels, but his feelings had
turned to pure hatred after a Hells wannabe named Dany
Kane had firebombed his bar, the Delphis, outside St-Luc
in early May 1992. Dupont, said to be *un vrai dur*—a
really tough guy—had taken it hard.

The Bandidos enjoyed a measure of karmic revenge two
weeks later when Nelson Fernandez, one of the three senior Rock Machine members to defect in early December,
suddenly succumbed to cancer. Fernandez, Sasquatch

Porter, and Salvatore Brunetti had been the targets of the Bandidos' venom in the online war of words, and many of his former colleagues were convinced that his diagnosis of advanced cancer just three days after he got his Hells Angel patch was retribution from a higher power for his treachery.

On the whole, however, there was no denying that if a higher power was involved, it was on the side of the Hells Angels. In early February the Bandidos' Toronto chapter defected en masse to the Hells' Woodbridge chapter. Leading the way was Billy "Velcro" Miller, so named because he had worn four different patches—Outlaws, Rock Machine, Bandidos, and Hells Angels—within eighteen months.

The major sweep of arrests originally planned for early autumn 2000 had been put on hold after police authorities examined the documents that Kane had secured, a week before his death, from Normand Robitaille's satchel. Their contents opened up a new avenue of investigation, one that delved into the Hells Angels' complex financial affairs and promised to lead to dozens of additional arrests and scores of additional charges. In the meantime the police could continue to harass the Hells in small busts without jeopardizing the larger case. In early February there were several roundups of low-level dealers associated with the gang in and around Montreal. A criminal telemarketing operation in which the Hells Angels had a stake—perhaps the one Kane was to profit from—was also shut down.

At mid-month the upper echelon was targeted when police got word that the members of *la table*—all except the jailed Boucher—were meeting at a Holiday Inn in downtown Montreal. They quietly arrested Richard

Mayrand as he left with his chauffeur and bodyguard, then grabbed the Nomads prospect and the Rocker who were doing watch. All were carrying unlicensed firearms. Inside the hotel room where the gathering was breaking up, police found Denis "Pas Fiable" Houle, Normand Robitaille, Gilles "Trooper" Mathieu, and Michel Rose, likewise carrying illegal handguns and almost $40,000 cash among them.

The bikers had been studying a collection of photos of senior and mid-level Bandidos, evidence that the Hells were hunting their enemies again. Along with Dupont's murder in January and an attempt on the life of the head of the Bandidos' Kingston chapter, Alain Brunette, just two days before, it appeared the biker war had resumed. Brunette's photo was there in the pile.

The Nomads were all charged with firearms and gangsterism offences. Just five days later, at their earliest possible opportunity, they agreed to plead guilty to illegal possession of restricted weapons. The more serious gangsterism charges were dropped. The deal raised some eyebrows, conveying as it did that police regarded the anti-gang law on the books, C-95, as unworkable: too much proof was needed to make it effective against organized crime. By then, however, the new anti-gang law set in motion by Michel Auger's shooting—one that demanded a lower burden of proof and meted out harsher penalties—was before Parliament. Although it wouldn't be in force for almost a year, its very existence seemed to confirm that C-95 was inadequate. Still, considering that police had nabbed the five men, all well-known members of the elite chapter of the Hells Angels, armed, in a hotel room, poring over photos of their rivals, with gang associates standing guard outside and in the lobby, it's

probable that prosecutors could have made the gangsterism charges stick. Instead they chose to let the charges
slide; the Nomad elite would soon face a slew of more
serious indictments.

By mid-February almost everything was in place for
Opération Printemps 2001, the concerted series of arrests
and seizures against the Hells Angels. Since mid-October
police had been inside the Nomads counting house, a
small apartment in a nondescript building in east-end
Montreal that was their drop-off point. Concealed cameras
and listening devices had been planted inside the apartment; outside, police surveillance teams monitored and
videotaped the coming and goings of an endless parade of
runners, all delivering shopping bags full of cash.

On the floor below, in a flat used by the Nomads to
store the cash, police found a computer zip disk. Copying
it, they discovered a spreadsheet itemizing cocaine and
hash transactions worth tens of millions of dollars. While
police had the apartments under observation, it was calculated that between $24 and $36 million passed through
every month.

24

TAKEDOWN
AND TRIALS

Wednesday, March 28, 2001, began early for the two
thousand police officers and other officials who had been
gathered from the SQ, the RCMP, Montreal police, and
various local squads to take part in Opération Printemps.
Dozens of arrests and seizures were planned across the
province and in Ontario, the objective being the apprehension of every member of the Nomads and the Rockers,
as well as dozens of other Hells Angels members and
associates. First there were the pre-dawn briefings held
in secrecy at various locales in Quebec; a five-thousand-
seat hockey arena was requisitioned for the purpose in
Montreal. Then teams of police swung into action in a
coordinated series of raids.

The operation went off with barely a hitch. Of the
142 members and associates of the Hells Angels and
puppet gangs who were targeted, 128 were in jail by the
end of the day, all arrested without resistance. Mom
Boucher was already behind bars, awaiting a second
trial for the prison guard murders, as were the members
of *la table*—Richard Mayrand, Denis Houle, Normand
Robitaille, Gilles Mathieu, and Michel Rose—who were
serving time for illegal possession of weapons. Now they

were joined by virtually everyone else in their criminal coterie, including Pierre Provencher, Guillaume Serra, René Charlebois, Donald Stockford, Francis Boucher, and Gregory Wooley. Walter Stadnick, vacationing in the Caribbean on March 28, was soon arrested with the help of Jamaican police. Others were believed dead, including jail-guard killer Paul "Fonfon" Fontaine, Louis "Melou" Roy, and two Rockers who had run afoul of the gang, Stephen Falls and Stéphane Hilareguy. A handful, most notably Wolf Carroll, who was in Mexico when the raids occurred, gave police the slip.

But the missing few didn't detract from the operation's overwhelming success, and it was portrayed as such by the media in the days following. The various police forces did not hesitate to congratulate themselves on a job well done. However, a short article in the March 30 edition of *Le Journal de Montréal* quoted one honest if unidentified source who couldn't refrain from giving credit to the investigators' secret weapon, a biker said to have taken his own life more than six months previously, a man named Dany Kane.

The revelation of Kane's double life was not the shock to his fellow gang members that it was to his family. Although they might never have guessed his treachery while he was alive, they were fully aware that the milieu was riddled with informants. It was like a game where the stakes—life, death, or long stretches in prison—were high, and Kane had beaten them at it. In retrospect some close to him wondered how they could have been so blind as not to have recognized him as a police source months, even years, earlier.

It explained his steady supply of cash in the absence of a viable business. It explained the Halifax mistrial when the police seemed to have him cold on a murder charge. It explained his eagerness to take on extra responsibilities and bothersome chores, like reserving hotel rooms or restaurant halls for gang meetings. And it explained why that most intuitive of all Hells Angels, Denis Houle, had always distrusted Kane for reasons that he could never quite articulate.

What it didn't explain, however, was Kane's death. In the weeks following the discovery of his body on August 7, 2000, only his family questioned the coroner's ruling of suicide. Their doubts were fuelled by many factors, not least by his own behaviour in the days just before his death. The renewed driver's licence, the dental work, the new in-line skates, the plans for Jesse's baptism all pointed to a life in everyday progress.

The scene at the house presented equally puzzling contradictions. Why would he have left his glasses in the bedroom—the glasses he needed to find his way even to the toilet—when he went into the garage? Why was his pager on the floor of the hallway? Why did he bother to take that new driver's licence out of his wallet and place it on the seat beside him as he turned the Mercedes' ignition and waited for the carbon monoxide to do its work? And where was the Palm Pilot that he used constantly, keeping track of phone numbers, personal notes, and his crowded schedule? It had vanished, and the police insisted they hadn't taken it. Then there was the mysterious silk pillow on the garage floor, the strange footprint halfway up the garage door, and the cat that had dashed out when Patricia forced open the door to the garage. There was no entry the cat could have used, and if it had been in the garage the whole time, it surely would have died as well. Cats have no higher tolerance for carbon monoxide than do humans, and the level in Kane's blood was far above a fatal level.

Furthermore, both his parents and Gisèle saw him the day of his death and were quick to recall his upbeat good humour. Ghislain "Coyote" Guay, the designated president of the Road Warriors with whom he had driven to Kingston on August 5, told them that Kane had filled the hours on the 401 singing every song that came into his head and regaling him with stories of his misspent youth. He might have been grumpy and perhaps preoccupied on Sunday evening, but hardly suicidal. And then there were the visions of the clairvoyants, information that would be dismissed by any inquest but that held a lot of credence for the Kanes. A woman with a reputation for supernatural insight visited their home within days of Kane's death and told them that their son had been murdered. Gemma says she later contacted Dany by using a Ouija board. The board revealed that four people, including a woman, had been in the St-Luc house at the time of his death, that there had been a struggle, and he had been pinned down on a coffee table.

For his family the suicide note that the police eventually released to them was hardly convincing either. To begin with, the most intimate and difficult letter he would ever write was found by police on his laptop computer. Patricia and the family maintained that Kane used the computer exclusively for surfing the net. All the notes he had ever written to them—and he scribbled notes compulsively—were by hand in his cramped script.

The contents of the message also struck them as uncharacteristic. Translated, with numerous spelling errors corrected but its erratic punctuation retained, it read:

Goodbye to my children what I have done you will probably never understand but I can't bear being pulled by one side and the other. No matter what you might hear about me I can tell you that I love you all equally and I love you more than anything in the world.

Patricia, I can tell you without any hesitation that you were the woman of my life you were the only one who I can say without hesitation understood me. I love you and please forgive me this act.

The letter was unsigned, even though Kane invariably ended his notes with "Dany," and a string of X's and O's. He addressed Patricia by her full name, when he always called her Pat, and he speaks of her as the "woman of my life." Gemma and Jean-Paul say it was a phrase he often used but only in reference to Josée. Kane's parents and sisters—Gisèle, in particular—were surprised that they weren't even mentioned in this last communication, further proof in their minds that Dany didn't write it.

Immediately after Kane's death the family had been told there were two suicide notes; the second, police said, was also written on the computer and was directed to Kane's friends. But when Gisèle pressed for a copy of it as well, the story changed. The officers had made a mistake, they said. There was one letter only. Then in April, a few weeks after the Opération Printemps raids, *Allô Police* published what it claimed was Kane's second suicide note, a document that the family found as peculiar as the first.

Who am I? That is the question!
Am I a biker?
Am I a p_____? [policeman]

Am I good or bad?

Am I straight or gay?

Am I rich or poor?

Am I honest or dishonest?

Am I loved or feared?

Am I exploiter or exploited?

Do I take advantage of people or do others take advantage of me?

With everything that I do am I aware or unaware?

Do I do what I do for myself or for a society which itself is sick and violent?

Who is honest these days, I ask WHO?

What will it change if we finish what we began about six years ago?

Is the only thing that will change the hell that I will live in afterwards or the hell that I will make those close to me live in when it has all ended? After all, does society really want me to do what I am doing and if so why is it that I have all the weight on my shoulders. Not only am I alone in torturing myself for the results of what I do but none of the others have even half the weight that I have on my shoulders (and I say it to you in all modesty). From my earliest childhood I wanted to do what I am doing and more than that, I am probably the envy of many people but today everything has taken a completely different turn. I am myself 100% satisfied with what I have done up to now but it is not enough to blah blah in what I do concrete actions are required, when it is not just a question of money to perhaps save a society in danger is it important to know how to count?

Am I a LEMON?

Yes I am like most of us!

I would really have liked to be able to have continued in my lead role but I no longer have the strength to continue!

I hope I can serve as an example to a society that is always complaining about everything and nothing, you are a biker you are a criminal, you are a cop you are an asshole. So what is good and what is bad. I have difficulty playing my role and not because I am not a good actor but actually because I don't have the budget and the command of my own role. I have 3 roles at once and not 1 but really 3. I have to play a scene in a film and afterwards come back on that scene and begin it again another time because there is a little gentleman sitting on his fat ass who himself decides that it will be this way that we will act in this scene, but the problem is that this little gentleman has never seen the filmscript and even less the film that we are in the middle of shooting.

So I say to you SHIT!!!!!!!!!!!!!!!!!

Good luck to BOB, TINTIN, GAETAN, RENE and others.

All of you mentioned above are in shit with the little gentlemen with big asses who want everything for nothing.

This letter suggests that Kane was in yet another conflict with SQ bigwigs over money and that he was suffering a crisis of confidence in what he was doing—both quite plausible. The spelling errors in the original French version are also fairly convincing in that they are consistent with the egregious spelling in the notebook Kane kept while working for the ERM. He continually confused *c'est* (it is) with *ces* (these) or *ses* (his) and *n'est* (is not) with *n'ai* (don't have). Even so, the letter is full of words and expressions he never used, according to his family. Nor had they ever heard him express a concern for the health of society.

All of these doubts and concerns remained within the family circle. Kane's parents were visited only once by his handlers, as was Patricia. Their concerns were never solicited, their suspicions neither forcefully expressed nor taken seriously.

When his former biker colleagues learned that Kane had been a long-time police informant and, according to press reports, the key to the Opération Printemps raids, they began to look at his death in a different light. They were inclined to agree with his family that it was unlikely he had died by his own hand. But the consensus among the bikers did not favour murder. Instead most were convinced that Kane was very much alive, an assumption that fitted with their paranoid suspicions, especially where the police were concerned. With no real evidence to support such a conspiracy, it became an article of faith in the milieu that Kane was living in Florida, British Columbia, or perhaps even in Quebec, rid of those problematic tattoos and wearing a new face, thanks to cosmetic surgery.

In the spring and summer of 2001 Kane's fate was among the most discussed and mulled-over subjects inside Bordeaux jail. All but one of the Nomads, Hells Angels, and Rockers arrested in Opération Printemps had been refused bail, and the enforced idleness while they awaited trial gave them ample time to dwell on Kane. When their high-priced legal help came to visit, the bikers were quick to share their theories. Before long, Kane's complicated relationship with the ERM, the SQ, and the RCMP and his questionable death were on their way to becoming a key part of the bikers' defence strategy.

The mass arrests presented an unprecedented challenge to the Quebec justice system: how to prosecute so many people charged with the same crimes, including the crime of belonging to the same criminal organization? One option was to proceed biker by biker or in small groups of two or three. This was the careful, deliberate approach, though one that would have presented enormous logistical problems when it came to assembling the requisite teams of prosecutors and jury members.

The more ambitious option was the mega-trial in which as many of the accused as possible would be tried in the same courtroom at the same time. This had the benefit of requiring only one prosecutorial team, and it guaranteed media attention, no small concern given the need to restore battered public confidence in the government's handling of biker gangs. But a mega-trial would, by definition, be unwieldy and susceptible to interminable procedural wrangles. There would be at least a dozen defence lawyers involved in the case, each with his or her own agenda. If such a trial went off the rails or gradually revealed itself to be utterly unworkable, the damage would be considerably greater than if one or two smaller trials fell apart.

Confident its cases against the bikers were solid, the Quebec justice department chose to proceed by two mega-trials, a decision that necessitated the construction of an ultra-secure, $17 million courthouse adjacent to Bordeaux jail that might never be used again. One mega-trial would bring to court those arrested as a result of Opération

Océan, the police investigation of low-level, peripheral associates of the gang charged with drug trafficking, money laundering, and gangsterism. The other mega-trial was for those pursued by Opération Rush, the pillars of the biker war—the forty-two Nomads, Hells Angels, Rockers, and senior associates who faced the same gangsterism and drug-trafficking charges. Most had murder or conspiracy to murder charges to deal with as well. Some were charged with as many as thirteen counts of first-degree murder.

The justice department decided to avoid a time-consuming and complicated preliminary hearing by proceeding by direct indictment, just as the Nova Scotia authorities had done when Kane was charged with Robert MacFarlane's murder in 1997. The case against the bikers arrested in Opération Printemps 2001 was, however, infinitely more complex than the case against Kane. It wasn't simply a matter of shipping two or three boxes of documents and videocassettes to the defence lawyers and saying, "We will build our case from these materials." Rather, the bikers' lawyers were given, among other evidence, the equivalent of 693,000 pages of documents stored on 177 compact discs plus 211 video-cassettes, some as long as six hours, and 1122 audiotaped wiretaps.

The lawyers immediately complained that the prosecution was trying to swamp them with paper in order to impede their preparation of a successful defence for their clients. The prosecutors knew very well that most of Quebec's biker lawyers worked on their own or in small offices in loose partnerships with other lawyers; none had large staffs of underlings to bore through all the documents, studying them, classifying them and picking out the useful nuggets. "At least 60 percent of the material they gave us was utterly irrelevant," says one lawyer.

Despite the antipathy that existed among many biker lawyers and the fact that the interests of their clients were often at odds, the lawyers chose to work as a loose-knit team and share the heavy burden of examining the evidence. Some would concentrate on the particular crimes the bikers were charged with. Others would examine general areas of police procedure, such as wiretaps or search warrants, probing for weak points and irregularities. From the start Dany Kane was identified as a potential Achilles' heel in the Crown's entire case against the bikers.

By this time all of those accused in Opération Océan had pleaded guilty, but the two-mega-trial approach was still deemed necessary. With respect to the forty-two Opération Rush defendants, the prosecution had been eager for one mass trial, but defence lawyers argued for several. Some bikers, such as Richard Mayrand, who wasn't charged with murder and who felt the evidence against him was weak, wanted to go to trial as quickly as possible. Others, against whom the Crown had a stronger case, wanted more time to prepare. Then there was the awkward case of Mom Boucher, who was scheduled to be retried for the prison guard murders while at the same time involved in the Opération Rush mega-trial.

Judge Réjean Paul, who had been given the onerous task of dealing with the Opération Rush defendants, eventually split the difference. He determined it would be impossible to handle all the bikers at once but said it could be managed in two separate trials. He himself would oversee the trial of the core group of Nomads and senior Rockers facing murder charges; another group of seventeen more junior, or at least more low-profile, members not accused of murder and for the most part more eager to get their trial under way, would be judged by Jean-Guy Boilard, the presiding judge in the main Lennoxville massacre trial and for Mom Boucher's trial for the prison guard slayings.

The Kane file was taken on by a lawyer in each trial: Louis Belleau, who represented Gilles "Trooper" Mathieu in the Judge Paul trial, and Lise Rochefort, who represented Ronald "Popo" Paulin, in the Judge Boilard trial. Separately the two lawyers went about finding out as much as they could about Dany Kane's life as a police source, his relationship with his police employers, and the circumstances of his death.

Belleau was the more dogged. In the hundreds of thousands of pages of documents dumped on the bikers' lawyers, Kane's chequered career with the RCMP was barely acknowledged. Belleau found a single mention of his work as a Mountie informant and that was in a police affidavit. Belleau suspected there might be more to it and eventually compelled the Crown to surrender the handlers' reports in early 2002, along with the contract that Kane had negotiated with the ERM. Reading them, he became convinced that Kane's relationship with the RCMP and with his ERM handlers had been not only highly irregular but had led to at least one miscarriage of justice.

Rochefort was more intrigued by Kane's death. The details provided were minimal; all she had was the publicly accessible summary of the coroner's report. Her request for the full report, made, she says, in December 2001, was not acted on until some six months later.

Both Belleau and Rochefort arrived at the same conclusion: Kane's death had been extremely convenient for the police. Were he alive he would certainly have had to take the stand at the mega-trials. Like most paid informants with an extensive criminal past he would have made easy pickings for the battery of very sharp defence lawyers.

But Kane was much more than a criminal cutting a deal. He had worked intimately with police for years; he'd committed some of the worst crimes in the criminal code while in their pay, and he knew precisely what information they had and when. Over the course of days and weeks of withering cross-examination, much of it was bound to come out, enough perhaps to jeopardize the Crown's case and almost certainly enough to raise critical questions about the forces' investigative techniques and source handling.

"He never could have testified," says Danièle Roy. "It would have been impossible. There would have been an *arrêt de procédure* like that." She snaps her fingers. "The crimes he committed while he was an informant were just too big, too serious, and there were too many of them for the trial to have hung together on his evidence."

Alive, Kane would have been the Crown's best gift to the bikers' defence and one the prosecutors could not have held tight. Given Kane's role in collecting their evidence, a judge could not have ruled against the defence's right to call him as a witness—which made the biker lawyers all the more curious about the circumstances of his death.

Yet apart from the weak point of Kane's relationship with police, the lawyers had to acknowledge that the Crown's case against the majority of their clients was discouragingly strong, so strong that it was barely worth arguing. In fact, at the urgings of their clients, many were feeling out the possibility of cutting deals with the prosecution. Dozens of lower-level dealers and runners who had been arrested in Opération Océan had done so, and their sentences weren't, in the larger scheme of things, so bad.

The Crown, however, had a very different attitude toward the men it regarded as the leaders of the biker war than it did toward its foot soldiers and flunkies. When, at their regular meetings with defence lawyers in the months leading up to the trial, they were approached about deals with full-patch Nomads, Hells Angels, or Rockers, the prosecutors weren't prepared to give anything away. They were confident of their case and they were conscious of the optics.

Quebec spends less per capita on its justice system than any other province, and its prosecutors have long laboured under the consequences of this parsimony, forced to make do without computers, basic reference books, or adequate support staff. One result is a staggering rate of burnout and stress-related ailments in their ranks. Another is a strong propensity among prosecutors to plea bargain as many cases as possible in order to reduce their workload and relieve the congestion in the province's courthouses. In the years before the mega-trials, the number of cases being plea-bargained—often to the advantage of an accused who everyone knew was guilty—regularly topped 95 percent. Confidence in the justice system suffered accordingly.

After the well-publicized violence of the biker war, after the bombing death of Daniel Desrochers, the attempted assassination of Michel Auger, and the vicious beating death of bar owner Francis Laforest, the Hells Angels were Quebec's most heinous villains. If the justice system was perceived as willing to bargain with these bad guys the public outcry would have been deafening, all the more so since the deputy minister of justice, Mario Bilodeau, had represented members of the gang in his earlier legal career. The bikers would literally get away with murder and the politicians would pay in the end. So the biker lawyers were eager to deal but found themselves without a willing player across the table. The challenge then became to change the Crown's mind, to convince the prosecution that a negotiated settlement wouldn't be such a bad resolution after all.

Pre-trial arguments before Judge Boilard began in earnest in January 2002, by which time the strategy of the bikers' lawyers had gelled. On the one hand they would exploit the inherent unwieldiness of the trial to drag it out and bog it down in the hopes that the jury would become impatient and the prosecution, fearing a mistrial, would lose heart. On the other hand they would hammer away at Kane's unorthodox relationship with the police and his perfectly timed demise in an effort to shake the Crown's confidence in its case and lead it to a plea-bargained settlement.

The lead biker lawyer in the Boilard trial was Jacques Bouchard, one of the old lions of Quebec criminal law and a veteran of the trials that followed the Lennoxville massacre. He was a formidable figure with his mane of grey hair, ever-present Gauloise, and gravelly baritone. He began with a barrage of motions. He asked that the anti-gang legislation be struck down as "unconstitutional, invalid, and inoperative." He called on the court to order a stay of proceedings on the basis that a direct indictment in such a case was "a violation of the rules of fairness and fundamental justice." When Boilard dismissed that motion Bouchard made another that proceeding by direct indictment in lieu of a preliminary inquiry was a fundamental breach of the Charter of Rights and Freedoms and should also be declared unconstitutional. Further, he requested that the charges against all the accused be made much more specific. None of these motions went anywhere, but they succeeded in stalling the work of the court.

A more serious motion was Bouchard's proposal that the so-called KGBs that Kane had recorded for the police in May be barred from being entered in evidence. The police have never explained why they had Kane videotape a reading of the contents of his notebook at that time, but one possible rationale was the murder of their other *agent source,* Claude De Serres, in February 2000. With Kane perhaps they thought it best not to take chances. The bikers' lawyers saw it differently. They regarded the KGBs as proof that the police knew in mid-May that Kane wouldn't be available to testify at a trial, and they had planned for that eventuality.

While raising this intriguing possibility the bikers' lawyers weren't eager to see Kane's videos entered into testimony for other reasons. On tape he gave no end of incriminating testimony about the Hells Angels and the associates he dealt with. He didn't, however, offer any compromising details about his relationship with the police that Bouchard and his colleagues would have tried to extract from him on the stand. Allowing the KGBs into evidence would be tantamount to allowing the Crown's star witness to testify while denying the defence the right to cross-examine. But Bouchard's arguments failed to persuade Boilard. He ruled that the KGBs were admissible.

It was April 22 when, with preliminary motions out of the way and the jury selected, the first trial finally got under way before Judge Boilard. The early going was stultifying, as the Crown had one policeman after another take the stand and testify about the particulars of an arrest, a seizure, or some other police operation. It was the entering-the-evidence phase of the trial, and as

often as not neither Bouchard nor any other biker lawyer
bothered cross-examining the witnesses.

Bouchard did have one surprise up his sleeve. On the
seventeenth day of a trial expected to last the better part
of a year, the Crown called Gaétan Legault to the stand.
All it sought from him were a few details about an arrest
he had made of a Nomads prospect, Jean-Richard "Race"
Larivière, in Boucherville in October 1999. The lead
prosecutor, Madelaine Giauque, had a total of six minutes
of questions for him. Bouchard, however, saw Legault as
his opportunity to bring Kane into the trial, and with a
splash. Legault was, after all, one of Kane's former handlers. For most of what remained of that afternoon and
much of the next three days of the proceedings, Bouchard
grilled Legault about his dealings with Kane, raising
along the way the suggestion that Kane's death wasn't the
simple suicide it had been portrayed as.

Bouchard's doubts were as sincere as they were strategic. He hadn't contacted Kane's family, but he shared
their skepticism and favoured the theory that he was alive
in an ultra-secret witness protection program. He wanted
to know what had become of Patricia, whether she was
still in Montreal or even in the country. But if Kane was
dead, he wanted to be sure that his clients hadn't been
involved in his demise.

Had the Hells Angels discovered that Kane was an
informant, they would certainly have killed him, and they
wouldn't have made it look like a peaceful suicide. On the
contrary, their interests—deterring others from even
thinking of working with the police—would be best
served by a death that appeared as painful and gruesome
as possible. That opened the possibility that Kane was
indeed murdered by bikers, but his death made to look

like a suicide by police. As far-fetched as it sounds, that course might have occurred to the authorities, who feared the influence of the bikers' message on other potential informants: first De Serres, then Kane. Playing both sides was a sure ticket to an early grave. Bouchard sent out feelers among the bikers in Bordeaux. Such inquiries weren't made directly, but the answer that came back was nonetheless unequivocal: the gang had nothing to do with Kane's death.

Bouchard couldn't expect Legault to resolve the big questions surrounding Kane's death, but cross-examining him would allow Bouchard to float the idea that Kane wasn't really dead or if he was, that he hadn't died by his own hand. Legault made few missteps in his testimony, though he couldn't deny that the ERM had hired Kane when it knew full well that while he had been an informant for the RCMP he had killed at least two men and committed countless other crimes. Likewise, Legault was so careful in what he said, so slow in formulating his answers, that it appeared he had secrets to keep.

Legault's cross-examination also allowed Bouchard to introduce into evidence and thus make public one of the more explosive documents that the Crown had provided the defence: Kane's $1.87 million *agent source* contract. The agreement generated some of the first front-page banner headlines of the mega-trial and left the police and Crown with much to explain about why an admitted murderer should deserve such a deal.

Legault's contortions in the witness box supplied the courtroom drama that Bouchard hoped to inject into the proceedings by pursuing the Kane issue. Behind the scenes he was working another angle: getting his hands on the fluid and tissue samples that had been taken from

Kane's body at the time of his autopsy. These had been tested by Quebec's Laboratoire de sciences judiciaires et de médecine légale, a government agency, and the expected results obtained: Kane had fatal levels of carbon monoxide in his **blood**. The two samples taken showed he had "saturation" **levels** of 63 and 69 percent. An average non-smoker **living in a** major city typically shows levels of between 0 and 3 percent, a heavy smoker between 8 and 12 percent. Levels between 25 and 50 percent are considered toxic; more than 50 percent is lethal. According to the lab report there was no evidence of alcohol, street drugs, or medication.

Bouchard wanted to have his own tests done to determine, first of all, that the samples were really Kane's blood. If that could be confirmed, the theory that Kane was hidden in a witness protection program would be disproved. If it was Kane's blood (and his ocular fluid, urine, and assorted tissue samples) Bouchard wanted it more thoroughly tested for other substances. The standard test performed by the Laboratoire on someone found dead in a garage with the car's ignition switched on looks for little more than alcohol and street drugs and, of course, carbon monoxide. Bouchard wanted an independent expert to look for traces of other substances that might have rendered Kane unconscious before he was placed in the car. He delegated another lawyer, Jacques Normandeau, to contact the coroner's office to obtain the samples, as well as the full coroner's report, which still hadn't been provided.

Phone calls and letters between Normandeau and the coroner's office date from May 7. Initially Normandeau was patient, perhaps even lax, in pursuing Bouchard's errand. By June 11, however, he was becoming more insistent. A stern letter written that day itemizes all the documents and samples the bikers' lawyers were after, including the photos taken at Kane's autopsy. It ends with Normandeau threatening to take the matter up with the court if "we cannot have a favourable response by June 15th."

That favourable response was not forthcoming. On June 20 Justice Boilard, finding it inexcusable that the coroner's office was taking so much time, signed a subpoena requiring the chief coroner's appearance at the megatrial on July 8 with all documents and samples requested.

The Crown didn't object. It had been blindsided by Bouchard's questioning concerning Kane's suicide. "The prosecution lawyers never thought that anyone would think that Kane wasn't dead," says Randall Richmond, deputy chief prosecutor of the Organized Crime Prosecution Bureau. Eager to get the issue out of the way, the prosecutors even helped the defence draft the subpoena to the chief coroner.

On July 8 the chief coroner did not show up, but his lawyer was at the mega-trial courthouse before 9 a.m. When he appeared before Boilard, he claimed to have everything that Bouchard and Normandeau had requested "and more." That, however, was far from the case. The blood, urine, and ocular fluid samples were nowhere to be found. The coroner's lawyer admitted he had no idea where they were or whether they still existed. If anywhere, they were at the Laboratoire de sciences judiciaires et de médecine légale, the lawyer said; the coroner's office had made no effort to obtain them, even though that office and the lab worked together closely.

It took two more days to sort out the confusion. Finally, on July 11, two officials from the lab—André Bourgault, the pathologist who oversaw the autopsy of Kane's body, and Pierre Picotte, the toxicologist who ran the tests on the samples—appeared in court. Picotte admitted that the samples had been destroyed sometime in the previous week or so, two months after the bikers' lawyers had initially requested them.

Under cross-examination by Bouchard, Picotte explained the lab's procedure regarding samples taken from people whose deaths are considered suspicious: they were kept a minimum of eighteen months after the toxicologist's final report was written. Then, "depending on the space available in our freezers and how busy the personnel" they were boxed and put aside for pickup by a firm specializing in the disposal of biomedical waste. Picotte's final report on Kane was completed September 14, 2000, so the samples were eligible for destruction anytime after March 14, 2002. But either the lab's staff were overworked or the freezers had room to spare because Kane's samples were not boxed for at least two months, until June 7 or a few days earlier—a month or so after Normandeau first requested them.

Even after his insistent letter to the coroner threatening legal action was faxed on June 11, the lab could have retrieved the samples: they were not collected by the biomedical waste company until June 18 or July 2—the lab wasn't sure which. Indeed, Picotte testified that the coroner's office didn't contact the lab about the samples until June 18 or 19, six weeks after Normandeau's first request. And yes, Picotte testified, the coroner's office was in constant contact with the lab in the course of its work, and under normal circumstances all it took was a phone call from the coroner for samples to be withdrawn from the disposal schedule. According to Picotte, such requests came frequently, but there was none in the case of Dany Kane.

Bouchard and his colleagues were astonished. This sequence of events seemed to confirm their conviction that Kane's death wasn't the simple suicide that police and the coroner's office maintained. The disappearance of the samples suggested to them one thing: a cover-up. It meant, too, that their efforts to prove definitively and scientifically that Kane had not died by his own hand had hit a wall. But the disappearing samples might yet work to their clients' advantage. The day after Picotte testified, Bouchard made a motion for a stay of proceedings due to destruction of evidence.

Judge Boilard refused to be drawn down that path. He promptly ruled that after four months of hearings and 1013 pieces of evidence he wasn't going to derail the trial because of the defence's "fantastical, speculative, even *rocambolesque* opinions" about Kane's death.

Bouchard, who had known Boilard for years and had great respect for his work on the bench, was hugely insulted by the ruling. It wasn't so much the final conclusion—no legal expert would have given the motion much chance of success—as the way it was phrased. Boilard's words dripped with contempt and sarcasm, and Bouchard decided to get his own back. Within a matter of days, Radio-Canada television aired an exclusive report based on a document leaked to their reporter covering the biker mega-trial: the outspoken Jean-Guy Boilard had been severely censured by the Canadian Judicial Council for demeaning and derisive remarks he made from the bench about a lawyer involved in the same trial.

Boilard learned of his censuring from the media. The council had sent its decision to his office at the main Montreal courthouse rather than the special courthouse where he was working. Feeling ambushed, he impetuously quit the mega-trial, walking away from those four months of hearings and hundreds of hours of testimony he had been so intent on preserving.

His resignation greatly disheartened the Crown. "The prosecution felt that things had been going very well, very smoothly with the case," says Richmond. "We were taken completely by surprise." Their disappointment only grew when the judge named to replace Boilard determined that there was no way he could pick up where his predecessor had left off and ruled that the case would have to begin anew. Soon thereafter, a disheartened Crown began serious settlement talks. Within weeks seven of the defendants, including Francis Boucher, pleaded out. The nine remaining took their chances in front of the new judge, Pierre Béliveau. (The seventeenth, Normand Bélanger, was dismissed from the trial and granted bail because of an AIDS-related terminal illness. He died in 2004.)

From the start, Jacques Bouchard's principal Hells Angels client was Denis "Pas Fiable" Houle, who, charged with multiple murders, was to be tried in the court of Justice Réjean Paul. Houle had "lent" Bouchard to Richard Mayrand and Luc Bordeleau for the Boilard trial, where he had been designated by the judge and by his colleagues as the principal litigator for the defence. It wasn't a job he could have kept up while also representing Houle in Judge Paul's court, where preliminary motions were filed in the early summer of 2002.

But Bouchard's work before Boilard was more or less accomplished. He had made the Crown very uneasy about Kane and planted the notion that a settlement with the bikers was an acceptable outcome. Even so, he couldn't just abandon Mayrand and Bordeleau. A lawyer needs a compelling reason to walk in the midst of a trial, and Bouchard didn't have one. A client, however, can fire a lawyer whenever he wants. Mayrand and Bordeleau obligingly dismissed Bouchard so he could go back to his principal client, Denis Houle. Bouchard was soon in Réjean Paul's courtroom. There the Kane file was being handled by Louis Belleau and in a very different way.

Belleau was as skeptical as anyone of the official line on Kane's death, but he didn't believe that questioning it would be a wise strategy. That line of inquiry might seem too paranoid, too desperate, and the likelihood of obtaining objective, physical evidence that Kane's suicide had been faked was extremely slight.

A more fruitful avenue to pursue was Kane's dubious relationship with the police, Belleau decided. In particular, the MacFarlane murder and what had happened at the trial in Halifax. During the spring and summer of 2002 Belleau researched and wrote a mammoth stay-of-proceedings motion detailing, among other things, the many crimes Kane committed while serving as a police source and alleging that it would have been almost impossible for his handlers to have been ignorant of his activities. The motion bore no resemblance to those put forward by Bouchard in the Boilard trial. Those rarely exceeded two or three pages and perhaps a dozen paragraphs. Belleau's was a thumping forty pages and 401 paragraphs, followed by a thirty-two-page appendix chronicling the spotty and inadequate response from the Crown to the defence's demands for additional documentation on Kane, everything from police reports of assorted bombings to the officers' correspondence and notes.

Judge Paul forced the release of some of the documentation but refused to sign twenty-seven subpoenas that

Belleau had prepared to compel the players in the Halifax case—most of them RCMP officers—to testify at the mega-trial. "I will not turn this trial into a commission of inquiry on Dany Kane," Paul said.

One of Belleau's main arguments was that the RCMP had committed an obstruction of justice in the MacFarlane murder trial by insisting that Kane's role as a police informant be kept secret. Gaetan St. Onge could have confirmed that Kane was in the Maritimes with Aimé Simard around the time of the murder and so should have testified on behalf of the Crown. Keeping Kane's relationship with the RCMP a secret and preventing St. Onge from testifying thus got in the way of a conviction—oddly enough with the help of the Crown.

Justice Paul gave more consideration to Belleau's stay-of-proceedings request than Boilard did Bouchard's. In the end, however, it was rejected with the clear message from Paul that the mega-trial was meant to decide the guilt or innocence of Dany Kane's biker colleagues, not investigate his relationship with police or answer the many questions about his death.

Kane was effectively kicked out of that courtroom, too, though not before exerting an influence on the Crown. Much of the evidence that Kane had personally provided police, including the KGB videos and his notebooks, were quietly withdrawn from the evidence that would ultimately be entered by the Crown in both mega-trials. Kane, the prosecutors seemed to conclude, was nothing but a hornet's nest. Ultimately they too lost the stomach to pursue nine of Quebec's most notorious Nomads and Hells Angels associates, including Normand Robitaille and Denis Houle, as thoroughly as the law would allow. They took up the standing offer from the defence for a plea-bargained settlement, a process that ended in September 2003 with the Crown dropping all the murder charges levelled against the bikers two and a half years earlier.

In the end Kane once more played a double role. He helped police and prosecutors nail Quebec's top Hells Angels and dozens of their underlings, people who had been his mentors, role models, and closest friends for years. Then he helped those same close friends and long-time associates get the best deal they could.

The murder charges against them withdrawn, Kane's former Hells Angels bosses were convicted for a range of drug, conspiracy, and gangsterism charges and sentenced to lengthy prison terms.

Long-time Nomads Walter Stadnick, Normand Robitaille, Denis Houle, Gilles Mathieu, Richard Mayrand, René Charlebois, Michel Rose, and Donald Stockford received minimum terms of twenty years each. Mom Boucher, who was finally convicted in May 2002 for the prison guard murders and received a double life sentence, was expected to receive the same when his case was judged or when he chose to plead out. Only Salvatore Brunetti, the Rock Machine veteran who defected to the Nomads a scant three months before the Opération Printemps 2001 sweep, drew a light term. He was sentenced to just over six years and was out on parole by mid-2004.

Two dozen Rockers and Nomad prospects, including Pierre Provencher, Guillaume Serra, Daniel St-Pierre, and Francis Boucher, received sentences of between ten and twenty years each. But these sentences, like the Nomads' twenty-year terms, sound more punitive than they are. Time served awaiting trial counts double against the final sentence, and all will be eligible for parole after serving half their terms. It is unlikely any will spend more than a decade in prison, some just half of that.

During their years inside they will be joined by colleagues who eluded arrest in March 2001 but whose luck eventually ran out. Among them are André Chouinard, the

Nomad who was expelled from the gang shortly before Kane's death, and who was in Mexico when the sweep took place. In April 2003 he was arrested at a chalet in the Eastern Townships.

Chouinard's capture occurred within hours of that of Richard Vallée, a Nomad who had been on the run since making his escape from prison authorities in 1997. Vallée had been behind bars awaiting extradition to the United States on murder charges after a witness who was due to testify against him in a drug-smuggling case had been blown up along with his Porsche. While in prison Vallée was assaulted and taken to hospital for treatment of a broken jaw. There an accomplice burst out of a cupboard and held a gun on the accompanying guards while Vallée made his escape.

The biker hid out in Costa Rica for several years before sneaking back into Quebec. He was stopped for drunk driving in Montreal on April 11, 2003, and found carrying a loaded gun and a large amount of cash. But he gave police a false name and was released after being fingerprinted and arraigned on charges. The fingerprints soon gave him away, and he was arrested under his proper name a week later.

Two other bikers once assumed dead were found by police very much alive in the spring of 2004. Paul Fontaine, Stéphane Gagné's accomplice in one of the prison guard hits, and Stephen Falls were thought to have been eliminated by their fellow gang members. But in early May police received a tip that Falls was living quietly in the Montebello region, an hour up the Ottawa River from Montreal. They moved quickly and within a day or two arrested him. Fontaine was found a few weeks later.

Dany Kane had told his ERM handlers in October 1999 that contrary to milieu gossip, Fontaine had not been killed but instead rewarded for his service to the gang with a full Nomads patch. His story was supported by Serge Boutin, another *délateur* who had operated a drug business with Fontaine. Boutin testified in 2002 that he had met with his ex-partner at Quebec City's Château Frontenac hotel in December 1999. Boutin had supported Fontaine's wife and children to the tune of $1000 a week for eighteen months after his disappearance and Fontaine trusted him to engineer a Christmas reunion with his family. But Boutin also testified that a year later, in 2000, Normand Robitaille had led him to believe that Fontaine was subsequently killed.

In late May 2004, likely as a result of a tip, police arrested Fontaine as he left a restaurant in a lower-town Quebec City neighbourhood. The former Hells Angels hit man had recently opened Sweetie's Fashions, a clothing stand at a local flea market. "He seemed a really good, nice guy," remarked a neighbouring stall owner. "He seemed more like a gardener than a murderer." Fontaine, however, didn't seem to have shaken all his Nomad ways. Another merchant claimed he had pressured her not to carry Pepe jeans; he wanted a monopoly on the brand at the flea market.

The apprehension of Fontaine and Falls followed the mid-March arrest of a much more notorious former biker, one whom Quebeckers had likewise regarded as gone for good, even though they knew he still walked freely among them: Yves "Apache" Trudeau.

Trudeau had been released from detention in 1994 after serving eight years—four in prison, four in halfway houses—for the forty-three murders he confessed to as part of his controversial *délateur* deal. Living under a new name, Denis Côté, and with a new life story, the short, slight former assassin had settled with his wife and children in Valleyfield, an industrial town off the western tip of Montreal island. Through the years the SQ kept a discreet eye on Trudeau to ensure he didn't revert to his old ways, but their vigilance failed to protect a young boy whom Trudeau began sexually molesting in 2000. The abuse continued until early 2004, when Trudeau was arrested and charged with ten counts of sexual assault, sexual interference, sexual exploitation, and invitation to sexual touching. Trudeau defended himself—no lawyer was interested in representing him for the meagre money he could afford—ended up pleading guilty, and received a four-year sentence. "You've killed more people than did the Canadian army during the Gulf War," admonished the judge. "You have a deplorable past and a pitiful future."

Outside Quebec, another figure from Dany Kane's world gave the RCMP its long-awaited conviction in the case of Robert MacFarlane. MacFarlane's murder had led to two related deaths. When William St. Clair Wendelborg, a cocaine-dealing associate of the Halifax Hells Angels chapter, talked too freely about the hit being Paul Wilson's contract, Wilson put out another. He offered a pair of Nova Scotia career criminals $20,000 and two kilograms of hash to kill Wendelborg. Then he changed his mind: Wendelborg's death would draw too much police attention to himself, he decided. But the hit men either didn't get the message or they felt that a contract was a contract. Wendelborg was beaten and injected with a lethal dose of cocaine. A hunter found his body in October 1998. It wasn't long before the killers were themselves ratted out and charged with Wendelborg's murder. Bizarrely, one of the men, Billy Marriott, committed suicide in the Halifax Correctional Centre on August 7, 2000, the same day that Dany Kane died, an apparent suicide, in St-Luc.

In flight from the police and from Wolf Carroll, who had Wilson on his hit list for, as Kane had reported, "chattering" about the involvement of Wolf and Kane in MacFarlane's death, Wilson hightailed it first to British Columbia and then to the Caribbean. He lost a great deal of weight and passed himself off as Paul Michaud, hoping to live a secluded life in Grenada. He held on to some habits, however: when police arrested him in November 2000 they reportedly found him in possession of more than twenty kilos of cocaine.

Wilson was deported back to Halifax and, after protracted legal wrangling, pleaded guilty in early 2004 to reduced charges of second-degree murder in the MacFarlane case, conspiracy to commit murder in the Wendelborg case, and a long string of drug-related and proceeds-of-crimes infractions. He was sentenced to twelve years in jail.

By the time Wilson was charged for commissioning MacFarlane's murder, the man who had actually fired the fatal shots was three years into his minimum twelve-year term. For Aimé Simard, it hadn't been easy time, and true to his nature, Simard hadn't been an easy prisoner. Informants are not looked on any more fondly by police and prison guards than they are by fellow inmates; along with child sex offenders, they are regarded as the lowest of the low. Simard was particularly loathed. He'd banked no good will with justice authorities since his testimony had failed to convict a single person. And he was openly gay and indefatigably irritating in a hypermacho institution where everyone's nerves were already stretched taut.

Simard was in the habit of telephoning journalists to complain about his treatment or to offer his opinions of the shoddy performance of police and prosecutors against the Hells Angels. He also made calls to companies that operated toll-free order lines and attempted to bilk them of various goods using the fraud-artist techniques he'd mastered as a young man. In one case, he persuaded a nutritional supplements company to invoice the prison administration for hundreds of dollars' worth of supplies shipped to him. Simard's provocative and obstreperous behaviour meant that he often found himself not simply in protective custody—the isolated state of almost all informants within a prison—but also in punitive solitary confinement, "the hole." For the same reasons, he was shuffled from one institution to another. After testifying against Kane, he was sent to the modern, maximum-security institution in Port-Cartier on Quebec's remote North Shore. Initially he took courses and demonstrated enough interest in Islam to convert, at least for a few months. Within the protective custody unit he seemed to make friends and even find love; he and another inmate, Tommy Berger, went to great lengths to try to marry each other in May 2001 using fraudulent documentation provided by a Montreal pastor who specialized in civil unions between gay couples. But by that fall, Simard's conduct had deteriorated, and he spent increasing amounts of time in "segregation"—solitary confinement—because of threatening remarks and actions directed against other prisoners and staff, especially, a Correctional Services report noted, the female guards. Twice during this period, Simard attempted suicide, on one occasion necessitating a three-day stay in hospital in Sept-Îles.

In June 2002 Simard was transferred to the Kent institution in British Columbia's Fraser River Valley. It was termed an "involuntary transfer," but Simard didn't oppose it; he knew that in Port-Cartier he was a marked man. As he told an interviewer from a Quebec gossip magazine, "Ever since the bikers put a contract of $100,000 on my head, some people here look at me like I'm an automatic teller."

Prison authorities hoped his reputation hadn't preceded him to B.C. and that he would be able to circulate in the wider prison population. It took all of a day for officials to change their minds: an altercation erupted in the cafeteria lineup, and Simard was placed in segregation once again. He remained there for virtually his entire stay in Kent. On the rare occasions he was allowed contact with other prisoners, officials noted that Simard was involved in "muscling, gambling and trading in contraband (tobacco)." He whined incessantly about prison conditions and launched a campaign to be allowed phone calls to his boyfriend back in Port-Cartier.

After little more than six months in Kent, Simard requested another transfer, this time to Saskatchewan Penitentiary in Prince Albert, Saskatchewan. "It is the safest institution for me because there is almost (or none at all) no bikers and I have no incompatibles," Simard explained in his request, using the Corrections Canada term for known enemies. He wanted to take that institution's course on anger management, Simard said, and he admitted to spiritual and romantic motivations as well. "I am embrasing [sic] the native way since 1999 and I have a native boyfriend who's going to be there. I am with him since 1999 and we intend to get married ASAP."

Corrections authorities were initially cool to the idea, but after he threatened to kill himself if he wasn't relocated, they relented. He was transferred in early June 2003. Simard was repeating the pattern of his youth, migrating from place to place, leaping from dream to scheme, firm in the belief that his problems were not self-inflicted but rather the fault of circumstance.

As was the case when he first arrived at Kent, Simard wasn't placed in protective custody at Saskatchewan Penitentiary. That was the way he wanted it, but there was no surer guarantee of a violent confrontation with other prisoners, a fact that should have been well known to prison authorities. He was put in a cellblock with fifteen other men, many if not all of them convicted murderers, in a special maximum-security unit within the larger medium-security facility. While its prisoners were kept separate from those in other wings of the unit, they could socialize among themselves. His fellow inmates soon figured out who Simard was, and again he became a marked man. This time, however, getting at him wouldn't be nearly as difficult as it had been in Port-Cartier or Kent.

In mid-July another inmate at Sask Pen told guards that attacks on Simard and three other prisoners were planned. Simard himself seems to have been aware that the vague threat he had always lived with in prison was now a very real and imminent danger: he asked for yet another transfer on July 16. Two days later, as guards made their rounds shortly after 10 p.m., they discovered Simard on the floor of his cell, stabbed more than seventy times. There was so much blood that guards lost their footing as they tried in vain to revive him. When the commotion drew the attention of other prisoners in the cellblock, they began chanting, "Another dead rat!"

On the face of it, finding Simard's murderer wasn't much of a challenge. There were a limited number of suspects who had the opportunity, and a trail of bloody footprints led to the cell of a convicted killer with strong links to an aboriginal gang and, through that gang, to the Hells Angels. Still, it took more than two years before any charges were laid in connection with Simard's death.

By early 2005, the only person involved in MacFarlane's murder who wasn't either in jail or known to be dead was the man who could have been called its fixer: Wolf Carroll. He was also the only Nomad still at large.

Like Chouinard, Carroll was in Mexico on March 28, 2001, and eluded Mexican police. But unlike Chouinard, Carroll either didn't develop a case of homesickness severe enough to tempt him back to Canada, or if he has returned, he has been careful not to be caught. Sightings have been reported in Halifax and British Columbia, but such stories are the norm in a milieu that is rife with unreliable rumours. Speculation about how Carroll managed to be out of the country at the time of the Opération Printemps raids and how he has avoided arrest ever since is taken more seriously. Invariably, as was the case with Kane's friend Claude Grégoire McCarter, suspicions are raised when someone is as uncannily lucky as Carroll has been throughout his criminal career.

Fuelling these suspicions are several known facts. One is that Carroll's brother worked as an RCMP agent in the Atlantic provinces, a situation not as anomalous as it might seem. Wolf was not the only Hells Angel to have close relatives in law enforcement. Indeed, the father, brother, and uncle of one member of the Sherbrooke chapter held positions in, respectively, the SQ, the local municipal police, and the RCMP. (Despite those familial ties, the biker still ended up in jail for loan sharking.)

It is curious, though, that Carroll has never been placed on the RCMP's most wanted list, even though he is being sought by the force on numerous charges of first-degree murder, conspiracy, and drug and gangsterism offences. The list, distributed in poster form and easily accessible on the web, alerts police forces at every level of the Mounties' highest priority targets. None of the twenty-odd individuals featured face such serious charges. Several are cited for conspiracy to traffic or import drugs, some for armed robbery. The crimes of others go back years, including one Hells Angel who is wanted for his participation in the Lennoxville massacre.

Questions were also raised about a police visit to Carroll shortly before the Opération Printemps sweep and his departure for Mexico. Some biker lawyers say that the police were simply making an effort to coax Carroll into becoming a police informant, but others suggest that during the visit he may have been tipped off—inadvertently or otherwise—that the arrests were imminent.

Similar suspicions surround Pat Lambert who has never been charged or raided by police. Lambert, however, seems to have had the good sense to begin withdrawing from the orbit of the Hells Angels in 1997, early enough to be off the police radar when the raids occurred. But not everyone accepts this version. When asked what Lambert was doing in 2004, one biker lawyer answered acidly, "Living off his police pension."

Outside the confines of the special courthouse constructed for the mega-trials, beyond the legal manoeuvrings of the prosecutors and lawyers, the biker war came to a

shuddering but conclusive end in the years following
Opération Printemps 2001. Only a handful of murders in the
province were attributed to hostilities between the gangs
thereafter, and a minority of these occurred in Montreal,
once the main battlefield of the conflict. Almost all were
personal settlings of accounts, not part of a larger dispute.

That is not to say that Quebec's Hells Angels had been
devastated by the raids, only the gang's most high-profile
and bellicose element, those members who had been intent
on securing a monopoly of the illegal drug trade and who
were prepared to go to the most murderous extremes to protect it. With these men in jail, the more level-headed, if less
ambitious, Hells took charge. The gang's control over the
drug trade in Montreal and elsewhere was loosened, with
results that any economics student might have predicted:
prices fell and quality rose. Supply was hardly affected. As
police grimly acknowledged, no one found it impossible to
score in the days following the March 2001 sweep.

Beyond Quebec, the gang continued to expand its drug
network through the consolidation of distribution operations that came as a result of the patch-over of the Ontario
bikers. New territory was conquered, some thanks to
another of Dany Kane's legacies, the Hells puppet club
known as the Road Warriors.

A little more than two years after Kane's death, the Road
Warriors were moving three kilograms of cocaine every
week through Belleville—some $250,000 worth at street
level. The gang's success was due partly to their association
with the undisputed rulers of the biker scene in Ontario, the
Hells Angels, and partly to a talent for instilling fear among
locals. Those who refused to pay a drug debt, or otherwise
crossed the Road Warriors, were severely punished. An
OPP officer testifying at the bail hearing of one member of

the gang described the kidnapping and torture of a Cornwall man who had failed to settle his unpaid drug account. "He was restrained while his toenail was removed with pliers, and then bleach was poured into the open wound," the officer said. "He was also beaten with a blunt object, whipped, and kicked repeatedly."

The gang suffered a setback in late April 2003 when seventy police officers launched a coordinated series of raids in the Belleville area, arresting sixteen Road Warriors and associates and seizing an impressive inventory of drugs, weapons, and explosives. But it wasn't a mortal blow; such raids and arrests are part of the cost of doing business for criminal organizations, and the Road Warriors ride still.

The careers of Kane's police handlers, both in the RCMP and the ERM, have been marked by more lows than highs in the years since they worked their prized source. Far from adding lustre to the professional lives of Mounties Pierre Verdon, Gaetan St. Onge, or, to a lesser degree, Jean-Pierre Lévesque, C-2994 contributed only controversy and doubt to their records. For Lévesque, the blemish stemmed from his much frowned upon letter to Kane while he was in prison in Halifax. That and his often poor relations with biker investigators from other forces, particularly those in Quebec, may have contributed to a loss of confidence among his superiors. At one time among the most visible RCMP spokespeople, he was increasingly restricted in his contact with the media and obliged to limit himself to more bureaucratic responsibilities at the biker desk of the Criminal Intelligence Service of Canada. He was scheduled to retire from the force in early 2006.

The careers of St. Onge and Verdon, more intimately involved with Kane, were more adversely affected. The report by J.H.P. Bolduc cast a cloud over their management of an important source and over their integrity as Mounties. But despite Bolduc's call for a wider investigation into the handling of C-2994 and his relationship with St. Onge and Verdon, none was ever carried out. Instead, after the Mounties submitted their rebuttal to Bolduc's eviscerating evaluation, the force seems to have done its utmost to put an end to the controversy. In June 1999, Supt. Rowland Sugrue, the designated referee in the matter, issued an inconclusive report that managed to be complimentary of both Bolduc's analysis and the efforts of St. Onge and Verdon. The handlers, he concluded, "did good work in difficult and stressful conditions." Even if the hoped-for results weren't realized, "this experience will serve us in the future and confirm to us that we must be extremely careful with a source who infiltrates the biker world or with a person from the milieu who offers us his services."

Despite this official exoneration, neither St. Onge nor Verdon saw his star rise within the RCMP. Instead of assignment to important projects like Carcajou, they found themselves involved in more routine investigations such as tobacco smuggling. St. Onge eventually retired in summer 2005 while Verdon was seconded from the Mounties to help train civilian police in Haiti.

The handling of Kane by Benoît Roberge and Gaétan Legault of the ERM was never scrutinized as thoroughly as that of their RCMP predecessors. Nevertheless, their careers suffered setbacks at least as serious. Following allegations of improprieties made by another biker informant he handled through much of the 1990s, Roberge became the subject of an internal investigation and was pulled from active service on the biker beat pending its outcome. He eventually returned to investigative work but not the organized crime squad. Legault, meanwhile, continued to pursue the Hells Angels but not without mishap. A 2003 investigation ended in a major raid on the organization in the Trois-Rivières area, after which Legault and fellow officers hit the bars to celebrate. At the end of the night, Legault was at the wheel of his vehicle when it was stopped by police. He was charged with impaired driving and since his return to work has been limited to administrative duties.

When Patricia learned that Dany had been the ERM's key *agent source* against his own gang, she became determined to find out more. In particular, she wanted to see the contract he had signed. She made phone calls and wrote letters to the Sûreté du Québec, arguing that as his common-law widow and mother to one of his children, she should have the right to review the full document.

She approached the SQ's Witness Protection Service but was rebuffed. The contract, she was told, was confidential to the parties concerned. She turned to the access-to-information division of the Department of Public Security, which oversees the province's police forces, including the SQ. She was again refused. Capt. Bruno Beaulieu, who took part in the negotiation of the contract, told the access official that "in committing suicide, [Kane] provoked a breach of the contract, thus putting an end to any obligations of the Sûreté du Québec. It is important to underline that the agreement only concerns Kane and the Sûreté." Beaulieu added that the contract couldn't be released because it was "an investigative document," and he cited an article of Quebec's law on evidence and five articles in the access-to-information legislation that allowed the SQ to deny Patricia a copy.

Either Beaulieu had forgotten the contract's terms or he was resorting to a very flexible interpretation. Nowhere did the agreement suggest that the SQ and ERM were freed from their obligations in the event of Kane's death, by suicide or otherwise. Rather, article 93 stipulated that "[t]he Sûreté will remit to the agent source's estate any indemnities which are owed at the time of his death, if it occurs."

But the SQ seems to have understood its position was shaky and probably anticipated that the contract would one day become public. After Patricia began asking to see it, the force engaged a law firm to provide it with a legal justification for its refusal to pay Kane's estate the monies it had promised for his work and the arrests that resulted. The legal opinion was delivered to the SQ on May 23, 2001, a week after Beaulieu declined Patricia's request for a copy of the contract. It argued that since the arrests hadn't been made at the time of Kane's death, the force owed him nothing.

That opinion did not impress many, including some within the SQ. When a heavily edited version of the agreement was made public a year later and after Patricia had studied its pages, she consulted a lawyer. The lawyer advised her to team up with Josée, the legal guardian to three of Kane's four heirs; together they wrote a demand letter to the SQ insisting that it honour the contract. The SQ offered to settle for a neglible amount, but Patricia and Josée refused and filed a lawsuit. The SQ played hardball and filed a defence, requiring Patricia to testify in an examination for discovery. But after the women's lawyer grilled Beaulieu and handler Gaétan Legault, the SQ yielded. Jacques Bouchard's work at the mega-trial had brought them enough bad publicity on the subject of Dany Kane. In late 2003 the SQ agreed to pay Kane's heirs a substantial but undisclosed amount. Before the money was released, Patricia, acting as the estate's executor, was obliged to pay back taxes on Kane's income during those years when he received $2000 cash a week from the RCMP and, later, the ERM.

Well before the settlement was reached, both women had taken steps to remake their lives. Patricia, graced with strong survival instincts, took a job in the internet industry and began laying the groundwork for the start-up of her own company. With Patricia's mother and sisters playing a large role in their lives, Steve and Jesse thrived.

For Josée, life without Kane was more complicated. She admitted that when first informed he was dead, she had felt a flood of relief. "My initial reflex was to cheer. He couldn't scream at me or insult me anymore. Then I realized it also meant that the kids didn't have a father." Raising three children without his financial support, however meagre, would be a challenge, as would remaining in St-Jean-sur-Richelieu, where she had to endure the whispers and stares of townsfolk who had read the stories in *Allô Police* and elsewhere. She considered changing the children's last name to spare them schoolyard teasing. And as ever, she yearned to move away from St-Jean, ideally to a house in the country. The settlement may allow her to do that.

As for how Dany died, there is no resolution, no clear answer, for either Patricia or Josée. Both will speak of his death as a suicide one moment and as a murder the next; both seem resigned to never knowing the truth about what really happened, perhaps a necessary concession in order to put it behind them and move on.

Others are less equivocal about what may have taken place that night in St-Luc, however thin the hard evidence. Outlandish as it seems, there are many, both within and outside the biker milieu, who are convinced that the police played a hand in Kane's death. They believe that the police had a motive—to rid themselves of a potentially damaging witness—and the means and opportunity. Several biker lawyers who know the case intimately find the timing of Kane's death just too convenient, mere days after he had procured the Rosetta Stone to the Nomads' financial dealings, just as he was going from being an invaluable police asset in their fight against the Hells Angels to a major witness-stand liability. Those who subscribe to this theory maintain that the police have the know-how to make a murder look like a suicide and, if need be, the power to lean on a coroner or make bodily fluid samples disappear. They dismiss the possibility of a gang hit: no murder designed as a warning to others would ever be mistaken for suicide. But just as many people refuse to countenance such speculation: Canadian cops don't do that sort of thing, they believe. Perhaps in Latin America, Eastern Europe, or in countries in Asia—but not in Canada. Even if there may have been an institutional interest in Kane's disappearance, these people argue, what individual police officer would carry it out?

After the autopsy photos were shown in court, in response to Jacques Bouchard's questions during the Boilard mega-trial, fewer observers persisted in believing that Kane's suicide was a piece of theatre and that he might still be alive in an elite witness protection program. Not that the photos didn't raise questions of their own: why all the blood oozing from his mouth, nose, and eyes? Why the electrode patches on his torso if there had been no attempt at resuscitation? Some are still convinced that Kane is alive. These include a professional infiltrator who has worked closely with the RCMP and with police forces in Canada and abroad for twenty-five years. He claims to have participated in faked suicides on at least two occasions.

Yet if Kane's suicide were an elaborate cover-up, it would have involved a substantially wider circle of conspirators, including presumably the coroner and his staff as well as St-Luc police, any one of whom could have exposed the plot. There is also the question, Why bother? If Kane had to be eliminated for the sake of a successful prosecution of his former gang mates, why go to such lengths to keep him alive? It is not likely that police imagined using him in similar operations elsewhere. His usefulness was almost certainly limited to Quebec.

After his role on Opération Printemps 2001 was revealed, Kane's parents grasped at the hope that he might still be alive, but gradually that dream dissipated. He would have contacted them somehow, they're sure. They don't believe he killed himself, however. The family's list of suspects is long and varied, fuelled as much by what seers have told them as by the circumstances of their only son's life and death. Their reluctance to move on has not brought them any closer to Patricia or Josée.

Relations between Kane's immediate family and the two women were further chilled by the financial settlement. Gemma and Jean-Paul felt left out financially and emotionally; it had all been negotiated without their knowledge. Only when the children insist on seeing their grandparents do Patricia and Josée now make their way to the wood-frame duplex in the old neighbourhood of St-Jean-sur-Richelieu.

There have been a few changes since Dany's death. A fresh coat of paint has brightened up the exterior of the house, and Gisèle is now ensconced in the apartment upstairs. There is new flooring on the main level, and in the rarely used living room a few pieces of tropical hardwood, some of Dany's African furniture, mingle with the family's conventional sofa and chairs.

It's hard to miss the photos of Dany, squeezed into cheap, ill-fitting frames, on almost every available shelf and end table. Some are from his smiling childhood and scrawny adolescence. Others are taken later in life, when Kane was tattooed and bulked up on steroids, projecting the image of the heavy-hitting biker he so wanted to be. A stranger might have difficulty guessing that all of these pictures are of the same person. To the camera, as to everyone in his life, this man was a chameleon.

Finally, the visitor might notice the square, red urn on a shelf beside an oversized stereo speaker. Inside is all that remains of Dany Kane: a litre or two of ashes and an enduring mystery.

A NOTE ON SOURCES

The information in this book was drawn overwhelmingly from two main categories: interviews with dozens of lawyers, police, and other justice officials, and with Dany Kane's family, friends, and associates; and hundreds of police, court, and other documents, some publicly accessible, others not, including land titles, family notes and letters, and newspaper reports. Institutionally, I had very little cooperation: the RCMP refused to allow any of its members to talk to me about Kane, and other forces were barely more forthcoming. Nonetheless, a number of Mounties, as well as members of other police corps, agreed to be interviewed on the condition that I not reveal their identities. Most of the police documents I consulted and refer to in the book came from the thousands released to defence lawyers before and during the mega-trials. Others were obtained in other ways.

There are relatively few books on the subject of biker gangs, and a short bookshelf would hold all that are worthwhile—an odd deficiency, given the fascination that popular culture has reserved for bikers since they first rode out of California in the 1940s. It is explained by the fact that most self-respecting outlaw bikers would never permit a journalist or researcher to observe their lives up close, let alone take him or her into their confidence. Outlaw biker gangs are notoriously insular groups, their members bound together as much by contempt and mistrust of straight society as anything else.

This secretiveness is most evident in the dearth of solid sociological and anthropological study. Only one North American researcher has truly succeeded in penetrating outlaw biker culture and documenting it from an academic perspective, and his circumstances were unique. The late Daniel Wolf ended up as a psychological anthropologist at the University of Prince Edward Island, but he grew up among the working-class poor in Alberta. He financed his studies by labouring in factories and meat-packing plants. Along the way he bought a motorcycle and found himself occasionally rubbing shoulders and sharing drinks with members of various biker gangs. When it came time to select a subject for his doctoral thesis, he decided to examine that same "ethnographically unexplored" subculture.

He observed the rules of the culture, adopted its dress code, and took a nickname. Eventually he won acceptance with Edmonton's Rebels, a club that had formed in the late 1960s and many of whose members joined the Hells Angels when they moved into Alberta in 1999. In the early 1980s, when Wolf rode with them, it would have been an exaggeration to call the Rebels "organized crime," but they were moving in that direction.

The book that was developed from his doctoral dissertation, *The Rebels: A Brotherhood of Outlaw Bikers* (University of Toronto Press, 1991), is a thorough study of the values and rituals of the outlaw biker world. At the same time Wolf maintains a disingenuous academic distance. The lifestyle clearly held an immense attraction for him, and like many bikers he saw it as a means of redefining and adding value to his life, yet he resists turning the lens on himself and the book is poorer for it. Nonetheless, it stands out for its effort to understand bikers as human beings, where they come from, and what motivates them—insights that most popular writing on the gangs lacks entirely. There are exceptions, notably Hunter S. Thompson's remarkable, if dated, *Hell's Angels: a Strange and Terrible Saga* (Random House, 1966) and Mick Lowe's *Conspiracy of Brothers* (Macmillan of Canada, 1988). The first is a classic of new journalism, almost as well known as the gang itself, and profiles the California Hells Angels when they were more a fraternity of hard partiers than an organized crime group in their own right. The second is a sprawling and fascinating look at Ontario's Satan's Choice and an investigation into the police railroading of several of their members for a 1978 murder in Port Hope, Ontario.

Books that deal with the biker world in Quebec tend to be thinner in substance if not shorter in length. The Toronto journalist Yves Lavigne has made a specialty of writing about the Hells Angels in Canada. Lavigne's *Hell's Angels: Taking Care of Business* (Deneau, 1987) is a sensationalist but informative and entertaining work in which everything is either black or white, usually black. The book aimed to raise the alarm about the threat the gang posed around the world; still, Quebec bikers occupy a disproportionate place in the book, and Lavigne's account of the Lennoxville massacre makes for its most compelling chapter. His later *Hells Angels at War* (HarperCollins, 1999) is a similarly Manichean treatment of the early years of Quebec's biker war, as well as the Hells Angels–Bandidos conflict in Scandinavia. It lacks the narrative energy of his earlier book and relies heavily on news reports and his own prescriptions for dealing with the biker threat.

Two *délateurs* in the Quebec biker war—Peter Paradis of the Rock Machine and Serge Quesnel, a Hells Angels hit man—have participated in tell-all books that are interesting for the insider accounts they provide. Both Paradis's *Nasty Business* (HarperCollins, 2002) and Quesnel's *I Was a Killer for the Hells Angels* (McClelland & Stewart, 2003) by Pierre Martineau focus almost exclusively on their personal escapades with, respectively, the Rock Machine in southwest Montreal and the Hells Angels in the Quebec City and Trois-Rivières area, omitting the larger story.

The Road to Hell: How the Biker Gangs Are Conquering Canada (Knopf Canada, 2003) by Julian Sher and William Marsden, two of English Montreal's top investigative journalists, provides a sound overview of the biker menace in Canada and a solid account of the war in Quebec from the police perspective. It makes no effort to understand the gang members' human complexities and doesn't question Dany Kane's death.

ACKNOWLEDGMENTS

This book began life as an article for one incarnation of *Saturday Night* magazine and was published in another. I owe thanks to the editors Dianna Symonds and Mark Stevenson, who encouraged my initial research, as well as to Matthew Church, Cynthia Brouse, Jay Teitel, Dré Dee, Josh Knelman, and Chris Debicki, who edited, fact-checked, and ran the resulting story.

Several reporters from the Montreal media who covered the mega-trials were very generous with their knowledge—George Kalogerakis, Christiane Desjardins, and Stéphane Giroux, in particular—if sometimes skeptical of my fascination with Dany Kane. Likewise, thanks to Bernard Tétrault of *Allô Police,* a Zen font of information and helpfulness about Montreal's criminal past and present, and Gary Francoeur, whose website—Google wiseguywally to find it—is the best and most comprehensive one-stop shopping site for information on Montreal organized crime. From further afield, Dan Kerslake of Saskatchewan CBC, Richard Dooney of *The Halifax Daily News,* Bill Hunt of the Belleville *Intelligencer,* and Rob Roberts of the *National Post* in Toronto have my gratitude for their contributions to different parts of the story.

For the obvious reasons, I can't thank most of the people from the legal and law enforcement world, or from the milieu, who helped me, often very extensively. Top of the list of those I can thank is Guy Ouellette, formerly of the Sûreté du Québec; were he a biker, his nickname would surely be "Encyclopedia." Others include the prosecutors Randall Richmond and Keith Riti of the Organized Crime Prosecution Bureau, along with their colleague Annie Lemieux, as well as the lawyers Peter Jacobsen of Toronto, Peter Girard of Belleville, Narissa Somji of Ottawa, Kurt Johnson of Montreal, and Michael Cooke of Halifax. France Côté of Montreal's Palais de Justice evidence room was the most helpful and pleasant of overworked government employees; the clerks at the Gouin Palais de Justice, not so put upon, were similarly accommodating.

Carlo Morselli of the Université de Montréal's criminology department provided fresh ways of thinking about organized crime in general; his student Nadine Deslauriers was generous in sharing the best nuggets gleaned from sifting through thousands of mega-trial documents.

From the movie world, thanks to Pierre Gendron, Christian Larouche, and Eric Canuel in Montreal for their interest and encouragement and to Pat Sherman in Los Angeles.

From the book world, thanks to Michael Schellenberg, formerly of Penguin, for buying the idea, Sara Borins-Angel for connecting us, and Diane Turbide for picking up where Michael left off. Special thanks to my editor, Jan Walter, for her rigorous attention to detail and helping me say more with less.

Many good friends were encouraging as I wrote the book; some did special service. These include Max Wallace, Robbie Dillon and Julien Feldman, and, in particular, Eric Siblin and Alex Roslin, who read early drafts of the manuscript. Babak Salari, my favourite photographer, showed me that taking photos of photos is also an art.

Finally, particular gratitude to Alex the part-time pony for his insights, Patkevco Inc. for its openness, and Catherine, Ariel, and Augie for their warmth and support.

A book with no redeeming characters is not the sort to dedicate to anyone, but if it were, this would be for Penny and Clyde, for the example set.

INDEX

Note: Josée and Patricia, respectively the first and second common-law wives of Dany Kane, asked that for reasons of personal safety their surnames not be included. They appear, therefore, in the index under their first names. The same applies to Patricia's son Steve and Josée's brother Dominique.

DK in this index stands for Dany Kane, *HA* stands for Hells Angels, and *SQ* and *SPCUM* for the Quebec provincial and Montreal City police respectively. The numerals in italics refer to photographs.